The Philosophy of Religion of Alexander Campbell

The Philosophy of Religion of Alexander Campbell

J. Caleb Clanton

The University of Tennessee Press • Knoxville

First Edition.

The paper in this book meets the requirements of American National Standards Institute / National Information Standards Organization specification Z39.48-1992 (Permanence of Paper). It contains 30 percent post-consumer waste and is certified by the Forest Stewardship Council.

Library of Congress Cataloging-in-Publication Data

Clanton, J. Caleb, 1978–
The philosophy of religion of Alexander Campbell / J. Caleb Clanton. — First edition
p. cm
Includes bibliographical references and index.
ISBN-13: 978-1-57233-946-0 (hardcover)
ISBN-10: 1-57233-946-2 (hardcover)
1. Campbell, Alexander, 1788–1866.
2. Religion—Philosophy.
3. Christian philosophy.
I. Title.

BX7343.C2C53 2013
210—dc23 2012040201

For my wife, *Sophia*
You have made me a philosopher—in the best sense

Contents

Preface

I will never forget my first encounter with W. David Baird, that great Oklahoman dean who recruited me to Pepperdine University in 2007. Toward the end of our negotiations, he squeezed my hand, looked me square in the eye, and with all the gravity in the world said, "Barton W. Stone and Alexander Campbell *are calling you from the grave* to come to Pepperdine." I confess, Baird's otherworldly intercession nearly doubled me over in laughter. But I suspect that it also planted something of a seed in the back of my mind, even if (as I would later find out) I was hardly the first person to whom Baird had relayed this summons-from-beyond.

So began my scholarly interest in Alexander Campbell.

At previous stages in my career, I could never have predicted that I would write a book about Campbell's philosophy of religion. For one thing, until just a few years ago, most of my research had centered on issues in social and political philosophy and classical American pragmatism. And like most other people—even many of us affiliated with the Stone-Campbell Restoration Movement—I had no clue that Campbell had much of anything to say about philosophy of religion as opposed to, say, theology or biblical interpretation. But because I found myself working at an institution to which I had apparently been called by Campbell himself (an amusing thought, I admit), it seemed only fitting that I should reacquaint myself with his work. And because I have always been drawn to the give and take of a formal debate, I started by thumbing through the transcript of Campbell's eight-day exchange with skeptic Robert Owen over the evidences of Christianity. While reading this debate, I eventually concluded that I had stumbled upon something that was not only historically intriguing but also potentially unique, at least as far as natural theology goes. On the first pass, I was tempted to view Campbell's case for God's existence—the one he showcased in the Owen debate—as little more than a rewarmed version of Descartes's so-called trademark argument. But the more I looked at it, the more I noticed that my initial impression was not quite accurate. For starters, Campbell clearly fancied himself a bit of a Lockean empiricist, and Descartes's trademark argument goes hand in hand with his rationalism. So, alas, my curiosities were unleashed, and I went in search of what scholars had to say about this unfamiliar argument for God's existence and about Campbell's philosophy of religion more generally. But aside from a few cursory treatments of his philosophical views, I returned from the library virtually empty-handed.

This book is effectively my attempt to write what I was hoping to discover when I went looking. And if I may torture a line from Santayana: should readers be tempted to smile when they find this book, I assure them that I smile right along with them. At the least, I hope that this book provides a decent enough starting place for those who are curious about whether there is anything in Campbell's philosophical thinking to smile upon. Admittedly, in many respects, this book raises more questions than I set out to answer here. But I trust that it is nonetheless an evenhanded, albeit critical, treatment of Campbell's philosophy of religion and that it points readers in the right direction for finding some satisfying answers—or, at any rate, that it raises the right sorts of philosophical questions to which Campbell and his followers should attend.

Many people have been helpful to me in the process of writing this book, and I owe them a great debt of gratitude. For their insightful comments on parts (or the whole) of this book, I thank Jon Atkins, John Mark Hicks, Michael Hodges, Mason Marshall, Kraig Martin, Garrett Pendergraft, Rubel Shelly, and the reviewers and editors at the University of Tennessee Press. I am also especially grateful to my former students Jacob Perrin and Peter Zuk for their comments on the manuscript, for their help editing the notes and bibliography, and for all their work as my research assistants. For helpful conversations about several points covered in this book or for their helpful historical tips along the way, I thank Scott Aikin, David Baird, Michael Ditmore, Chris Doran, Ron Highfield, Loretta Hunnicutt, Mark Wiebe, John Wilson, and Darryl Tippens. For their research assistance to me during July 2011, I am grateful to the staff at the Disciples of Christ Historical Society Archives in Nashville, Tennessee, and for her research assistance at Payson Library at Pepperdine, I thank Elizabeth Parang. For the opportunity to present portions of the book to the faculty and students at Lipscomb University in November 2011, I thank Richard Goode and Tim Johnson. Needless to say, any remaining infelicities or errors in the book are entirely my own fault.

Parts of two chapters of this book draw from material first published as journal articles. In particular, part of chapter 2 draws from material first published as "Alexander Campbell's Revealed-Idea Argument for the Existence of God" in *Restoration Quarterly*. Part of chapter 4 draws from material first published as "Alexander Campbell on the Problem of Divine Hiddenness" in *The Stone-Campbell Journal*. I thank the publishers of these articles for their kind permission to draw from them.

I am also deeply grateful for the various sources of funding that enabled me to do much of the research for this book, and I thank Lee Kats and Maire Mullins in particular for their generous travel assistance and research support. I am also thankful for the funds provided to me by Pepperdine University's Summer Undergraduate Research Program and for the opportunity to involve undergraduates in my work as a scholar during the summer of 2011. The initial stages of this project were completed during my time as a Seaver Fellow in the Humanities at Pepperdine (2010–11), and I benefited greatly from the research funds associated with that fellowship.

When I first floated the idea of writing this book in the winter of 2010, I received a hearty dose of encouragement from friends, colleagues, and administrators in the Pepperdine community. That encouragement proved to be powerfully motivating, and I am deeply grateful to all those who offered their kind words of support along the way. In the summer of 2012, I was recruited to join the faculty at Lipscomb University, where I was able to put the final touches on the manuscript. I am deeply grateful to my colleagues there for their support in completing this project.

Lastly, for everything she does and has done to make my life better, I am especially grateful to my beautiful wife, Sophia. Without her, even southern California days would lack sunshine. This book is dedicated to her with all my love and affection.

J.C.C.

Chapter 1

Campbell the Philosopher and His Philosophical Influences

Alexander Campbell (1788–1866) was a man of extraordinary status in his day. His contemporaries would not have been surprised to learn that while traveling on a speaking tour in Europe in 1847, he carried a letter of introduction in which Henry Clay, the former secretary of state, described him as "among the most eminent citizens of the United States, distinguished for his great learning and ability, for his successful devotion to the education of youth, for his piety and as the head and founder of one of the most important and respectable religious communities in the United States."[1] And indeed Campbell was distinguished in a variety of ways. As a successful sheep breeder and farmer, he would become one of the wealthiest men in the new state of West Virginia by the time he died at his home in Bethany.[2] And as an author, debater, religious reformer, itinerant preacher and lecturer, statesman, Christian apologist, and college founder and president, Campbell would become one of the most respected and influential figures of nineteenth-century antebellum America. Yet as is often the case, even the towering giants of one age can slip quietly into the shadows of the next, and much about Campbell's life and thought, particularly his philosophical views, has simply faded from memory in the past 150 years. But despite this partial eclipse, he deserves attention. His importance in American history is incontestable, and his influence can still be seen today, thanks to the important and distinctively American religious movement he helped found, a movement that would survive him and eventually come to bear his name.

This book is an effort to reconstruct, explain, and evaluate the main contours of Campbell's philosophy of religion. In the chapters that follow, I critically examine his unique argument for the existence of God, his case for the resurrection of Jesus and the truth of Christianity, his reply to David Hume's famous argument against belief in miracles, his responses to the problem of evil and the problem of divine hiddenness, and his view about the relationship between religion and morality. First, though, to cast these arguments in the proper light, I should say more about Campbell himself. Because he is little known these days among contemporary philosophers, for example, in the rest of this chapter I discuss who he was and why he is worth considering today. After offering a brief biographical sketch (**§1.1**), I consider why scholars in recent decades have largely ignored Campbell's philosophical views (**§1.2**). Because it is understandable to ask whether Campbell actually qualifies as a philosopher, I go on to explain why he plainly was (**§1.3**). Both to underscore the extent to which he was a philosopher and to provide some context that will be useful in later chapters, I then discuss which figures in the history of philosophy most influenced Campbell's thought (**§1.4**). Finally, I provide an overview of chapters 2–5 (**§1.5**), and then I speak more fully to why the project of this book matters (**§1.6**).

1.1. The Life and Career of the "Sage of Bethany"

A Scots-Irishman born in 1788 in County Antrim, Ireland, Alexander Campbell was educated in his early years by his father, Thomas Campbell, a learned Presbyterian minister and educator. He eventually followed in his father's footsteps to study for a short period at the University of Glasgow in the months immediately leading up to his immigration to the United States.[3] Soon after his arrival in 1809, Alexander joined his father in an effort to unify Christians and restore a primitive New Testament-based understanding of Christianity. Thomas had immigrated to the United States two years before the rest of his family for health-related reasons, and he shortly thereafter distanced himself from the Seceder Presbyterian synod of Pennsylvania amidst some controversy over his ministry. He soon penned the *Declaration and Address of the Christian Association of Washington*, a text now widely regarded as one of the most important founding documents of the American Restoration Movement, also known today as the Stone-Campbell Restoration Movement.[4] In what some have construed as the religious analogue to the Declaration of Independence,[5] Thomas's *Declaration and Address* called for local church autonomy, exclusively biblical requirements for church membership, the unity of Christians around biblical essentials, and an end to sectarian creeds and ecclesiasticism.[6] Eventually, Alexander embraced these aims and became the leading and most articulate voice in the religious reformation that his father's vision had helped initiate. The younger Campbell's leadership would prove to be nothing short of remarkable, as his movement enjoyed an almost unparalleled growth rate during his lifetime, and it played a significant role in the Christianizing of American society that took place during the first half of the nineteenth century.[7]

According to some estimates, just four years after Campbell died in 1866 there were as many as 350,000 followers of his religious movement.[8] By the close of the century, those numbers had more than tripled, making this religious community, at that time, one of the largest Protestant groups in America.[9] Campbell's movement would continue to grow in the next century, although, ironically, it would fracture into several distinct groups thereafter. Today, there are several denominations that trace their heritage to the Stone-Campbell Restoration Movement, including most notably the Churches of Christ (a cappella), the Christian Church (Disciples of Christ), and the Independent Christian Churches/Churches of Christ.[10] To the extent that these denominations today represent the different trajectories of Campbell's religious influence, there are at present nearly three million Americans—and an estimated four to five million people worldwide—who are in some way associated with the movement Campbell helped found.[11]

But even aside from the continuing significance of his religious movement, Campbell's life was marked by extraordinary accomplishment and reputation in its own right, facilitated no doubt by an unusual degree of discipline and dedication in almost all his undertakings. Unsurprisingly, several interesting anecdotes abound. One is that he kept a bowl of water at his desk for the purposes of dunking his head, if ever he faced the temptation to slack off or doze.[12] Another is that a certain type of crappie fish was named after him. (One wonders whether the "campbellite fish" earned its name because it dies quickly outside of water—reflective, perhaps, of what would become Campbell's signature doctrinal commitment to adult baptism by immersion.)[13] Yet another story, told by his second wife, is that he had some sort of quasi-mystical encounter while at Glasgow—the very kind of experience he was prone to dismiss as only so much "enthusiasm"[14]—with a tongueless, earless woman who, before suddenly vanishing into thin air, predicted (accurately) that he would be shipwrecked while immigrating to America, that he would preach before large crowds, and that he would be married twice.[15]

Ordained as a minister at the Brush Run Church in Washington County, Pennsylvania, in 1812, Campbell served as an itinerant preacher for numerous congregations, a service for which he never accepted remuneration or reimbursement.[16] He eventually became a highly sought-after lecturer, traveling to colleges and literary societies throughout the United States and Europe to address an array of topics, ranging from capital punishment and war to demonology and public education to a variety of religious and philosophical issues.[17] It can raise a few eyebrows these days to learn that although Campbell reportedly never spoke for less than two hours—and in some cases for much longer than that[18]—he apparently never failed to draw a crowd and keep it, if for no other reason than his sheer eloquence as a speaker.[19] In fact, it would be difficult to *over*estimate Campbell's celebrity as a speaker in his day. Commenting on the "prodigious excitement" that Campbell's visit to Hannibal, Missouri, apparently stirred, Mark Twain saw fit to spin a characteristically irreverent yarn about Campbell in his autobiography, noting that when "the great Alexander Campbell" came to town, "many had to be disappointed, for there was no church that would begin to hold all the applicants; so in order to accommodate all, he preached in the open air in the public square, and that was the first time in my life that I realized what a mighty population this planet contains when you get them all together."[20] Yet Campbell's reputation as a preacher was by no means limited to commentary on the numbers he managed to pull. James Madison, for example, said that Campbell was "the ablest and most original expounder of the Scriptures" that Madison had "ever heard"—no small compliment from a former president trained in theology at Princeton.[21]

With his pen and his printing press, Campbell was no less prolific. From 1823 through 1830, he edited and published (and wrote the majority of) a monthly journal entitled *Christian Baptist.* In 1830, Campbell launched his second journal, *Millennial Harbinger,* for which he served as editor and contributor for nearly four decades. These publications proved an important tool in expanding the sphere of his influence and that of his religious movement, and Campbell likely welcomed with open arms his appointment as postmaster, a position that allowed him to take full advantage of the franking privileges. Although his journals were geared toward promoting Christian unity in keeping with his vision to restore "the ancient order of things" found in the New Testament, they also eventually helped make a name for Campbell as an outspoken critic of the ecclesiasticism and religious clergy of his day. Rarely inclined to pull his punches, he found abundant targets for criticism, including authoritarian structures in various religious groups; the status and social position of clergy; creedal tests for church membership; speculative theology and the nonscriptural traditions, superstitions, and customs of established churches; sectarianism; religious enthusiasm; the union of church and state; and any vestige of Roman Catholicism insufficiently purged by the Protestant reformations of previous centuries.[22] And his censures were hardly reserved for long-running religious traditions. For example, in a pamphlet entitled *Delusions,* Campbell let fly at the Book of Mormon, just as the Church of Jesus Christ of Latter-day Saints (popularly known as the Mormon Church) was emerging on the American frontier.[23]

In all, the tenor and spleen of Campbell's criticism of other religious groups made him appear, at times, to have strange bedfellows. As one scholar notes, Campbell was "willing to go, and actually did go, far with all opponents of revealed religion," as his critical stances frequently paralleled those of the deists, natural religionists, skeptics, and atheists of his day.[24] Not surprisingly, Campbell's self-appointed role as a religious flyswatter courted some measure of controversy—from which he never exactly ran, especially in his earlier years—and, in turn, he was greeted on occasion with a bit of mudslinging. His critics showered him with accusations of heresy, and he was reportedly called everything from infidel to freethinker, deist, Universalist, Unitarian, Arian, Socinian, Arminian, Pelagaian, Antinomian, Sebellian, Sandemanian, Haldanian, and Calvinist. One college president went so far as to call him the Devil.[25] To say the least, Campbell's views were often as misunderstood as they were polemical, and he was persona non grata to many people.

Throughout his career, Campbell exemplified and honed his skills as a religious thinker and stylish rhetorician by participating in public debates with important religious leaders such as John Walker, W. W. McCalla, John Purcell, N. L. Rice, and Dolphus Skinner. And over the span of eight days in April 1829, Campbell debated the prominent skeptic and protosocialist reformer Robert Owen.[26] Attended by more than 1,200 people, this debate in particular received a good deal of attention in the newspapers, and it played a pivotal role in catapulting Campbell into the national spotlight as a Christian apologist. In addition to the transcripts of these debates, Campbell published a number of monographs and pamphlets, including *The Christian System*; *Christian Preacher's Companion, or Infidelity Refuted by Infidels*; *Christian Baptism: Its Antecedent and Consequents; Life of Thomas Campbell*; and *Popular Lectures and Addresses*; as well as an edited translation of the New Testament he entitled *The Living Oracles*,[27] his own translation of the book of Acts, and a (lucrative) two-hundred-page hymnal.[28]

Nor were Campbell's accomplishments limited to the realm of his religious reformation. In 1818, he tried his hand as an educator by launching a boarding school known as the Buffalo Seminary. Though this initial venture would be relatively short-lived, Campbell eventually made a lasting mark as an educator in 1840 by founding Bethany College, where he served as president and professor until his death. During this time, he became a prominent advocate for public education, as well as for the education of women.[29] And his views on the role and nature of education were not overlooked. For example, Campbell was invited to address the state legislature of Missouri on the subject of public education.[30] And the president of then Washington College—none other than the former general Robert E. Lee—would some years later comment in a letter to a friend that Campbell's "Address on Colleges" in *Millennial Harbinger* (1854) was "read with much interest" and was "among the ablest productions" Lee had ever read.[31]

Although Campbell never set out to be a political icon, and in some respects may have even opposed the thought of being one,[32] he nonetheless did garner a measure of political influence in antebellum America. He reluctantly served as a delegate to the historically important Virginia Constitutional Convention of 1829–30, which was also attended by such luminaries as former presidents James Madison and James Monroe, future president John Tyler, Chief Justice of the Supreme Court John Marshall, and John Randolph.[33] As a noteworthy though somewhat controversial presence at the convention, Campbell crossed swords with several of these men and unsuccessfully lobbied for efforts to further democratize Virginia by expanding the representation of western counties to weaken the power-grip enjoyed by slave-owning elites in the eastern counties.[34] Reportedly, Campbell also wanted to initiate an effort to gradually end slavery in Virginia, but ultimately his intentions failed to materialize.[35] Despite the fact that he had once owned slaves (whom he eventually freed), Campbell publicly opposed slavery, not on scriptural grounds but for political and economic reasons. Although his public stances on slavery moderated and became more nuanced in an effort to preserve the Christian unity he had sought to engender,[36] as late as 1849 he followed his friend Henry Clay in urging the Kentucky legislature to end slavery.[37] (The similarity of Clay's and Campbell's reconciliatory stances with respect to slavery, together with their various points of personal contact, may even be suggestive of mutual influence.)[38] A pacifist and conscientious objector, Campbell held an aversion to war that would also lead him to promote something like the United Nations or a world court.[39] Related to other matters, in 1850 Campbell became the first religious leader in history to be invited by Congress to address a joint session of the House and Senate—an invitation he accepted, despite what he had said nearly a decade earlier about the "worldly pomp and splendor" of Washington, DC. Apparently, Campbell addressed that audience for only an hour and a half, on the topic of church-state relations.[40]

Given the scope of his involvement during his lifetime, and given that his career spanned the generations of the American Revolution and the Civil War, it is unsurprising that someone of Campbell's stature would come to make the acquaintance of an impressive list of personalities in nineteenth-century America. And if one were to hypothesize about the full scope of Campbell's influence, the company he kept provides a great deal of fodder for speculation. He was welcomed into the White House by President James Buchanan, and he took note of (and eventually replicated) the wallpaper patterns of the Hermitage while visiting former president Andrew Jackson in Nashville. He was a close personal friend to future president James Garfield, who also served as a trustee of Bethany College. Overnight guests at Campbell's Bethany mansion included Henry Clay, Daniel Webster, John C. Calhoun, and Jefferson Davis—the very men who took center stage in negotiating America's political reality in the days to come. But perhaps Campbell's renown is most eloquently captured by Robert E. Lee, who wrote of him in a letter to a friend:

> As Dr. Symonds said of the great Milton, so may I say of the late President of Bethany College, "That he was a man in whom were illustriously combined all the qualities that could adorn or elevate the nature to which he belonged. Knowledge, the most various and extended, virtue that never loitered in her career, nor deviated from her course. A man who, if he had been delegated as the representative of his species to one of the many Superior worlds, would have suggested a grand idea of the *human race.*" Such was President Campbell.[41]

When Campbell died at his home in Bethany shortly after the Civil War in 1866, his graveside monument would memorialize him as the "Sage of Bethany." For his efforts at combating religious skepticism and restoring the ancient order of the New Testament church, he was named there the "Defender of the faith once delivered to the saints."

1.2. Overlooking Campbell

To say that Campbell was an important antebellum figure is to make a claim at which few would balk. Yet to discuss his work as though he were a *philosopher*—and one whose work is worthy of analysis and evaluation—will perhaps inevitably strike some as a bit odd, if for no other reason than that there is almost no precedent for doing so. In fact, some scholars—mostly historians—have been quick to dismiss Campbell as being somehow "disinclined toward philosophical thinking."[42] Naturally, then, contemporary philosophers may find it surprising that I regard Campbell as a philosopher in this book. If he is even known at all by philosophers these days, he is typically viewed by them almost exclusively as a theologian and religious leader.

Of course, in some sense, this view is perfectly understandable. For one thing, there exists next to nothing about Campbell in the philosophical literature of recent decades. To my knowledge, there is only one article on Campbell appearing in a professional philosophy journal (from 1982), and it mostly surveys the issue of freedom and determinism discussed in Campbell's debate with Robert Owen.[43] Likewise, there are only a handful of books and unpublished dissertations that discuss Campbell's philosophical work in any detail, and most of them were written more than fifty years ago.[44] And those studies leave much to be desired, as the discipline of philosophy has certainly matured in scholarly practice and argumentative rigor since those works were published. Admittedly, there are a host of articles and book chapters written by nonphilosophers, and occasionally they offer some useful reflection on Campbell's philosophical views. But generally speaking, the attention his work has received is, understandably, less than penetrating in its philosophical analysis, as it is aimed at accomplishing other scholarly objectives. In sum, most of the treatments of Campbell's philosophical work over the past fifty years have been written by nonphilosophers—typically theologians, historians, and rhetoricians—and, perhaps predictably, most of that work has been indexed to an audience identifying with the Stone-Campbell Restoration Movement in some way or another. When attention is given to his philosophical work at all, it is typically by way of quickly positioning Campbell's theology at the receiving end of his main philosophical influences. As a result, the vast majority of the literature on Campbell tends to be religious or intellectual history, with little or no analysis and critical assessment of Campbell's philosophical views. Moreover, the vast majority of this literature appears in publications not typically cited by professional philosophers or even those outside of Restoration-related circles. While all of this work is certainly worthwhile and often quite illuminating, it simply does not provide the analysis and assessment Campbell's philosophical work calls for.

That professional philosophers have overlooked Campbell's work is understandable for at least one additional reason: his philosophical views tend to be scattered about in his voluminous writings of nearly five decades. And many of those writings appeared in what some scholars have brushed aside as "fugitive literature,"[45] and almost all of them can be relatively difficult to locate these days.[46] To add to that, often when Campbell addressed philosophical topics—as he did in his debate with Owen[47]—his philosophical positions and arguments were intermingled with sometimes tedious historical, theological, or biblical excursuses. In fact, Campbell admitted with some regret that he was not able to take the time to organize, systematize, or even make explicit his views as carefully as he would have liked. For example, in the closing remarks of the last issue of his journal *Christian Baptist,* Campbell says:

> Many subjects introduced into this work have not been fully and systematically discussed. General views have been submitted, rather than full development and defences. Not a single topic has received that finish, or that elucidation which it is in the compass of our means to bestow upon it. I have thought if life should be prolonged, and an opportunity offer, that I would one day revise this work, and have a second edition of it published, with such emendations as experience and observation might suggest.[48]

With these considerations in tow, we can certainly understand why philosophers in recent years have largely passed Campbell's work by. Edward and Dennis Madden further speculate that this lack of attention can be attributed to the fact that Campbell was "early on the scene, before the great rush to Scottish realism and the systematic development of that position" in America.[49] But whatever accounts for this inattention—and even though it might seem perfectly understandable—it is nonetheless unfortunate and worth correcting. Given his stature as an intellectual figure in his day and given that he helped found one of the largest indigenously American religious groups, we are right to take a closer look at his philosophical views and arguments pertaining to religion.

Along similar lines, some contemporary Christians (particularly those affiliated with the Stone-Campbell traditions) may find it peculiar, and perhaps even somewhat problematic, to contemplate and examine Campbell as a Christian *philosopher.* Why might I think this? For one thing—at the risk of being repetitive here—most of what has been written about Campbell in Restoration-related publications (with only a few exceptions)[50] has been either entirely inattentive to his philosophical views or, alternatively, philosophically decaffeinated in its treatment of them. For another thing, the Restoration traditions have tended to neglect the discipline of philosophy in general. Consider the following. First, at the dozens of colleges and universities historically associated with the Stone-Campbell movement, there are at present relatively few professional philosophers on faculty in comparison to the number of philosophers on faculty at comparable institutions affiliated with other religious traditions.[51] And at each of those same schools, there are relatively few philosophers on faculty in comparison to the number of faculty members representing other academic disciplines (such as biology and history). Second, there have been very few philosophical works published by the presses and journals associated with these Restoration-related institutions. Third, to my knowledge, there has not yet been anything like a steady stream of professional philosophers hailing from these schools.[52] So we have at least some decent prima facie reasons for thinking that the discipline of philosophy has received less attention in Restoration-related circles than one might otherwise expect or wish.

Of course, we are right to wonder about what accounts for this inattention to the discipline of philosophy in general, and to Campbell's philosophical thinking in particular. Although there are probably several historical phenomena that could explain this feature of the Stone-Campbell traditions, I will mention only three here.

First, it is very likely that the founding vision of the Restoration Movement was articulated in such a way that was, ironically enough, conducive to a suspicion of, and antipathy toward, philosophy as a whole. Edward Scribner Ames—one of John Dewey's doctoral students and a Disciples minister in the first half of the twentieth century[53]—noted that by the time he was ordained in 1890, "nothing was heard" of the distinctively Lockean views of the movement's founders.[54] Ames speculated that this silence was "due to the tendency to minimize human influences in the formulation of the 'plea' [of the Restoration Movement] and to emphasize the direct authority of the New Testament."[55] There is certainly something to Ames's speculation here. Indeed, much of the rhetoric employed by the founders of the movement was aimed at restoring a view of Christianity that was uncontaminated by philosophical and theological theorizing beyond the biblical texts. Consider, for example, the "Last Will and Testament of the Springfield Presbytery" signed in 1804 by Barton W. Stone, the other half of the Stone-Campbell duo. The signers of this "Last Will and Testament," which is widely regarded as one of the founding documents of the movement, affirmed that "candidates for the Gospel ministry [will] henceforth study the Holy Scriptures with fervent prayer . . . *without any mixture of philosophy,* vain deceit, traditions of men, or the rudiments of the world."[56] These sorts of platitudes by no means evaporated in Stone's day, and in fact they may have snowballed in unintended ways throughout the nineteenth century. For, in some sense, difficulties in relating to the study of philosophy seem to shoot through the entire Restoration tradition—and this leads to my second point.

As early as 1856, there was a heated public squabble between Tolbert Fanning and Robert Richardson—two of the most prominent early leaders in the Restoration Movement—over the relationship between philosophy and Christianity.[57] Consistent with much the same spirit of the "Last Will and Testament," each party raced to prove his Restorationist bona fides by trying to outdo the other in showing he had fewer extrabiblical, philosophical commitments. Eventually, Campbell chimed in publicly to denounce Richardson for "placing faith and philosophy in any real or formal antagonism."[58] But the Fanning-Richardson affair in particular probably caused a bit of ripple effect in the tradition following it.

Third, the uncharitable reader might gain the sense that Campbell was opposed to philosophy; with some frequency, Campbell speaks rather disparagingly of various schools of philosophy, particularly of the ancient Greek and Scholastic schools of thought. For example, he says that those schools in particular have "filled the human mind with darkness and confusion, and the world with mythology, scepticism, and libertinism; till the very name of Philosophy . . . disgusted every lover of true wisdom and morality."[59] But, as I think is quite clear to anyone who bothers to read these sorts of passages in their proper context, it is a complete misreading of Campbell to conclude that he opposed all schools of philosophy or philosophical thinking in general. In fact, that view is simply false. Nonetheless, many affiliated with the Restoration traditions have confused Campbell's rejection of one area or school of philosophy with a rejection of philosophy *simpliciter*.[60] In speaking negatively of some schools of thought, Campbell had as his purpose simply to toss out the rubbish to make room for the new, true philosophy (as was characteristic of many Enlightenment-era thinkers).

Regardless of why those affiliated with the Restoration traditions have historically underappreciated the discipline of philosophy and have tended to avoid reading Campbell as a philosopher—and despite how understandable this inattention may seem—the fact that such tendencies should exist among Restorationists in particular is unfortunate, for at least three reasons. First, such tendencies can encourage one to overlook the degree to which Campbell was very much a philosopher and a vociferous proponent of philosophical inquiry. A failure to recognize this fact can lead one to fundamentally misunderstand who Campbell was. Second, a failure to appreciate Campbell as a philosopher can leave one unable to appreciate the degree to which the Stone-Campbell tradition has a philosophical substance and center of gravity all its own. And third, those tendencies can encourage contemporary Restorationists to miss out on something very important to the religious movement Campbell helped found: such tendencies can diminish one's ability to acknowledge, appreciate, and critically evaluate the various strands of philosophical influence Campbell helped introduce into his religious movement.

1.3. Campbell as a Philosopher

As for why one would be inclined to view Campbell not just as a religious leader or theologian but as a philosopher, there are a variety of reasons. Most obviously, Campbell received the training one might expect of a philosopher. By nearly all accounts, during his early years under the tutelage of his father, Campbell cut his teeth on John Locke's *Essay Concerning Human Understanding* and the *Letters Concerning Toleration*.[61] (Apparently, Locke's *Essay* in particular would become something of a safety blanket for several of the early Restorationists: many of them are reported to have carried a copy of it in their saddlebags at all times, along with a copy of the New Testament and a hymnal.)[62] In due course, Campbell studied philosophy briefly at one of the key schools of the day, the University of Glasgow, during a period many regard as Scotland's golden age of philosophical thinking. At Glasgow, Campbell studied under George Jardine, whom he considered a special friend and through whom Campbell would become acquainted with the Scottish common sense philosophers. But not only did he receive a fairly straightforward education in philosophy, Campbell's writings show him to have been a critical reader of many of the important philosophical figures of the Enlightenment period, including Francis Bacon, John Locke, Thomas Reid, George Jardine, James Beattie, Dugald Stewart, David Hume, Rene Descartes, Francis Hutcheson, Adam Smith, William Paley, Joseph Butler, Blaise Pascal, Samuel Clarke, Thomas Hobbes, George Berkeley, Thomas Paine, Gabriel Mirabeau, Denis Diderot, Pierre-Simon Laplace, Jean-Jacques Rousseau, Edmund Burke, Baruch Spinoza, and Voltaire, as well as Anaximander, Democritus, the Stoics, Pythagoras, Plato, and Aristotle, among others. And Campbell clearly viewed himself as a philosopher. For example, he not infrequently referred to himself in the third person—or at least he was referring to an imagined interlocutor with whom he was clearly sympathizing—as a "Christian *philosopher*."[63] In a move that probably most explicitly reveals his self-conception, Campbell appointed himself to the position of professor of mental and moral philosophy upon the founding of Bethany College, and his introductory address at the founding event was about the nature and state of the discipline of philosophy.[64] In the years that followed, he lectured on moral philosophy, logic, apologetics (particularly Paley's and Butler's), and political economy.[65] And if a man's book recommendations say anything about how he views himself, Campbell's clearly reiterates his self-identification as a philosopher. Campbell saw as sine qua non titles by Pascal, Bacon, Locke, Newton, Beattie, Paley, Butler, Hume, Berkeley, Smith, Jonathan Edwards, Reid, George Campbell, and Baron D'holbach, among others.[66]

Of course, the case for Campbell's being a philosopher by no means rests, nor should it rest, upon the books he read, the people he cited, or the titles he gave himself. The main reason one can properly regard him as a philosopher is that, in addition to offering some interesting and even novel arguments in philosophy of religion, Campbell's manner of thinking is saturated with an honest concern for truth, a respect for open inquiry and careful analysis, and a high view of the give and take of critical deliberation with opposing parties. He clearly took it as the duty of an interlocutor to try to clarify his terms and justify his positions noncoercively by offering reasons and evidence, and not simply rhetoric.[67] For, in Campbell's view, a person "who will not reason is a bigot, he who cannot is a fool, and he who dare not is a slave."[68] He understood well that the proper exchange of reasons requires social institutions that are supportive of the freedom of expression, even of the religious skepticism and atheism that he opposed. This conviction in particular drove him to say that "if our most pure, holy, and heavenly religion can be defended . . . by no other weapons than iron blocks, swords, and faggots, I wish not to be in the rear or van of its advocates. No! on our banner is inscribed, *reason, argument, persuasion*."[69] Never one to shy away from combative exchanges with those who disagreed with him, Campbell expressed optimism that engaging in conversation with opposing parties was productive of at least as much as light as heat: "[C]ontroversy . . . is only another name for error, and there can be no improvement without controversy."[70] This attitude led him to publish his opponents' views alongside his own in his journals; in general, Campbell was receptive to anyone wishing to challenge his thesis or critically engage his views.[71] What is more, he understood that genuine inquiry requires that one practice the virtue of epistemic humility and that one be willing to refine his position in light of better reasons and evidence. For example, in a passage reminiscent of Socrates's dialogue with Gorgias (in which the former confesses that he would rather be refuted than to refute),[72] Campbell states,

> It is always more or less detrimental to the ascertainment of truth to allow our previous conclusions to assume the position of fixed and fundamental truths, to which nothing is to be at any time added either in correction or enlargement. On the contrary we ought rather to act under the conviction that we may be wiser today than yesterday, and that whatever is true can suffer no hazard from a careful and candid consideration. In this manner I am accustomed to examine all questions.[73]

In sum, then, there are several reasons to read Campbell as a philosopher: (1) he took himself to be a philosopher; (2) he studied philosophy and was conversant with the leading philosophers of his day; (3) he taught philosophy at Bethany College; (4) he offered philosophical arguments in defense of his religious views; (5) he conducted himself like a philosopher in his thinking; and (6) he promoted philosophical inquiry, even as he acknowledged its limitations.

1.4. Campbell's Primary Philosophical Influences

If anything is much known these days about Campbell qua philosopher, it is typically concerning his indebtedness to Francis Bacon, John Locke, and the Scottish common sense school of thought most typically associated with philosophers such as Thomas Reid, Dugald Stewart, James Beattie, and others. This point is fairly well documented in the scholarly literature on Campbell.[74] However, we should bear in mind that although he was deeply influenced by Bacon, Locke, and the Scottish common sense philosophers, Campbell was neither an uncritical sycophant nor a helpless parrot, as some interpreters might leave us thinking.[75] None of these philosophers and their philosophies, Campbell says, can "be adopted as a complete and perfect text book."[76] In fact, he took himself to be "no special advocate" of any particular school of thought, and he sought "to be an eclectic," at least as far as consistency would allow.[77] Indeed, Campbell viewed himself as something of a motley peacock: reflecting on his own influences, he channeled John Newton in saying, "[W]henever I [saw] a pretty feather in any bird, jackdaw like, I plucked it out, and plumed myself with it until I became so speckled that not a single species would own me."[78] With that said, although my primary aim in the following chapters is to offer a direct engagement with Campbell's philosophical arguments and positions—and not to cast yet another intellectual-historical narrative in which he simply plays wide receiver—it will be useful nonetheless to note some of the more important philosophical deposits in his thinking.

Perhaps the chief influence on Campbell's methodology and his views about the norms of inquiry was Bacon's *Novum Organum*. Following Goethe, Campbell praised Bacon for having drawn "a sponge over the table of human knowledge" to make way for the new sciences,[79] and he repeatedly credited Bacon with having laid the groundwork for correct reasoning and proper inquiry.[80] In Campbell's view, Bacon brought to the fore the primacy of empirical observation and the importance of compiling and comparing facts, with a fact being defined as something said or something done. Accordingly, after considering these compiled facts, one could come to discover causes of phenomena and the laws of nature by means of induction. Following Bacon, Campbell sought to distance himself from a priori approaches to inquiry that begin with some set of abstract ideas, first principles, or conjectures and employ observation as a means to either substantiate or elucidate those ideas. Thanks to Bacon, so he averred, gone are the days of Aristotelianism, as well as the dubious search for the "philosopher's stone, the perpetual motion, or the abstract essence of any thing; or of looking into the penetralia [*sic*] of Nature's sanctuary" by means of deductive syllogism, disputation, and dialectical reasoning.[81] Campbell not only took Bacon's inductive method to be the proper procedure for investigating the natural world but also thought it was the appropriate method with which to undertake religious inquiry: one's hermeneutics should be governed by the same epistemic norms.[82] Proper biblical interpretation, in Campbell's view, requires that one begin with an acquaintance with, and comparison of, the textual facts—textual facts from which one can make inductions about divine matters. Theological speculation and theorizing beyond the parameters of the observable biblical data is, in Campbell's view, deeply problematic because it is conducive to the same sort of problems generated by Aristotelian syllogistic inquiry in the natural sciences. This view naturally positioned Campbell to harbor a deep suspicion of extrabiblical language, creeds, systems, and theories. For, just as Bacon's "idols of mind" can blind us to proper scientific induction,[83] so too can sectarian creeds and speculative theological commitments impair one's ability to properly understand scripture and hence God's revelation to humanity.[84]

Although Bacon may have provided the methodological norms for Campbell's thinking and the philosophical framework for his hermeneutics, Locke and the Scottish common sense philosophers influenced nearly every other feature of Campbell's epistemology and philosophy of religion.[85] His indebtedness to Locke in particular is not difficult to spot, in keeping with what one might expect of a man who kept the *Essay* close at hand, and Campbell consistently referred to Locke's work throughout nearly all of the fifty years of his publications. In fact, he clearly viewed Locke as *the* philosopher for the Restoration Movement, calling him "*our* Christian philosopher,"[86] to whom, he says, "we are more indebted than any other."[87] In general, Campbell adopted many of the basic contours of Locke's theory of knowledge, including his rejection of the theory of innate ideas, his tabula rasa theory of mind, and his view about the so-called way of ideas. Campbell agreed with Locke that our simple ideas are "furnished to the mind"[88] only by way of sense perception and reflection, a point that Campbell found particularly crucial—in combination with the Lockean and Humean view concerning the limits of the imagination—in formulating his own unique argument for the existence of God. Yet despite all Locke's influence, Campbell did *not* adopt Locke's version of the cosmological argument for God's existence. In short, Campbell took Locke's case for theism to be a virtual abandonment of some of the central tenants of his empiricism, to which Campbell sought to remain faithful. And because Locke was not Lockean enough for Campbell in his argument for God's existence, Campbell tried to take the baton and run the course properly on that track.

Campbell did, however, follow Locke fairly closely in emphasizing the limits of human knowledge as well as the role of divine revelation in matters beyond reason's reach. For Campbell, philosophical reasoning effectively plays a supportive role to revealed theology by showing the shortcoming of many arguments in natural theology and thus the need for divine revelation. Furthermore, he thought that we must examine the historical and philosophical evidence to determine whether the biblical texts are truly divinely revealed and to determine what those purportedly revealed texts mean. And Campbell believed that we should use reason to defend the content of revealed propositions against objections and to underscore the harmony between the biblical texts and the natural sciences.[89] Indeed, Campbell adopted several features of Locke's view on the relationship between faith and reason, and he agreed that revelation may extend beyond or above the scope of reason but that revelation is ultimately never contradictory to it.[90] Consequently, like Locke,

Campbell thought that testing revelation by reason was crucial: before one accepts a claim as divinely revealed, one should have good reason for thinking that it was actually revealed by God in the first place.[91] This conviction led Campbell to view religious enthusiasm and metaphysical/theological speculation with the same sort of antipathy Locke was prone to view them with.[92] And although the role Locke's theory of language plays in Campbell's overall philosophy of religion is not clear, Campbell was clearly influenced by it, and he agreed with Locke that speech was furnished by God.

Whether he consciously adopted them or not, there are several Lockean features to Campbell's theology. He agreed with Locke about the central linchpin claim around which Christians should unify (that Jesus is the Messiah and the son of God), and he agreed with Locke about many other important doctrinal positions, including his emphasis on ordinances such as baptism and communion; his pneumatology; his understanding of the church as a voluntary association; his rejection of apostolic succession; and his rejection of the doctrine of total depravity.[93] Campbell also shared Locke's critical attitude toward clericalism and authority in the church. Extending the sentiment a bit, Campbell seems to have been of the mind that the main problem with the Protestant Reformation was that it had not gone far enough: individual believers still needed to have deep and direct contact with the scriptures for themselves, a connection that was unmediated through the pope (whom he repeatedly christened the "Man of Sin")[94] or his Protestant counterparts. In keeping with his desire to make the Bible even more accessible to laypeople and to render it more easily interpreted in its proper literary context, Campbell actually produced what Locke had only hoped for in the preface to *An Essay for the Understanding of St. Paul's Epistles*: a printing of the Bible made less cumbersome by doing away with the typical "chopp'd and minc'd" chapter and verse indentations. [95]

Campbell clearly read, and held in especially high regard, Locke's *Letters Concerning Toleration*,[96] and this affected not only his views about religious and civil liberty but also his theology.[97] Whereas Locke encouraged agreement on the central soteriological claims of Christianity and forbearance on other points of theological disagreement, Campbell believed that a lack of certainty vis-à-vis inferences about theological issues not directly expressed in scripture provided the space for tolerating a certain degree of doctrinal diversity in the church. This toleration, so Campbell hoped, could aid Christians in uniting around that which is explicitly revealed in the biblical texts. He, in turn, took up the mantra that would come to define the Restoration Movement: unity on essentials, liberty on nonessentials, and charity in all things. Similarly, Campbell's efforts to overthrow unscriptural church authorities, traditions, and creeds so as to restore the church to its original New Testament model seems to have been informed by Locke's theory of justified revolution.[98] Additionally, Campbell's philosophy of education—aimed, as it was, at cultivating the faculties of the student so she can achieve autonomy—is reminiscent of Locke's *Some Thoughts Concerning Education.*[99] And in his role at the Virginia Constitutional Convention, Campbell displayed Locke's influence on his views of social contract theory, rights, and the separation of church and state.

Most likely, the Scottish common sense philosophers were introduced to Campbell during his days as a student under George Jardine (a friend and sympathizer of Thomas Reid) and through a close reading of Reid's popularizer, James Beattie.[100] Although his references to them are less frequent and less overt, the Scottish common sense philosophers were clearly still influential on Campbell's thinking.[101] He explicitly acknowledged his indebtedness to them in his confession "that with many of these opinions I agree as I do with . . . Mr. Reed [*sic*],"[102] and he cited Dugald Stewart affectionately as "the greatest of all metaphysicians."[103] In Campbell's introductory address to the students at Bethany College, he tipped his hand even further by asserting that after "a long and violent controversy between Philosophy and Common Sense, they have at length amicably adjusted their differences, and entered into a solemn league and covenant never to be dissolved."[104] He went on in that address to list the crucial lessons to be learned from the common sense philosophers: we should reason from what we already do know to what we do not know; we should employ the five senses in ascertaining sensible facts; we should regard the testimony of others as veridical unless there is positive reason not to; we should accept that the "internal sense of consciousness will always be regarded as a faithful and competent witness of the mental and moral facts of the inner man"; we should never "build a system" on a priori reasoning; we should never accept something as a law of nature if it has not actually been observed; and we should proportion our beliefs to the evidence.[105]

Although Campbell borrowed many of his philosophical moves from Locke, he seems to have drawn upon the Scottish common sense philosophers in reacting against the skeptical implications that some, like Hume, wanted to draw out of Locke's empiricism.[106] For example, though he nowhere elaborates on this point, Campbell seems to have adopted the Reidian doctrine according to which there is no overwhelming defeater of the "vulgar" or common sense view about sense-perception.[107] Accordingly, Campbell seems to have followed the Reidians (as opposed to Locke) in thinking that we have been fitted by God with certain intellectual powers that, when they are functioning properly, allow us to come into direct contact with real objects in the external world—as opposed to some intermediate thing, namely, the *idea* of an external object.[108] (In similar ways, Campbell thought that it was possible to directly perceive the meaning of biblical texts).[109]

Importantly, following Reid on this point allowed Campbell to circumvent Hume's skepticism (if all we have access to are our ideas, then how can we infer anything about their external-world causes?) and Berkeley's idealism (if all we have access to are our ideas, then why think there is anything else?), both of which Campbell clearly and squarely opposed.

In other ways as well, Campbell seems to have appropriated the general philosophical outlook of the Scottish common sense philosophers. Whereas Reid and Beattie thought that we cannot help but take for granted, or regard as basic, certain principles of common sense (even if we cannot provide arguments for doing so),[110] Campbell tended to appeal to the common mind among the church as a way of discerning what is correct about matters of theology—a modified *vox populi, vox Dei.*[111] And in much the same way that Reid tried to state the first principles in philosophy, Campbell tried to lay down the first principles of Christianity and thereby specify the theological essentials around which there should be unity. Indeed, he thought that insofar as we have good reasons to accept the Bible as containing God's revelation, we should effectively regard revealed truths as axiomatic, "not to be tried by reason, one by one, but to be received as new principles, *from which we are to reason* as from intuitive principles in any human science."[112]

In other, more specific ways, Campbell seems to have betrayed a Reidian influence. Similar to Reid, Campbell held that the will or volition plays something of an active role in the process of sensation—active, that is, in the limited sense of directing one's attention or focus. When it came to his view of memory, Campbell also seems to have sided more with Reid than with Locke. Whereas Locke viewed the memory as being little more than an active power to revive perceptions once entertained in the consciousness, Campbell drew a distinction between the active faculty of recollection on the one hand and the passivity of memory on the other, where the latter was viewed more along the lines of a great marble tablet on which ideas get etched with some permanence.[113] This view of memory naturally inclined Campbell to side more with Reid than with Locke in matters of personal identity.[114] Campbell also seems to have sided with Reid over Locke when it came to his view of freedom and moral responsibility.[115]

Hume's influence on Campbell's thinking is also worth a mention. Even though Campbell opposed Hume on nearly every point at which he engaged him, he did not simply dismiss Hume's criticism of Lockean empiricism, natural theology, or the rationality of belief in miracles. Rather, he was responsive to many of Hume's criticisms, and he tried to adjust some of his own views to be properly concessive to the better angels of Hume's philosophy, despite the fact that Campbell certainly took pleasure in bad-mouthing Hume along the way. (All the same, Campbell thought enough of Hume to visit his gravesite while traveling in Edinburgh.)[116] The dialectical resistance provided by Hume's skepticism was formative in Campbell's thinking, and certainly Hume was his main foe when it came to thinking about miracles, supernatural phenomena that Campbell saw as the primary external evidence that a particular proposition had been revealed by God. When responding to Hume's famous essay on miracles, Campbell took his cues from yet another Scottish common sense philosopher and theologian, George Campbell, whose translations the former saw fit to include in his own compilation of the New Testament.[117]

1.5. The Nature and Outline of This Book

It may be helpful to the reader for me to pause here and briefly outline the remaining chapters of this book and to say a bit more about what this project is—and what it is not. First, this book is not primarily meant to be intellectual history per se, although in some sense it may serve in that capacity. That is, my primary goal in this book is not to spell out any more than I already have the conceptual influences bearing on Campbell's philosophy of religion, the intellectual milieu in which his thinking resides, or the various streams of thought that flowed from his views. Nor does this book emphasize the historical landscape surrounding Campbell's life or how that may have affected the development of his positions. Obviously, such a historical approach can be helpful in teasing out a person's views, but I refrain from that approach in the following chapters, except in those cases where doing otherwise is required for reconstructing and evaluating his philosophical positions. Rather, this book is organized thematically, and it focuses on the arguments and positions in Campbell's thinking; very little attention is given to chronological issues. On another note, this book by no means represents an effort to somehow effusively praise or stand in condemnation of Campbell (as though he is "our hero" or just another religious zealot) any more than his work may seem to deserve. By way of full disclosure, I confess to being a philosopher who identifies with, and has a great deal of respect for, several features of the Stone-Campbell Restoration Movement. Nonetheless, I try to give an honest and straightforward interpretation and assessment of the issues and arguments contained herein.

As for what this project *is*: first and foremost, this book is meant to offer an analysis and assessment of Campbell's philosophical case for Christian theism and its relation to morality. I submit that this analytical and critical approach to reading Campbell—while rarely undertaken—is fairly Campbellite in nature, as Campbell himself was far less concerned about the historical development of a view than whether it was actually correct. What I mean by way of *analysis* and *assessment* is fairly flat-footed: I aim to reconstruct and, in turn, break Campbell's arguments down into their constituent parts, examine the logical structure of his views, and assess whether his arguments can address the most obvious objections a critic might want to throw at them. At the least, I try to determine whether and where there is something worth fighting for in Campbell's arguments. Inevitably, the overall task here involves saying a little something about the general philosophical context in which a particular issue emerges, as well as presenting Campbell's stated (and unstated) positions, the likely objections, and the possible replies. As my primary aim in this book is to provide a critical survey of Campbell's philosophy of religion, I dedicate individual chapters to what I take to be the main themes of it.

In the next chapter, for example, I focus my attention on Campbell's unique argument for the existence of God, an argument about which he has a great deal to say in his famous debate with Robert Owen. While this particular argument—what I call Campbell's *revealed-idea argument*—is in some ways structurally reminiscent of Descartes's so-called trademark argument, Campbell's is nonetheless distinctive, and hence it represents an interesting and fairly novel contribution to the history of natural theology, despite the fact that it remains unconvincing. In presenting Campbell's case, I explain why he rejects Locke's cosmological argument and how this line of criticism leads him to think that his revealed-idea argument (or at least something like it) is sorely needed. I also emphasize the role that this argument plays in Campbell's overall philosophy of religion, particularly in how this argument serves, in his view, as something like a key to unlock other arguments in natural theology. In assessing his revealed-idea argument, I raise the most obvious objections a proponent of this argument would likely face, and I provide some reflections on how Campbell would and, in some cases, *did* respond.

Campbell was by no means satisfied with the prospects of vanilla theism, so he placed especial importance on making a case for his own preferred flavor, namely, that of Christian theism as informed by biblical revelation. For Campbell, the move from theism *simpliciter* to biblical Christianity in particular pivots on a set of historical considerations about the reliability of miracle reports, especially those concerning the resurrection of Jesus of Nazareth. Accordingly, chapter 3 is dedicated to Campbell's views on miracles, and I reconstruct his argument *from* miracles for the truth of Christianity and his argument *for* the miracle of Jesus's resurrection. Of course, Campbell understood that Hume's influential argument against belief in miracles poses a potential defeater to his overall case for Christianity, so I reconstruct Campbell's fourfold response to Hume. While his response to Hume is not exactly unique—he draws fairly explicitly from George Campbell's *Dissertation on Miracles*—it does provide a competent, if not compelling, response to the general worry Hume raises, and it anticipates some of the moves made by contemporary philosophers such as Peter van Inwagen, Richard Swinburne, and J. L. Mackie.

One of the standard arguments for atheism—hence, against Christian theism—stems from a consideration of the evil and suffering in the world. In chapter 4, I examine Campbell's reply to the so-called argument from evil by examining a series of exchanges he had with a young skeptic about suffering and hell. To position this discussion within the proper philosophical context, I consider the two most prominent formulations of the argument from evil—the *logical* and the *evidential* formulations—and I show how Campbell was inclined to respond to them. In my view, Campbell offers a free will defense against the logical formulation of the argument from evil, and he offers the resources for something of a "skeptical theist" response to the evidential formulation of the argument from evil. Although I do not think that Campbell's views on the problem of evil are particularly novel or fully developed, his views gesture in the right direction for the most part, and in some cases, they anticipate the general strategy employed by contemporary philosophers such as Alvin Plantinga, William Alston, Stephen Wykstra, and others. Also in this chapter, I examine Campbell's anticipation of, and response to, what is known these days as the argument from divine hiddenness. My view is that Campbell's discussion of what he calls the "understanding distance" is helpful in getting a sense of why, in his view, some people do not think there is sufficient evidence for believing that God exists.

Chapter 5 represents something of a shift in this book, as I turn my attention away from Campbell's positive and negative apology for Christianity and toward his view about the relationship between morality and religion. Specifically, I try to reconstruct his moral epistemology and his views about the metaphysical grounding of morality. In Campbell's view, all non-revelation-based approaches to moral theory are deeply and inevitably flawed. He believed that humans could not have originally discovered moral truths in the first place without the aid of divine revelation. Although he nowhere carefully or explicitly spells out a divine command theory of ethics, Campbell seems to me to have been nonetheless committed to it on some level, especially given certain features of his moral epistemology. Given his commitment to a divine command theory of right conduct, I take up a discussion of the central philosophical problem facing such a theory of ethics, a problem stemming from what philosophers typically label Euthyphro's Dilemma. Because Campbell offers no direct consideration of this problem, I try to imagine on his behalf how he *could* have replied (or may have *wanted* to have replied or even *would* have replied) to such a problem.

In these chapters, I draw from a variety of Campbell's written works in an effort to piece together and reconstruct his arguments, as well as his replies to various objections. This reconstructive task is necessary because Campbell did not always give a thoroughly systematic presentation of his philosophical views on a given issue—at least, he did not always give one that was conveniently located in a single place. Thus, I had to piece together his take on various issues and even to connect the dots in several places by making some speculative subjunctive guesses. And although one should expect that a thinker's views would change and develop over time, I have generally aspired to interpret Campbell's work nondevelopmentally and as a unified whole—that is, I have aspired to do so as much as possible, and I note those places where this approach is abandoned. To be sure, in some cases it was necessary for me to speculate about Campbell's views a bit more than one might wish. But I have taken the liberty to do this because, in some cases, it was far more interesting and philosophically productive to reconstruct what Campbell may have been trying to say—or even *should* have said—than simply to report what he actually did say. However, in those cases where this approach has proven necessary, I have tried to remain faithful to Campbell's writings, and to the overall spirit of his philosophical outlook, in order to provide the most charitable interpretation of his views allowable by the text.

1.6. Why This Project Matters

It remains for me to say a little something at this point about why the project undertaken in this book matters and why it might be worth reading. There are at least five reasons, some of which will be relevant to professional philosophers who are not terribly familiar with Campbell's work already, and some of which will be relevant to other scholars and nonacademicians who are interested in Campbell because of the important role he played in the American Restoration Movement that emerged during the Second Great Awakening.

First, a common concern is that Americans in general do not know very much about their own religious, philosophical, and intellectual heritage. If that is correct—and I suspect that it may be—then there are some epistemic goods to be had in learning something about one's intellectual forerunners, even those figures who, for whatever reason, have been tucked into the weeds. Growing acquainted with this heritage is more than just simple nostalgia, as it is also about gaining a kind of self-knowledge. Those individuals who turn a blind eye toward their own past run the risk of deliberating in ways that are sullied with misinformation and prejudice. As John Cottingham aptly puts it, "[O]nce we accept the basic psychoanalytic insight that the partly forgotten past colours the significance of what we do today, then if we refuse to scrutinize the past, the risk is that we will lack a proper awareness of the true motivational structure of our present activities, decisions, and projects, and that the resulting distortion may have highly damaging consequences."[118] If Cottingham is right about this, then Santayana's well-recycled epigram is probably apropos: ignorance of our past positions us to repeat it.

A second reason this book might matter is that the received view of a thinker that gets passed down through the years is sometimes inaccurate or incomplete, even if that interpretation is inspiring or useful in some other way. My deep suspicion is that Campbell's philosophical work is no exception here, as it is often altogether unknown, misinterpreted, or incompletely understood. Accordingly, this project is meant to help readers understand the views of this historically important American a little better than we already do.

Third, having a better understanding of Campbell's philosophy of religion should serve to help theologians and religious historians to gain a better overall picture of his theology and hence a better overall view of the important religious movement he helped spark.

A fourth and parallel reason is wrapped up with the simple hope that this book can offer scholars who may be unfamiliar with Campbell's work at least a starting place for understanding the philosophy of one of America's most important and influential antebellum religious figures.

And last, but not least, it may be the case that Campbell's philosophy of religion actually helps shed light on some perennial philosophical questions of great importance to the human condition, particularly for those who are affiliated today with the several traditions of Campbell's Restoration Movement. We stand to learn what his philosophical thinking can contribute, and at the least, we can learn how to avoid the philosophical mistakes Campbell inevitably made. Whether the lesson learned is more by way of the latter or the former is ultimately a matter left for the reader to decide.

Chapter 2

The Revealed-Idea Argument for the Existence of God

Francis Bacon once famously said that "a little philosophy inclineth man's mind to atheism; but depth in philosophy bringeth men's minds about to religion."[1] Alexander Campbell held a similar view. He thought that, done poorly, natural theology can push a person toward atheism, or least skepticism; but done properly, natural theology can point you toward the very thing it stands in need of, namely, supernatural revelation. One of the clearest traces of this view of Campbell's is his unique argument for the existence of God—what I call his *revealed-idea argument*. My primary aim in this chapter is to reconstruct and critically examine that argument. But first I need to set the stage. Campbell's seemingly split attitude toward philosophy—his view that certain sorts of philosophical argumentation about God's existence are pernicious and other sorts are vital—can be confusing. It leads him to decry some sorts of philosophizing about religious matters even while he engages in others, whereupon he can appear hostile to natural theology as a whole. So to see his revealed-idea argument in the proper light, we first have to get clear on what he thinks of natural theology in general.

In this chapter, I start by addressing the common misperception that Campbell was somehow opposed to natural theology (**§2.1**). I then explain why he rejected John Locke's cosmological argument for God's existence, since Campbell's reasons shed light on why he thought we need his revealed-idea argument in the first place, as well as why he thought it serves as a corrective to previous efforts in natural theology (**§2.2**). The next task is to reconstruct Campbell's argument in detail (**§2.3**). I end by considering some of the more obvious objections to the revealed-idea argument and some replies that Campbell could offer (**§2.4**). Although Campbell's argument remains unconvincing, it nonetheless represents an interesting and genuinely novel contribution to natural theology, or so I will argue.

2.1. Was Campbell Opposed to Natural Theology?

The term *natural theology* typically gets defined in contrast to *revealed theology*, where the former is generally seen as a project for philosophers and the latter for theologians. For our purposes, we can think of natural theology as, roughly, the effort to gain warranted beliefs about God's existence (or nonexistence) or about God's attributes (or other divine matters) without recourse to any purportedly revealed sources such as the Bible or the Qur'an. Accordingly, a natural theology argument for God's existence would not contain any premises that rely on the authority of some supernaturally revealed source of information. In contrast, revealed theology places no such methodological constraint on itself. Accordingly, revealed theologians would take themselves to be free to construct theological arguments on the basis of a given religious text. Some theologians—Karl Barth most notably[2]—want to eschew the project of natural theology altogether, insofar as they see it as somehow distasteful, unnecessary, or otherwise problematic.[3] In their view, we need not (and perhaps ought not) try to do anything other than understand, and draw out the implications of, the received divine revelation. By contrast, natural theologians tend to think that revealed theology alone, while perhaps crucial in other respects, simply cannot provide noncircular arguments for the most fundamental claims of religion. Not surprisingly, then, natural theologians typically begin with questions such as, What reasons do we have for thinking that God exists?—and, What reasons do we have for thinking that a purportedly revealed source is actually of supernatural origin? Bearing this distinction between natural and revealed theology in mind, we can now turn our attention to Campbell.

Much of the literature on Campbell can lead readers in the direction of supposing that he had a low opinion of, or was even opposed to, natural theology.[4] And it is easy enough to see why interpreters might be tempted to draw this conclusion. For one thing, this temptation is amplified by the fact that a chief aim of his religious movement was to restore Christianity to the *revealed* model of the New Testament—and to that biblical model exclusively. In addition, Campbell offers ample textual fodder for such a misperception: he is often aggressively critical of natural religionists and their undertakings, and he repeatedly comments on the failure of unaided human reasoning in acquiring knowledge about God. For example, recalling a lecture he gave to a group of religious skeptics at Tammany Hall in 1833, Campbell bemoans the "perfect inadequacy of reason to originate or decide any thing regarding religion," and he says that "reason, however enlightened and cultivated by natural science, [is] altogether incompetent to guide men."[5] He claims elsewhere that "with no other guide but the light of nature," humans are simply incapable of producing even the *idea* of God in the first place.[6] "Nothing astonishes me more," Campbell says, "than the impotency of philosophy in all matters and things pertaining to a spiritual system."[7] Accordingly, in his view, the apologetics of William Paley, Joseph Butler, Thomas Reid, and Dugald Stewart are all "equidistant from the equator of truth," insofar as "the new science[s] of mental and moral philosophy are equally at fault in their attempts to deduce from their own premises a system of natural religion . . . worthy of God or of man."[8] Elsewhere Campbell says that by "the light elicited by our reflections upon the universe, 'without any supernatural aid,' we can 'know absolutely nothing of God and a future state.'"[9] He goes as far to say that "natural religion is a figment of human invention,"[10] and he even calls the skeptics of New Harmony "good philosophers" for remaining agnostic about what we can know of God's existence on the basis of human experience alone.[11] Given passages of this sort, one can certainly understand why some of Campbell's interpreters have been inclined to think that he was generally hostile toward natural theology.

But even if such an interpretation might seem well grounded at first glance, it is inaccurate nonetheless. To see this, one needs to appreciate the distinction Campbell draws in his writings between natural theology and natural religion. Following Henry Lord Brougham, Campbell stresses that the terms *natural theology* and *natural religion* are not synonomous,[12] despite the fact that they are, as he says, "frequently, and rather unceremoniously used as verbal equivalents" by some authors.[13] Admittedly, these two terms can be easily conflated, so getting clear on this distinction will be helpful. Fundamentally, the distinction Campbell has in mind is one of scope. When he refers to natural religion, he seems to have in mind the task of applying the methodological constraints of natural theology to each and every religious inquiry. In other words, in his view, the natural religionist maintains that the *entirety* of one's theology and all of one's religious doctrines ought to be formulated exclusively on the basis of arguments that do not appeal to the authority of any purportedly revealed sources. Accordingly, the natural religionist would refuse to accept—at any level—anything other than human reasoning and the experience of the natural world as an appropriate basis for grounding any feature of one's religious dogma; appeals to revelation would be ruled out entirely. And Campbell is indeed squarely opposed to natural religion, so understood. His opposition is rooted in his view that, sans revelation, our unaided human reason and the limited scope of our sensory experience can tell us far too little about divine matters. For Campbell, revelation is indispensable when it comes to having a complete theology.

However, to be sure, Campbell does not take natural theology and revealed theology to be at odds with one another. Accordingly, he is *not* opposed to what I define above as natural theology, particularly when it comes to the task of offering an argument (with no revealed premises) for the existence of God.[14] In fact, he is committed to the view that a natural theology argument is *needed* in order to justify both the belief in God's existence and the belief that one has a divinely revealed source appropriate for grounding the remainder (and hence the vast majority) of one's theology. Admittedly, Campbell spills a great deal of ink carping about other natural theology arguments for God's existence—but only to the extent that he sees those arguments as flawed, not because he takes natural theology as such to be an inappropriate undertaking.

As it turns out, Campbell thinks that all previous attempts to provide a natural theology argument for God's existence have failed to do what they should. And, importantly, he thinks they have all failed for pretty much the same reason: none of them provides an adequate empirical account of the origination of the *idea* of God employed in the course of the argument on offer; instead, they simply begin with that inadequately explained idea as a given. Consequently, in his view, all previous stabs at natural theology have been misguided from the outset. As we will see later in this chapter, getting clear on how the idea of God originates is the fulcrum on which Campbell's own argument for God's existence pivots. In short, he thinks that there can be no explanation for the origin of our idea of God, short of saying that God himself revealed it to humanity. Accordingly, Campbell's revealed-idea argument is not offered as a reflection on some feature of the natural world per se. Rather, Campbell's argument is meant to be a reflection on a curious combination of two facts about *us*: the fact that we are limited in our ability to perceive supernatural objects or construct ideas about them, and the fact that we nonetheless possess the idea of God. By elimination, then, Campbell thinks that the only possible explanation for the origination of the idea of God is that it was revealed to humanity by God through some sensible means. Whereas traditional a posteriori arguments in natural theology (such as cosmological, teleological, or moral arguments) attempt to draw out implications from our first-order perceptions of the world, Campbell's revealed-idea argument is an attempt to draw out the implications of a second-order observation of sorts—that is, observations about *how we perceive* (and what we *cannot perceive*) when we have our first-order experiences. And whereas traditional arguments typically attempt to reason from something true about the natural world, Campbell's argument tries to draw out the implications of something true about ourselves, namely, that we have certain perceptual and creative limitations, and yet we also have an idea of God. But note that his kind of argument nowhere relies on a premise drawn from a purportedly revealed source. So, contrary to what some of Campbell's interpreters might lead us to think—and contrary to what some of Campbell's own words might even suggest when taken out of context—he does, in fact, offer a natural theology argument for God's existence. Thus, it is safe to say that he was not altogether opposed to natural theology; in fact, he practiced natural theology, though perhaps in atypical ways.

Still, some interpreters may be thrown for a loop by the fact that Campbell's revealed-idea argument is chiefly aimed at grounding *revealed* theology—and that fact might appear to be indicative of some deep-seated hostility toward natural theology. He does comment, for instance, that "as it appears to us, the notion of natural theology as *prerequisite* to the revelation of God . . . robs the Bible of its supreme glory as making God known to us."[15] But, again, Campbell's aim here in the given context is simply to stress the fact that some philosophers mistakenly think that by reflecting on the natural world we can come to have knowledge of God. Accordingly, their *particular* approaches are misguided, not the overall task of doing natural theology. So to drive the point home, we might ask, What would it mean for Campbell's revealed-idea argument to be one of revealed theology, as opposed to natural theology? His argument would need to rely on a premise that could be endorsed only by presupposing the truth of a putatively revealed text. But while Campbell's revealed-idea argument is aimed at justifying the belief in a particular source of divine revelation (namely, that contained in the Bible), the means by which he makes his case does not rely on the authority of a revealed source. Again, a revealed theology argument for God's existence would appeal to a purportedly revealed source as a premise. But, of course, doing that would beg the question all the way down insofar as such an argument would assume the existence of a revealer as a way of supporting the very revealed premise that is supposed to provide warrant for believing in the existence of the revealer—round and round we go. Campbell certainly did not think such an argument could withstand the challenges of atheists, agnostics, skeptics, or deists—challenges that he took himself (and other Christians) to have a duty to address.[16] Accordingly, his revealed-idea argument for God's existence appeals to secular, nonrevealed reasons as a way of arguing that the only way we can explain the origination of our idea of God is through divine revelation. Thus, Campbell's revealed-idea argument is properly interpreted as a natural theology argument for divine revelation—that we are the recipients of revelation and, hence, that there is a revealer. Whatever else it may be—and whether or not it is compelling—Campbell's revealed-idea argument is *not* a circular revealed theology argument for the conclusion that the revealed source has a divine revealer.

2.2. Why Campbell Rejected Locke's Cosmological Argument

As I mention above, Campbell thought that all previous attempts to provide an adequate natural theology argument for God's existence have been unsuccessful. To be sure, his view here can seem somewhat surprising. Given the extent to which Campbell's thinking borrowed from John Locke—and given the esteem in which he held Locke's *Essay*—one might expect that Campbell would at least view Locke's cosmological argument with a bit more optimism. Indeed, one might expect that Campbell's argument for God's existence would even mimic Locke's. Yet although Campbell took several important cues from Locke, it was not in the way of adopting his version of the cosmological argument. In fact, he unequivocally rejected Locke's argument. This is a significant point because Campbell's reasons for doing so give us insight into his general view of traditional natural theology arguments for God's existence and why he, in turn, felt the need to develop his own revealed-idea argument in the first place. Accordingly, it will be helpful to pause here to consider Locke's cosmological argument.

It is probably fair to say that among the array of arguments in the history of natural theology, Locke's cosmological argument is in a race to be among the least discussed by contemporary philosophers of religion.[17] And perhaps this is for good reason. As Nicholas Wolterstorff notes, "[W]hen compared to other variants, and formulations of variants, of the cosmological argument for God's existence, [Locke's] is surely among the weakest, making use at several points of premises whose questionableness Locke's subsequent discussion does nothing to eliminate, and making moves that are either fallacious or dependent upon unstated and dubious premises."[18] With that said, my present aim is neither to assess nor to bolster Locke's argument in light of the objections a critic might raise; nor do I seek here to provide any commentary on the role this argument is meant to play within the broader landscape of Locke's empiricism. Rather, my aim is simply to outline Locke's cosmological argument in order to highlight Campbell's response to it.

Locke thought that we can prove God's existence by means of a demonstrative argument premised on the intuitive knowledge of our own existence. Accordingly, if we simply employ our natural abilities properly, we can come to have knowledge of God's existence with math-like certainty. In book 4 of the *Essay,* Locke contends that because I know that something now exists (if nothing other than that *I* exist)—and because something cannot proceed from nothing—there must have always been some eternally existing being capable of bringing about the existence of something else. Furthermore, this eternal being must contain in itself all the perfections that could exist in anything else produced by it. Thus, Locke concludes, there must be some eternally existing being that is maximally powerful and maximally knowledgeable. And this maximally powerful, maximally knowledgeable, eternal being is, as Aquinas might say, what all men call *God* (though Locke says whether we call it by that name does not really matter).[19] Because this snapshot is a bit too compact to be of much use for our purposes, it will be helpful here to tease out a more detailed analysis of Locke's argument and to supply some of the suppressed premises that are needed for clarity. We can summarize *Locke's cosmological argument* in the following way:

(Lc1) I am certain of my own existence and that I am something as opposed to nothing.

(Lc2) Thus, something presently exists. (Let S_1 stand for this presently existing something.)

(Lc3) A nonentity cannot produce any real being. That is, something cannot be caused by nothing.

(Lc4) Whatever exists is either uncaused or (if it began to exist) caused by something else.

(Lc5) S_1 began to exist.

(Lc6) Thus, S_1 was caused by something else.

(Lc7) S_1 was either caused by some eternally existing and uncaused being, *E*, or it was caused by some other noneternal being, S_2.

(Lc8) If S_1 was caused by S_2, then S_2 must have been caused by either *E* or some other noneternal being, S_3. If S_2 was caused by S_3, then S_3 must have been caused by either *E* or S_4—and so on.

(Lc9) Either some *E* exists and is the first cause of everything else, or there is an infinite regress of causes (such that S_n is caused by S_{n+1}).

(Lc10) If there is an infinite regress of causes, then nothing would presently exist.

(Lc11) Because something presently exists, there is not an infinite regress of causes.

(Lc12) Thus, some *E* exists and is the first cause of everything else that began to exist.

(Lc13) Whatever is caused by something else cannot have more power or knowledge than is contained in what caused it.

(Lc14) The first cause must contain in itself all the power and knowledge that can ever exist.

(Lc15) Thus, there exists some eternally existing and uncaused being that is maximally powerful and maximally knowledgeable.

(Lc16) Thus, God exists.

Campbell was clearly very familiar with Locke's argument above, and he discusses it in his response to a letter to the editor printed in the *Christian Baptist* in 1827. (The author of that letter to the editor—listed only as "A Lover of Just Reasoning"—quotes directly from Locke's *Essay* as a way of supporting his opinion that the "Book of Nature" provides us with a way of knowing that God exists.)[20] While there are many objections that a critic might throw at Locke's argument, Campbell contends in his response to Lover that the argument suffers from one great and fatal error: the main problem, for Campbell, is that Locke proceeds in his argument with the *idea* of an uncaused eternal being in hand before he provides an adequate account of how that idea originates in the first place.[21] As Campbell puts it to Lover, "[Y]ou [the proponent of the Lockean argument] begin to work with the idea [of an uncaused eternal being] in your own mind, and fondly imagine you have acquired it by your reasoning."[22] But instead of starting out with such an idea in mind, Campbell thinks that the first task "should have been to show how a person without such an idea is to originate in his own mind the whole idea of God. You [the proponent of the Lockean argument] suppose him in possession of *a part of the idea* before he begins to reason at all."[23] With reference to the summary of Locke's argument above, Campbell's view here seems to be something like this: at premise Lc4—and, hence, at premises Lc7, Lc8, Lc9, and Lc12—the *idea* of an eternally existing and uncaused causer is made available to the arguer as a possible explanatory hypothesis, even though Locke has not yet provided an adequate empiricist explanation of the origination of that idea. Admittedly, Locke does attempt in the *Essay* to provide an empiricist account of the origination of the idea of God prior to developing his cosmological argument,[24] but Campbell thinks that it fails.

How did we first come to have the idea of an uncaused causer? Following Locke, perhaps we could say that we acquired it or pieced it together in the course of observing, and reasoning about, the usual sequence of events around us.[25] We certainly do observe A-events followed by B-events all the time. No one doubts, for example, that we observe excruciating pain (B-event) consistently on the heels of an unfortunate slip of the hammer (A-event). From there, so the thought goes, we acquired our ordinary ideas of cause and effect. And from those ideas, we then acquired our idea of an *un*caused causer. But in Campbell's view, such an account is deeply problematic because nothing about our empirical observations of the natural world *can* lead us to have an idea of an uncaused causer. Why? Campbell thinks that we simply cannot tease out the idea of an uncaused causer from our observations of the usual sequence of causes and effects around us, precisely because the sequence of causes and effects that we observe contains only *caused* causes—not *uncaused* causes. Along similar lines, in his debate with Robert Owen, Campbell says that some thinkers mistakenly try to "go upon the ladder of effect and cause, up to the first cause; but to reason *a posteriori* on this subject [in that way] is . . . fallacious."[26] Such a move is fallacious, he thinks, because "it is predicated of a *petitio principii* inasmuch as it assumes that the material universe is an *effect* . . . —the very thing to be proved."[27] In other words, Campbell thinks that we would be begging the question if we were to say that we acquired our idea of an uncaused causer by contemplating the universe as a whole as the effect.

To be sure, Campbell's last point above is somewhat unclear. Perhaps his view here can be further explained by means of the following illustration. We would not be begging the question if we were to say that we acquired our ideas of cause and effect from our observations of, say, an ill-swung hammer followed by a bruised thumb. We can legitimately deem the bruised thumb an *effect* because we observe that it invariably follows on the heel of the ill-swung hammer (the cause). Fair enough. But what about when we turn our attention to the universe as a whole—where the universe consists of the sequence of *all* observable causes and effects? If we *could* actually view the whole universe as an effect, then perhaps we could come to have the idea of an uncaused causer that produced the entire sequence of (caused) causes and effects that constitutes the universe as a whole. But do we actually have a vantage point from which to observe the universe as a whole? Clearly we do not. And so we ought not speak of the universe as an effect as though we are able to take a step back to observe its cause. What this means is that we lack any observation of an uncaused causer to which we can trace our idea. "All that the book of nature teaches," Campbell says, "is that every animal and vegetable is dependent on one of its *own* kind for its production."[28] Given that we can observe only *caused* causes, our empirical observations of the world can stimulate in us only ideas of things that are *caused by something else,* and we do not get to the idea of an *uncaused* causer. The same goes for the idea of creation ex nihilo: we nowhere observe that kind of thing, because we observe creation only from *something else*—we do not observe creation from nothing. Accordingly, Campbell asks, "[A]nd when have you seen any thing creating or producing something out of nothing, or forming any thing essentially unlike itself [in the sense of being uncaused]? And if such an object is no where presented you, can you have the image of it[?]!!!"[29]

Ultimately, then, Campbell thinks that Locke does not offer an adequate empiricist account of the origination of the idea of an uncaused causer.[30] And because he lacks an adequate account for how the idea of an eternal, uncaused causer originates, the rest of Locke's cosmological argument puts the cart before the proverbial horse: we first need to explain how the idea in question originated, and this is a task that Locke's empiricism cannot perform without also appealing to divine revelation, so Campbell thinks. So how did the idea of an eternal uncaused causer originate, in Campbell's view? In short, he thinks that this idea must have been divinely revealed by some sensible means precisely because there is no other empiricist way of explaining its origination. Specifically, he thinks that we can find only "*in the bible* the idea of all things being dependent on a Being unlike every other [in the sense of being uncaused], who produces no being like himself . . . and who produces all beings both unlike himself and one another."[31] And if Campbell is correct about that, then Locke's cosmological argument effectively sneaks in through the back door an unexplained idea—hence, a crucial premise—drawn from beyond the proper methodological constraints of natural theology. Accordingly, when one makes use of such an idea whose origin is unaccounted for, Campbell says, "you leap over [the] distance from earth to heaven in your reasoning, or rather, you fledge yourself with the wings of faith."[32] And he thinks the same goes for other traditional arguments in natural theology as well: they too dip their pens in stolen ink insofar as they, like Locke, unknowingly lift the idea of an uncaused causer from a divinely revealed source and then turn around to make use of it in their arguments, as though nothing suspicious had occurred. In a different context, Campbell makes a similar point concerning those thinkers who borrow divine ideas without sufficiently accounting for their origin:

> The first philosophers who presumed to theorize upon this subject, if they demonstrated anything, clearly demonstrated this, that their conclusions were *wiser* than their premises. In other words, that they were in possession of *previous information* upon the subject which they did not derive from reason; and in defiance of the rules of logic, they had more truth in the deductions than in the data which they assumed. They always remind me of a lad at school who had stolen a penknife, and when pushed by his examiners to account for the knife found in his pocket, in answer to the question *How he came by the knife,* answered, that he "*found it growing on a tree.*" As just and logical is the reason given for many of those ideas declared by philosophers to have been derived from their own reasonings [*sic*], but evidently stolen from other sources, either from the volume of Revelation itself or from streams flowing from it.[33]

Effectively, then, Campbell's criticism of Locke's cosmological argument—as well as other traditional arguments for God's existence—boils down to this: Locke makes use of an idea that is still empirically unexplained to the extent that he fails to recognize that the idea was divinely revealed through some sensible means. Hence, so Campbell thinks, the use of such an unexplained idea stands in tension with Locke's idea-empiricism, according to which *all* of our ideas are derived from sensation and reflection and are never innate. Another way of putting the problem here is that, for Campbell, Locke does not go far enough in his own empiricism when he makes use of an idea the origin of which his "way of ideas" does not and cannot provide an adequate account, short of appealing to divine revelation. Accordingly, for Campbell, even Locke's own cosmological argument proves to be insufficiently Lockean in nature.[34] And the problem for Campbell here is not with the Lockean way of ideas per se but with Locke's failure to recognize the revealed origin of the idea of God, and hence with Locke's use of an empirically unexplained idea in an argument aimed at demonstrating the reality of the object of the idea in question. Thus, the long and short of it for Campbell is that some altogether different approach to arguing for God's existence is needed. And he offers his revealed-idea argument to fill this gap.

My interpretation of Campbell on all of this is that he is trying to drive home a point about the *epistemic priority* of accounting for the origination of the idea of God. That is, Campbell thinks that we first need to explain how we acquired the original idea of God before we can ask whether the idea refers to something in reality or before we can offer an argument for God's existence. Once we have the idea of God satisfactorily in play—that is, once we know how the original idea of an eternal, uncaused, omnipotent, omniscient, and omnibenevolent person originates in the first place—then and only then can we start arguing about whether the object of such an idea actually exists. In other words, only *after* we successfully explain the origin of the idea of God can we determine whether traditional natural theology arguments (such as cosmological, teleological, moral, and ontological arguments) are worth their salt. If Campbell is correct about this, then his revealed-idea argument acts as the scaffolding that supports all other attempts to argue for God's existence. Accordingly, it seems to me that Campbell's final evaluation of Locke's cosmological argument might run something like this: perhaps Locke's cosmological argument (or some other traditional argument for God's existence) is actually sound at the end of the day, but we simply cannot know whether it is sound without first explaining the origin of the idea of God. Of course, Campbell thinks that getting clear on the origin of the idea of God actually does the work of demonstrating the existence of God. But we cannot, as good empiricists, truly determine the soundness of *other* arguments for God's existence until *after* we observe the soundness of the revealed-idea argument. Thus, if we assume with Campbell that the revealed-idea argument is sound, then all other arguments for God's existence become *unnecessary*: at best, they provide only additional confirmation of what we already know; at worst, they provide occasions for confusion.

Campbell's point about epistemic priority here seems to undergird his view that once we have the idea of God satisfactorily in play, our reflections on the natural world actually *confirm* God's existence—but the former is needed as a sort of key to unlock the confirmation provided by the latter. Once we see that the idea of God has been revealed to us by God, Campbell says, "[t]he proofs of [God's] existence, become as numerous as the drops of dew from the womb of the morning—as innumerable as the blades of grass produced by the renovation influences of spring; everything within us and everything without, from the nail upon the ends of our fingers, to the sun, moon, and stars, confirm the idea of his existence and adorable excellencies [*sic*]."[35] Elsewhere, Campbell comments that once we have satisfactorily explained the origin of the idea of God and once the proposition that *there is a God* is presented to us by divine revelation, "the universe, with its ten thousand tongues, addressed to the ear of reason, and its ten thousand times ten thousand designs submitted to the eye of reflection, is demonstration clear, full, and overwhelming."[36] And in keeping with this view, Campbell went on to lay out something akin to William Paley's well-rehearsed argument from design.[37] But again, having an adequate account of the origin of the idea of God is a task that must precede the confirmation of God's existence presented to us by the apparent design in the natural world.

Campbell recognizes that some Christians will perhaps inevitably take his view in this matter (about epistemic priority) to stand in conflict with the fact that certain scriptural passages suggest that the *heavens declare* the handiwork of God (Psalm 19) or that the invisible attributes of God are observable *in creation* (Romans 1:20). He responds to those concerns by reiterating his point about the epistemic priority of accounting for the origin of the idea of God. For example, he claims that

> when the proposition that '*God exists,*' or that '*there is a God,*' is offered to the mind—the heavens and the earth, with all their riches and glory, fully and satisfactorily prove it. But we affirm that the universe furnishes us not with both the *proposition* and the *proof*; or, in other words, the heavens and the earth are not the proposition and the proof.... When, indeed, the idea is once suggested [through revelation], the whole universe, in all its dominions, bears witness to the being and perfections of God. Our dogma ... then is, that the Creator himself suggests the proposition [through revelation], and the Universe proves it.[38]

Thus, in Campbell's view, we first need to provide an adequate account for the origination of the idea of God; hence, we need a different approach to arguing for God's existence—one that sufficiently addresses this need.

Of course, critics are right to ask Campbell the following sort of question at this juncture: Why should we think that we must have an adequate account of the origination of the idea of God before we can ask whether that idea refers to something? Typically, we do not need to explain how an idea originates before we can determine whether it has a referent or make use of it in an argument. For example, we do not need to explain how the idea of a unicorn first originated before we ask whether unicorns exist; there is no such worry here about epistemic priority. Why should we think things are any different when it comes to the idea of God? Unfortunately, Campbell does not attempt to justify his view here, so his point about the epistemic priority of explaining the origination of the idea of God seems questionable at best. At any rate, we do not need to determine whether his point about epistemic priority is actually correct to see how it fuels his criticism of Locke's cosmological argument and, in turn, how it motivates him to offer his revealed-idea argument as the corrective alternative to traditional natural theology arguments.

2.3. Campbell's Revealed-Idea Argument for the Existence of God

We can now focus our attention on Campbell's unique argument for the existence of God. Among the handful of scholars who have discussed his argument in any detail, there appears to be no consensus on how to reconstruct it. Nor is there much agreement on how to categorize it or on what its main philosophical influences are. Regarding the latter, some interpreters have suggested (unsurprisingly) that Campbell's argument for God's existence borrows almost everything of substance from Locke,[39] while others have hinted that it smacks of Thomas Reid and the Scottish common sense philosophers.[40] When categorizing the argument, some scholars have labeled it generically as a cosmological argument,[41] and some have suggested that it is a teleological or design argument.[42] One scholar has even christened it a modified ontological argument (though no account was given as to why we might call it that).[43] I submit that Campbell's argument does not fit neatly into any of these categories, particularly the latter. While it can seem sensible enough to think of his argument as a type of causal or cosmological argument, even those labels are less than satisfying because they do nothing to describe the more distinctive and novel features of Campbell's thinking. As noted above, I prefer to call his argument the *revealed-idea argument* because I think such a label probably best describes what Campbell is trying to get at.[44] In short, Campbell argues that we have an *idea* of God, the original acquisition of which we cannot explain except by an appeal to revelation from God himself. In Campbell's view, the original idea of God is not innate, nor do we receive it from sensation or reflection, nor could we have invented it, given the limits of our imagination. By elimination, then, the only possible cause of the original idea is divine revelation. Thus, God exists.

Before launching into a more detailed analysis and critical assessment of his revealed-idea argument, we should take note of how Campbell frames it in his own words. While he offers several variations on this argument throughout his writings, unfortunately he does so with fluctuating degrees of thoroughness and systematicity. Below, I quote the two passages in which Campbell seems to best describe the argument he has in mind. (Because these texts are probably unfamiliar to most contemporary philosophers and theologians, I quote these passages at greater length than propriety would normally allow.) First, in his 1829 debate with Robert Owen, Campbell says,

> Locke, Hume, and all the mental philosophers have agreed upon certain premises. . . . They all agree that all our original ideas are the result of sensation and reflection; that is, that the first senses inform us of the properties of bodies, that our five senses are the only avenues through which ideas of material objects can be derived to us; that we have an intellectual power of comparing these impressions thus derived to us through the media of the senses; and this they call reflection. . . . [B]ut if it be correct that all our simple ideas are the result of sensation and reflection, how can we have any idea, the archetype of which does not exist in nature?
>
> But the question is, whence are the ideas, which we call religious, derived to us? Neither our sensations, impressions, nor their combinations, have ever been able to shadow out an archetype of a God or Creator producing something out of nothing. All our ideas concerning creative power have exclusive reference to changes wrought upon created matter. . . . [T]he idea of changing a shapeless piece of wood into a chair, is easily derived to us—it is simply an idea of a change wrought upon the raw material, that being created to the hand of the maker. But we have an idea of God, of a Creator, a being who has produced the whole material universe by the bare exhibition of physical creative power. This idea, we contend, can have no archetype in nature, because we have never seen anything produced out of nothing. But we have the idea of the existence of this creative power. . . . If we appeal to traditionary [*sic*] or historic evidence, we shall find that all nations had originally some ideas of the existence of a Great First Cause. But

> the difficulty is—how did the idea originate? By what process could it have been engendered? Where was the archetype in nature to suggest (consistently with the analysis of the human nature) the remotest idea of a Creator, or any other idea concerning spiritual things? Locke and Hume admit the almost unbounded power of the imagination. It can abstract, compound, and combine the qualities of objects already known, and thus form new creations *ad infinitum*. But still it borrows all the original qualities from the other faculties of the mind, and from the external senses. Imagination can roam at large upon the properties of animals, and by abstracting from one and adding to another, and thus combining their respective qualities, it creates to itself images unlike anything in nature. Hence the Centaur, the Sphinx, and the Griffin. But our ideas of all the constituents of these creatures of imagination are derived from our senses and reflections. . . . But a man, some say, may imagine the idea of a First Cause, and may originate spiritual ideas. But this is impossible from anything yet known in experience or in philosophy. To form ideas concerning spiritual things, imagination has to travel out of her province. To form the very idea of a God, she must transcend the visible material world. . . . I therefore conceive that it develops upon [the opposing party] . . . to show that we possess those powers which can enable us to reason from sensible material objects up to spiritual, immaterial existences. It behooves him to show that ignorant men, or men in the rudest ages of the world, were competent to invent and establish religion. If it be so that man is destitute of power to create something out of nothing, or to originate the fundamental ideas and terms found in all religions—if he cannot clear up this matter, how can he affirm that all religion is founded upon the ignorance of men?[45]

Campbell offers a slightly different, reductio-style formulation of this argument in an 1835 article entitled "Evidences of the Gospel—No. 1":

> The Christian philosopher . . . interposes his dilemma—"You affirm, Mr. Atheist," says the Christian, "that the *idea* or the *name* of a supreme spiritual intelligence, called GOD, *did not* enter the human mind by supernatural revelation, and that it *could not* enter the human mind by reason; but the idea and the name are now in the human mind. . . . Will you, then, please explain to us how this name *God*, and the idea which it represents, first took possession of the human understanding?"

> "By imagination," promptly responds the Atheist. "Who," replies the Christian philosopher, "is this god IMAGINATION?—in what heaven does he dwell? He can create out of nothing the idea of one supreme spirit! . . . *Imagination,* the god of Atheists, creates the God of Christians! I believe not in this divinity, and will not believe in him, unless he can work one miracle at least. Let him create one new idea, or the model of one new idea, and I will believe in him. But it must be a *new* idea. I cheerfully assign to imagination the honor of being the chief artificer in the magazines of all the fine arts. It combines, compounds, new-modifies, and arranges all the materials found in the chambers of our perceptions, reflections, and memories. But as soon will the architect create the material for the house which he builds, as imagination furnish the materials for its own manufacture. . . . In all its patchwork we see how much it is indebted to the five senses;—that it is only *imitative.* If it could create a God, it certainly could furnish man with at least one new sense. But it has been asked in vain to suggest one original idea, and to try its strength in giving a name to a sixth sense. . . ."
>
> The Christian has two sources of original ideas; the unbeliever has but one. The Book of Nature and the Book of Revelation furnish the Christian with all his original simple conceptions. For the Book of Nature he is furnished with five senses. . . . His reflections on the objects of sense, and the impression these objects make on him, furnish him with ideas compound and multiform; but every idea properly original and purely simple, is a *discovery.* Its model, or that which excites or originates it, is found in the volume of Nature, or in the volume of Revelation. Sense fits him for the one, and faith for the other. Every supernatural idea found in the world, as well as the proper term which represents it, is directly or indirectly derived from the Bible. . . . [T]he Apostle Paul sanctions these conclusions by affirming that it is "by *faith* we understand that the universe was made by God"—and that "he that comes to God must *believe that he exists;*" for the world by wisdom did not know God.[46]

With these representative passages in view, we can now tease out a more formal summary of the argument Campbell seems to have in mind. To the extent that my goal is to interpret his argument in a way that invites the least amount of philosophical controversy, I take some liberties below in making explicit what I think are some important but suppressed premises in his thinking. Following this analysis, I provide a brief explanation of each of the premises and why Campbell sees fit (or would see fit) to endorse them. Although there are probably other useful ways of presenting *Campbell's revealed-idea argument,* the following reconstruction captures its basic logical structure.

(R1) Throughout history, people have possessed an idea of an immaterial, supremely intelligent, maximally powerful, uncaused creator-spirit called God. (Let *IG* stand for the *idea* of God.)

(R2) Whatever begins to exist within time has a cause.

(R3) The original *IG* began to exist within time.

(R4) The original *IG* has a cause.

(R5) The only possible causes of the original *IG* are the following:

[a] *IG* was innate;

[b] *IG* was acquired by directly perceiving the object of *IG* through sensation;

[c] *IG* was constructed through a combination of reflections and sensations;

[d] *IG* was invented in the imagination, either wholesale or in part; or

[e] *IG* was revealed by some source capable of revealing such an idea to humans.

(R6) The original *IG* was not innate, because the blank slate theory is true and all of our ideas are derived of sensation and reflection.

(R7) The original *IG* was not acquired by directly perceiving the object of *IG* through sensation, because such an object (were it to exist) would be beyond the grasp of our five senses.

(R8) The original *IG* was not constructed through a combination of reflections and sensations because either [a] reflection is constrained to operations on content provided to it by sensation or [b] reflections on internal operations of our minds (in combination with the sensations of external objects) cannot produce the constituent properties of *IG*.

(R9) The original *IG* was not invented in the imagination (either wholesale or in part), because the imagination is constrained to operations on content provided to it by sensation and reflection.

(R10) Thus, by elimination, the original *IG* must have been revealed by some source capable of revealing such an idea.

(R11) The only thing capable of revealing *IG* is something that possesses at least as much reality as *IG* represents God as having.

(R12) God revealed the original *IG* (through some sensible means).

(R13) Therefore, God exists.

I turn now to a consideration of Campbell's reasons for endorsing each of these premises.

Premise R1: Throughout history, people have possessed IG. Campbell's view here is fairly flat-footed and uncontroversial. In nearly every cultural context throughout history, there have been individuals who have possessed *IG*, or at least some variation of it.[47] Similarly, there have been those who have held other ideas that Campbell takes to be somehow derivative of *IG*, namely, ideas of spiritual entities beyond the observable natural world such as angels, demons, heaven, hell, and so forth. The claim made in premise R1 is merely that *IG* is and has been held, even if the individuals holding it do not think the object of *IG* actually exists. (As for those who do not possess *IG*, they, too, can come to hold it once it is explained to them.)

Premise R2: Whatever begins to exist within time has a cause. This premise is a fairly modest formulation of the so-called causal principle, and it plays an important role in getting Campbell's argument up and rolling. Obviously, if there were absolutely no reason to think that the original *IG* has a cause, then there would be no need for Campbell to identify that cause. So why should we think that the original *IG* has a cause in the first place? For Campbell, the thought here seems to be that we can know that the original *IG* has a cause because it began to exist within time, and whatever begins to exist within time has a cause. So the causal principle in premise R2 effectively stages the rest of the argument.

Although Campbell nowhere discusses any formulation of the causal principle in much detail, he clearly endorses some variation of it. Campbell says, for example, that one may correctly assert that "every effect supposes a cause," and he offers three reasons for thinking this. First, he thinks such a proposition is self-evident because "as soon as [it is] exhibited in words which be understood, the mind assents to [it]."[48] Second, he thinks that such a proposition functions as an "axiom" in rational thinking.[49] And third, Campbell seems to think that our experience continually leads us to affirm such a proposition. He says, for example, that "we have never seen anything produced out of nothing."[50] Rather, every time we have observed something being produced in times past, we have also observed (or could have observed) that there was something else that produced it. That is, the observed effect was always preceded by a cause. So, in general, our experience suggests to us that when something begins to exist, it does so because of *something else*—as opposed to coming about from nothing. Accordingly, given repeated observations of the world around us, we can infer through inductive generalization that whatever begins to exist within time has a cause.

To be sure, Campbell does not explicitly assert or defend the *specific* formulation of the causal principle I attribute to him in premise R2 above. Nevertheless, I think we can and should read him as endorsing it, because his argument relies on at least some variation of the causal principle, and the specific formulation offered in premise R2 is relatively modest and hence invites fewer objections than do more expansive formulations. In other words, the most charitable way of interpreting Campbell is to attribute premise R2 to him. It is worth noting here what premise R2 is *not* saying. Claiming that *whatever begins to exist within time has a cause* is not equivalent to claiming that *everything that exists has a cause.* I take it that Campbell is committed at the end of the day only to the more modest claim that whatever *begins* to exist within time has a cause. Consequently, he is not committed to saying that something that did not begin to exist within time (like, say, God) has a cause. Nor does Campbell appear to be committed to saying (perhaps with someone such as William Lane Craig)[51] that whatever begins *with or within time* has a cause. Generally speaking, the more expansive *with or within time* formulation of the causal principle invites objections from those who think that uncaused origination of the universe is possible.[52] But because Campbell's argument need not rely on anything more expansive than the claim that whatever begins to exist *within* time has a cause, it seems both charitable and appropriate for us to avoid wording his causal principle in a way that invites unnecessary concerns—even if those concerns can be adequately addressed.[53] I take Campbell to have no commitment to these more expansive formulations of the causal principle (for example, that *everything* that exists has a cause or that whatever begins to exist *with or within* time has a cause) because, as a would-be Lockean empiricist, Campbell would probably want to avoid saying that our experience or intuitions tell us anything about those things that did not begin to exist or about those things that began to exist *with* time. (I return to a consideration of the causal principle in the next section.)

Premises R3–R4: The original IG began to exist within time, and it has a cause. Campbell is clearly committed to saying that the original *IG* began to exist within time and thus that it has a cause. There are only two possibilities here: either the person who first possessed *IG* did so because it was innate in her mind, or she acquired it sometime after birth through some other means. If the former is true, then the original *IG* began to exist at that moment *she* began to exist. If the latter is true, then the original *IG* began to exist at some point thereafter. In either case, the original *IG* is something that *began* to exist within time. The only other option is that the original *IG* somehow existed prior to any mind. For Campbell, though, there could be no such thing as a free-floating, mind-independent idea—

that is, there could be no idea that was not possessed by some mind. He describes ideas as being "images" on the "glass" of a mind.[54] The implication of this view is that if there were no minds to possess the ideas, then there could be no ideas. If Campbell's view here is correct, then the original *IG* could not have existed prior to there being some mind to entertain it. Accordingly, Campbell would reject the claim that the original *IG* somehow existed before there was a mind to possess it.

One might be tempted at this juncture to think that the same tradition responsible for transmitting our *present IG* to us is also itself the cause of the *original IG*: over time, *IG* simply evolved piecemeal in the very same tradition that eventually passed it down to us. But positing that still leaves unanswered the question of how the original *IG* crystallized in the course of tradition. Did people somehow piece together *IG* by combining this or that constituent part of *IG*? If so, how did they acquire those constituent parts of *IG*? Sensation and reflection? Imagination? Those are the very same possibilities considered in premise R5, which is discussed below.

Alternatively, one might be tempted to think that the tradition of passing down *IG* spans indefinitely back within time; consequently, pointing to the tradition would provide a complete history of the original *IG*. But whatever one's preferred view about the eternality of the universe may be, no one thinks that human minds (capable of possessing ideas) have existed from eternity past. That is, even if the universe as a whole is eternal and did not *begin* to exist, all would agree that *human minds* began to exist at some finite point in the past. And if that is true, then it follows that the original *IG* (as well as the tradition that passes it down) began to exist within time and has a cause.

Premise R5: The only possible causes of the original IG are that [a] IG was innate; [b] IG was acquired by directly perceiving the object of IG through sensation; [c] IG was constructed through reflections and sensations; [d] IG was invented in the imagination; or [e] IG was revealed by some source capable of revealing such an idea. The list of possible causes given in this premise is meant to be exhaustive, and Campbell clearly thinks that this list covers all the relevant bases. Obviously, if this list is *not* exhaustive, then his argument falls flat on its face. So, because his argument proceeds by way of elimination, Campbell needs to be sure that there is not some sixth (or seventh) option. But to Campbell's credit, it is indeed difficult to imagine what other radically distinct options there might be. What other possible causes of the original *IG* might there be?

One might be tempted at this juncture to say that the existence of the original *IG* is just a brute, unexplained, and unexplainable fact. Adapting what Bertrand Russell says about the universe as whole,[55] one might say that the original *IG* was *just there* (either in whole or in part) in the tradition responsible for passing it down to the present—and no explanation of its origination is required or even possible. Of course, the problem with this brute fact hypothesis is that if human minds began to exist, then so did the tradition of passing *IG* down to succeeding generations. And if that is true, then the tradition as a whole has a cause if premise R2 is correct. And if the tradition containing *IG* has a cause, then so does the original *IG* embedded in that tradition. Still, those wishing to assert the brute fact hypothesis might just wish to bite the bullet and deny the claim that whatever begins to exist within time has a cause. In this case, the brute fact hypothesis about the original *IG* would serve as an objection to both premise R2 and premise R5. (And, as mentioned above, I return to a consideration of the causal principle in the following section.)

Alternatively, one might be tempted to think that the original *IG* exists necessarily, and that it somehow floats freely among the heavenly ether of Platonic forms (even if there is no mind around to possess it). But such an account would indeed seem far-fetched, and it introduces an explanatory fifth wheel, namely, something like the view that ideas are necessary, eternally existing entities that can exist even without a mind to possess them. Clearly, Campbell's view about what ideas are—the view that ideas are images before the glass of the mind—commits him to rejecting such an account.

Premise R6: The original IG was not innate. It is safe to say that Campbell follows Locke in thinking that we have no innate ideas and that, alternatively, all of our simple ideas about the material world are derived of sensation and reflection.[56] Accordingly, if there are no innate ideas in the first place, then the original *IG* could not have been innate. Concerning his rejection of innatism, Campbell unfortunately offers no explicit argument or elaboration of his own. Rather, he seems perfectly satisfied to cite the "well established article in the catholic faith of all mental and moral philosophers"—a clear reference to Locke's rejection of innatism in book 1 of the *Essay*.[57] Campbell simply asserts that the mind is born a "*cart[e] blanche*"[58]—an obvious reference to Locke's blank slate theory of mind. Given just how much Campbell relies on Locke to support premise R6, it might be helpful to pause here and briefly recall Locke's treatment of innatism.

In short, Locke offers a series of challenges to proponents of innatism, and ultimately he posits a better explanation for how we acquire our ideas.[59] Why, Locke asks, would we think that certain of our ideas are innate? That is, what evidence can we marshal in support of the theory of innate ideas? If a proponent of innatism attempts to answer this question by claiming that certain of our ideas appear to enjoy universal assent, Locke responds by saying that there is no such universal assent in the first place. After all, he says, children and "idiots" do not seem to be aware of the most obvious candidate for universal assent (namely, the idea that *what is is, and it is impossible for the same thing to be and not to be*).[60] But what if a proponent of innatism says that her theory is supported by the fact that there are certain ideas to which everyone would come to assent, if only they used their reason properly when the idea was proposed to them? Locke responds to this kind of move by pointing out that such a criterion for discovering innateness would imply that nearly *every* idea should count as innate, including complicated scientific theories. So that move will not work either. Of course, Locke also thinks that even if there were universal assent to an idea, that agreement alone would not entail that the idea in question is actually innate, because universal assent could have come about by some other means. Ultimately, given that innatism is unwarranted, Locke proposes a straightforward and much less mysterious way of accounting for our ideas: our minds start out as blank slates upon which ideas get etched. And our ideas are derived of sensations from external objects and reflections on the internal operations of one's mind. Campbell clearly accepts this Lockean account, and he regards innatism as only so much unwarranted metaphysical speculation.

In Campbell's view, the five senses are the sole avenues through which simple ideas about the material world come before the mind.[61] Accordingly, if a man were blind, he would have no access to ideas of colors; if a woman were deaf, she would have no idea of sounds. A blind man might *hear* someone describe the color of the Pacific, but without sight, he could not acquire the idea of the ocean's color. Alternatively, a deaf woman might *see* someone's fingernails scrape across the chalkboard, but she would have no idea of the horrible sound it makes. Such reasoning leads Campbell to conclude that "a man born without any one of these senses, must [for]ever remain destitute of all ideas derivable through it; that a man born deaf, dumb, blind, and without tactibility, has all these avenues to intelligence closed up, and must therefore remain an idiot all his lifetime."[62] Thus, prior to any sensation or reflection, a person could have no ideas before the mind—the slate would simply be blank, so to speak.

It is worth noting here that Premise R6 is what most plainly distinguishes Campbell's revealed-idea argument from Descartes's famous trademark argument in the Third Meditation. To be sure, Campbell's argument appears to mimic some of the basic moves of Descartes's.[63] Recall that Descartes argues something like the following: I have an idea of a perfect being, and hence I have an idea of God; I do not possess all the perfections that my idea of God represents God as having, nor do angels and other corporeal objects; and because every idea must have a first and principal cause that possesses at least as much reality as the idea represents its object as having, the first and principal cause of my idea of God must be God.[64] Now, one might be tempted to think that Campbell's revealed-idea argument is little more than a twist on Descartes's trademark argument, given the obvious resemblances between the two. (And because Campbell was clearly familiar with Descartes's *Meditations*, one might be equally tempted to think that the former simply borrowed from the latter.)[65] But I think we should be careful to note the important role that Campbell's Lockean idea-empiricism plays in his revealed-idea argument, and we should not downplay the extent to which he thinks that the original *IG* could not be innate. Descartes maintains that the idea of God *is* innate in us—it is the "mark of the craftsman stamped upon his work," he says[66]—and that innateness explains how the meditator first *acquired IG* about which he then meditates. As an idea-empiricist, Campbell wholeheartedly rejects the possibility that *IG* was innate, and he thinks it is necessary that we offer an empiricism-compatible explanation of how *IG* first originated in the human mind. Admittedly, both Descartes and Campbell think God is the ultimate source of our original *IG*, but they differ in how they explain the mechanism by which humans *acquire* the original *IG*: Descartes takes this idea to be innate; Campbell takes *IG* to be revealed by God through some sensible means, namely the Bible.

Premise R7: The original IG was not acquired by directly perceiving the object of IG through sensation. This premise emerges directly from Campbell's view concerning how we acquire our ideas of external objects. We must rely on our five senses to acquire simple ideas of external objects. But in Campbell's view, our five senses do not give us access to anything beyond the grasp of sight, sound, touch, smell, and taste. And given what the object of *IG* is supposed to be like (were it to exist), we simply have no means by which we could directly perceive God in sensation. Not surprisingly, then, Campbell's view is that if there is a realm of spiritual entities, that realm is one "of which these five worlds [of our senses] do not afford an archetype, or sensation, or perception."[67] And given the limited nature of our five senses, "no window or door has been opened to us in the department of sense" through which we could access that spiritual realm.[68] So how did we acquire our *IG* or our ideas of other spiritual entities? Campbell says that it was "not by eye, the ear, nor taste [etc.]; for these are our corporeal senses, and [they] cannot take cognizance of spiritual existences."[69] Thus, in his view, the original *IG* was not acquired by directly perceiving the object of *IG* in sensation. (I return to a critical assessment of this premise in the next section.)

Premise R8: The original IG was not constructed through a combination of reflections and sensations because either [a] reflection is constrained to operations on content provided to it by sensation or [b] reflections on internal operations of our minds (in combination with the sensations of external objects) cannot

produce the constituent properties of IG. Admittedly, the wording of this premise is not terribly lucid, but I word it this way to account for the ambiguity in Campbell's language about the faculty of reflection. Unfortunately, his description of reflection is not as careful as it could be, and as a result, it is a bit confusing. In some places, he describes reflection as a faculty whose powers are similar to those of the imagination.[70] In other places, he talks about reflection in ways that are more in line with how Locke describes it: reflection is the faculty by which we observe the internal operations of our own minds (observations of thinking, doubting, believing, reasoning, and so forth). Hence, premise R8 is worded in a way that can allow it to serve as an interpretative catchall, so to speak. Whichever way one might want to interpret Campbell's use of the term *reflection,* the end result will be the same for his argument. If reflection is supposed to be something akin to the imagination, then we would still be unable to construct *IG* through reflection (so understood), as it is constrained to operating only on what we receive through sensation. (I say more on this in the discussion of premise R9 immediately below.) If reflection is supposed to be something akin to the introspection of the internal operations of our minds, then in that case reflections (plus sensations) will not give us the resources with which to construct the original *IG.* For in Campbell's view, we do not perceive any of the constituent properties of spiritual ideas through either our perceptions of external objects or the observations of the mind's internal operations. We simply do not have available to us the materials out of which to construct the original *IG.*

Premise R9: The original IG was not invented in the imagination. As mentioned immediately above, Campbell thinks that the imagination is incapable of inventing *IG.* Why? In short, he thinks that the imagination has an unbounded functionality of a certain sort, but only within discrete limits. Following both Locke and David Hume,[71] Campbell describes the imagination as having unbounded powers to analyze, abstract, arrange, compound, combine, and "new-modify" all the various simple ideas presented to it by sensation, reflection, and the memory. But, importantly, Campbell thinks that the imagination has "no [utterly] creative power" all its own.[72] That is, the imagination can work only on (and with) the raw materials provided to it by sensation, reflection, and the memory; it cannot by itself create those raw materials from scratch. So, for example, the imagination has the power to abstract certain qualities from the idea of an animal—say, the body of a horse—and combine it with a quality abstracted from the idea of a human being—say, the torso of a man—to make a complex idea of a centaur. Additionally, the imagination has the power to "new-modify" the object represented in this idea of the centaur by picturing it as having a sensible quality—say, green—which is abstracted from the idea of grass. And so on. The important thing for Campbell here is that the imagination is limited to working on (and with) only those simple ideas presented to it by some other gathering-faculty. Naturally, then, he says that "nothing [is] so fantastic as the vagaries of imagination, and yet nothing is more circumscribed."[73] To illustrate the thought he says, "My imagination might picture to me a tree, the roots of which are *iron,* the stem *brass,* the leaves *silver,* and the apples *gold*; but if I had never seen a tree growing in the earth, could I possibly have conceived, in the wildest vagaries of imagination, an idea of this wonderful metallic tree?"[74] Campbell clearly thinks the answer to the question above is "no," as the imagination has to borrow all of its raw materials from sensation and reflection. Thus, given its circumscription, the imagination is unable to invent *IG* wholesale out of thin air: the qualities of the object of *IG* are simply beyond "her province," as they are also beyond the scope of sensation and reflection.[75] Nor, in his view, is the imagination able to create ex nihilo those qualities that, in combination with simple ideas it receives from sensation and reflection, could help piece together *IG*. Consequently, in Campbell's view, the imagination is simply incapable of inventing the original *IG* either wholesale or in part. (This is clearly one of the more controversial premises in the revealed-idea argument, and I return to a critical discussion of it in the following section.)

Premises R10 and R11: By elimination, the original IG was revealed by some source capable of revealing such an idea, and that source must possess at least as much reality as the IG represents God as having. If the original *IG* is not innate and if we cannot acquire that *IG* in sensation or reflection or invent it in the imagination, then for Campbell there is only one option left: the original *IG* was revealed to us (through some sensible means like, say, the Bible) by some source capable of doing so. And although he nowhere explicitly claims that the only thing capable of revealing *IG* would be something that possesses at least as much reality as the *IG* represents God as having, I think Premise R11 in particular is needed to close the loop for Campbell's argument. For without some such premise, we would be left wondering why the original *IG* could not have been revealed by some inferior deity, an angel, or even an alien from another planet. And if the original *IG* could have been revealed to us by, say, an angel, then perhaps there is no God after all, but only some inferior spiritual entity capable of revealing *IG*. Accordingly, we would not be able to infer that God exists on the basis of the fact that the original *IG* was revealed. So the question for Campbell is, Why think that the only thing capable of revealing the original *IG* is something that possesses at least as much reality as the *IG* represents God as having? Why would an angel or some other sub-god entity not be capable of revealing *IG* to us? Unfortunately, Campbell offers us very limited resources for answering these kinds of questions, despite the fact that his argument relies on this assumption to get us to the existence of God. I suspect that Campbell either consciously or unconsciously takes his audience to be on board with the principle of causal adequacy, according to which the cause of an idea must have at least as much reality as the object of that idea is represented as having.[76] And unless we accept something like this principle, we have no reason to infer that God exists from the fact that *IG* was revealed. So, given that Campbell says very little about this, I can only speculate about how Campbell might respond to critics.

Perhaps the thought here would (should?) be something like the following. Imagine that *IG* was revealed to the first holder of it by some sort of sub-god spiritual entity. (Let *Z* stand for this sub-god entity.) If *Z* revealed the original *IG*, then *Z* must have first acquired *IG* at some point in order to be able to pass it along to us (assuming entities like *Z* do not have innate ideas). So how did *Z* get *IG*? From some prior *Z*? From a direct perception of God? From invention? Obviously, we are off to the races again, and the problem of accounting for the origination of *Z*'s *IG* is now before us. I suspect that Campbell would need to say that *Z*, like humans, would be unable to invent *IG* or acquire it through sensation and reflection—and that *Z* has no innate ideas either. But there are difficult questions for Campbell here: Does *Z* have *no* innate ideas? Would *Z*, in fact, be unable to perceive God directly, given what *Z* is like? Would *Z*, in fact, be unable to invent *IG*, even if God did not exist? If the answer to any of these questions is "no," then there is going to be a problem for premise R11 of Campbell's argument. In any case, we would need to know a lot more about *Z* than we do, and Campbell would clearly want to deny that we can know anything about *Z*-like things in the first place.

Premise R12 and Conclusion R13: God revealed the original IG; therefore, God exists. If all of the premises up to this point are true, then premise R12 follows. Does the conclusion at line R13 follow from premise R12? Campbell clearly thinks so. One might wonder why the fact that God once revealed (and hence caused) the original *IG* implies that God *now* exists. Campbell's move here would need to be this: If God ever existed at some finite point in the past, then he must exist now. Why? Because our *IG* represents God as eternal.

2.4. Objections and Replies

Given how many different components are involved in Campbell's revealed-idea argument, I do not think anyone will (or should) be surprised by the number of objections it will occasion. Unfortunately, I cannot here canvass all of the possible objections a proponent of this argument would likely need to address. Accordingly, I limit myself to those that strike me as the most obvious and potentially devastating objections to Campbell's revealed-idea argument.

Objection 1: The causal principle is unwarranted. Recall that Campbell relies on something like the causal principle (as expressed in premise R2 above) to motivate the rest of his argument. Yet, arguments that rely on causal principles are not uncommonly greeted with a measure of suspicion by some philosophers, and perhaps rightly so. Why should we think the causal principle (and specifically the one given in premise R2) is actually true in the first place? Why should we think that the nature of reality is such that whatever begins to exist within time has a cause? While it can certainly seem odd to talk about uncaused origination, doing so does not appear to involve us in any contradiction straightaway. So, for example, while it seems odd to say that a kangaroo could just pop into being uncaused, precisely why such an occurrence is supposed to be *logically* impossible is not clear. Consequently, critics will want to hear more on why we should think it is true that *whatever begins to exist within time has a cause*. As I mention above in my brief explanation of premise R2, I take it that Campbell thinks that something like the causal principle is self-evident, axiomatic, and supported by inductive generalization. But is the causal principle in premise R2 actually self-evident? Is it supported by inductive generalization? Is it axiomatic?

Some philosophers will no doubt contend that the claim that *whatever begins to exist within time has a cause* is not actually self-evident.[77] If it were self-evident, as Campbell seems to think, then anyone who sufficiently understands this principle would find it to be true. For example, the claim that *something that is black all over cannot be white all over* seems to be self-evident; as soon as we understand the claim, we see that it is true and that it cannot be false. But some philosophers perfectly well understand the causal principle in premise R2 and nonetheless say that they do not see why the principle is supposed to be true—and some may even think that it is false. If that is the case, then, if Campbell maintains that premise R2 is self-evident, then his argument is going to court more controversy than he may be able to countenance.

Is the claim that *whatever begins to exist within time has a cause* supported by inductive generalization? Recall that Campbell thinks that every single time we have observed something that began to exist within time, we have also observed (or could have observed) a cause. Moreover, we have not experienced something that began to exist within time that did *not* have a cause. From those past observations, Campbell might say, we can infer that *whatever* begins to exist within time has a cause. In other words, Campbell might say that we can offer an enumerative induction of the following sort: All observed things-that-begin-to-exist-within-time have had a cause; therefore, *whatever* begins to exist within time has a cause. To be sure, an enumerative induction that has no obvious counterexamples is a good thing, and it certainly offers us good reason for placing bets on the conclusion. But the problem is that the observation at hand does not entail the *necessity* of the conclusion—that is, we could be correct in our observations about past experiences and the conclusion could prove to be false at the end of the day. That means that an inductive generalization would not justify the stronger claim that whatever begins to exist within time *must* have a cause, but only the weaker claim that whatever begins to exist within time *probably* has a cause. And that means Campbell's appeal to inductive generalization as a way of supporting premise R2 would not get him everything he needs. Accordingly, if we rework the formulation of the causal principle in premise R2 to reflect the fact that we are limiting ourselves to making assertions about only that for which we have inductive evidence, then premise R2 would need to be replaced by

(R2*) Whatever begins to exist within time *probably* has a cause.

Note what premise R2* is *not* saying: it is not equivalent to the stronger claim that something that begins to exist within time *cannot be* or is *never* uncaused. Campbell would not, I think, take himself to have had observations of the respective *nevers* and *cannots* that would be needed to support such stronger claims empirically. (Perhaps we will experience something coming to exist uncaused from nothing one day in the future—who knows?) Campbell's empirical claim is merely that we have not seen that yet—and not that we *cannot* or *never will.*

The problem is that if we accept the wording of premise R2* in place of premise R2 above, then we would also have to rework (among other things) premise R4 to read something like

(R4*) The original IG *probably* has a cause.

And if we make that change, then there will be a domino effect such that, mutatis mutandis, Campbell's argument (were it sound) would imply only the following conditional conclusion:

(R13*) If the original IG is not uncaused, then God exists.

Whether this more modest conclusion would be acceptable for Campbell at the end of the day, I do not know. However, I suspect that this conclusion would be a bit of a disappointment for a man who seems to think that we can know with certainty that God exists.[78]

Is there a way Campbell can avoid having to reformulate premise R2? Perhaps he means to say that the undiluted causal principle (whatever begins to exist within time *must* have a cause) is an axiom of rationality. In other words, we might read Campbell as saying that the undiluted premise R2 is something that all rational agents must *presuppose* whether they want to or not and whether they can produce reasons for doing so or not. In short, the thought here would be that rational agents must presuppose premise R2 in order to make any sense of the world around them.[79] And if premise R2 is an axiomatic presupposition of this sort, then *that* is reason enough to think premise R2 is true.

Of course, difficulties remain. It is indeed difficult to see—even if this causal principle is an axiomatic presupposition—how that fact alone entails the *truth* of premise R2. Even if we provisionally grant that premise R2 is an axiomatic presupposition, critics will argue that that only shows there is no way for us not to *believe* it to be true—and that fact alone does not show that premise R2 is itself actually true. After all, why should we think that our axiomatic presuppositions tell us anything about what reality is like? With William Rowe (and others), critics might contend that "nature is not bound to satisfy our presuppositions."[80] And if that is correct, the fact that we must presuppose premise R2 does nothing to entail that reality is such that whatever begins to exist within time has a cause.

My inclination is to think that Rowe and others are probably correct in pushing this point. Campbell's only recourse here may be to take a cue from the Scottish common sense philosophers and add something of a twist. Perhaps he could argue something like the following: if it is true that all rational agents cannot help but believe *p*—even if they cannot offer great reasons for the truth of *p*—then we should take *that* fact about rational agents as being somehow indicative of the truth of *p*. Accordingly, Campbell might argue that, contra Rowe, our axiomatic presuppositions do indeed tell us something about the nature of reality and hence about what is true. If—and this may be a very big if—Campbell could make good on this last claim, then perhaps the worries surrounding premise R2 could be put at bay.

Objection 2: We might be able to experience God directly. Recall that premise R7 claims that the original *IG* was not acquired by directly perceiving the object of *IG* in sensation, because such an entity (were it to exist) would be beyond the grasp of our five senses. But here critics might ask Campbell, What about the possibility of directly experiencing the object of *IG* by means of some super-sense-perceptual capacity? Whereas sense perception is our primary mode of accessing physical objects in the natural world, perhaps there is some other primary mode of accessing spiritual entities. And perhaps that mode is the mode through which one could directly experience God and hence acquire the original *IG*.[81]

Although Campbell does not directly take up a consideration of this possibility, it seems fairly clear to me that he would simply reassert his appropriation of the Lockean way of ideas and deny that we possess any such super-sense-perceptual capacities in the first place. On several occasions, he explicitly says that we cannot even imagine what a sixth sense (of any sort) would be like.[82] If it is true that the only means by which we can come to have our ideas of external objects is through the five senses, then of course we would be unable to directly experience spiritual entities such as God. Still, it would be nice to have some explanation from Campbell here as to why we should be confident in asserting the antecedent of the conditional immediately above. I suspect that Campbell's general antipathy toward mysticism and religious "enthusiasm" probably causes him to overreach just a bit here.

Why does Campbell rule out the possibility of directly experiencing God? Frankly, it seems to me that he does not really need to. After all, if it were admitted that someone *could* have direct experience of God, then that would provide an additional causal account for the origination of *IG*, thereby leaving us with the same conclusion of Campbell's revealed-idea argument—or at least something pretty close to that. (Admittedly, though, allowing for this possibility would problematize the elimination feature of Campbell's argument.) Perhaps prior to mankind's fall from Eden, humans had the capacity to experience God directly. Or perhaps humans were once able to experience God directly through one of their five senses. Interestingly, Campbell seems to toy with these possibilities when he says, "That man was, in his first estate, designed to *converse familiarly* with his creator, the scriptures teach us; and not until he became a transgressor was this familiarity interrupted."[83] The thought here (on which he does not elaborate, unfortunately) might be that prior to the Fall, humans had something akin to what Alvin Plantinga and others call a *sensus divinitatis*.[84] Or maybe the way to read Campbell here is that he is suggesting that, pre-Fall, humans had a capacity to hear God's voice audibly at wavelengths we can no longer detect (or some such account). If the first humans "heard" or otherwise experienced God directly, then they could have acquired the original *IG* in that way. Such an acquisition of the original *IG* could have initiated the tradition of passing *IG* down through the generations, thereby providing an adequate causal explanation of our present *IG*. Campbell's task, then, would be to explain why we can rule this possibility out.

Objection 3: We can construct or invent the original IG. If one is at all inclined to accept the basic setup to the revealed-idea argument (that is, premises R1–R5 above), and if one is inclined to accept the basic empiricist features of Campbell's thinking, then it seems to me that the biggest problem facing the revealed-idea argument probably centers on premises R8 and R9—the claim that we are simply incapable of either constructing (through a combination of reflections and sensations) or inventing the original *IG* in the imagination. The pivotal question for Campbell is fairly obvious: Why should we think that our imaginative and reflective powers are incapable of producing the original *IG*? As explained above, Campbell thinks the imagination is limited to operating on those materials provided to it by sensation and reflection. (And, of course, sensation and reflection are, in his view, incapable of yielding the materials needed to construct the original *IG*.) So despite how powerful the imagination (or reflection) may be in some respects, it is impotent in producing the *IG*. Of course, this claim is challenged by several of Campbell's fellow empiricists—in fact, the very same ones whom Campbell follows in thinking that the imagination is constrained to operating only on the raw materials provided to it by sensation and reflection. Hume, for example, claims,

> When we analyse our thoughts or ideas, however compounded or sublime, we always find, that they resolve themselves into such simple ideas as were copied from a precedent feeling or sentiment. Even those ideas, which, at first view, seem the most wide of this origin, are found, upon a nearer scrutiny, to be derived from it. The idea of God, as meaning an infinitely intelligent, wise, and good Being, arises from reflecting on the operations of our own mind, and augmenting, without limit, those qualities of goodness and wisdom.[85]

Locke offers a similar view when he says that

> the complex *ideas* we have both of God, and separate spirits, are made of the simple *ideas* we receive from *reflection, v.g.* having, from what we experience in ourselves, got the *ideas* of existence and duration; of knowledge and power; of pleasure and happiness; and of several other qualities and powers, which it is better to have than to be without; when we would frame an *idea* the most suitable we can to the supreme being, we enlarge every one of these with our *idea* of infinity; and so putting them together, make our complex *idea of God*. For that the mind has such a power of enlarging some of its *ideas,* received from sensation and reflection, has been already showed.[86]

The important point here is that if Locke and Hume are correct, then—contrary to what Campbell thinks—we do in fact receive from reflection and sensation all the materials we need to construct or invent the original *IG*. As I see it, the debate over premises R8 and R9 ultimately comes down to the question of whether sensation and reflection provide the raw materials out of which we could produce *IG*. And unfortunately for Campbell, there is something to the Lockean and Humean view that they do.

Perhaps the following illustration will be helpful. Take Campbell's idea of God and break it down into its constituent parts: immaterial, spirit, supremely intelligent, maximally powerful, uncaused, creator. We can even add some additional ingredients Campbell might have in mind: transcendent, eternal, personal, perfectly good, supremely loving, and worthy of worship. But do we not have some sensations or reflections to which we can trace each of these ingredients, so to speak? I can observe a loving mother, the goodness of my friend, and the awe and esteem associated with having a hero. I can reflect on my own mind and observe the faculty of having beliefs and knowledge. I can observe the power displayed by a climber and the creativity of a painter. And so on. My mind can then abstract these various observed qualities, amplify and combine them, and—alas—I construct my idea of God.[87]

If Campbell is going to stick to his guns and defend the revealed-idea argument, he needs to offer some sort of pushback here in defense of premises R8 and R9. I suspect that he might want to say something like the following: "Perhaps we can acquire ideas of *some* of the constituent properties of *IG* from sensation, reflection, and imagination—but not *all* of them!" That is, perhaps Campbell might concede that we can get the ideas of intelligence, power, creativity, goodness, love, and worthy of worship from sensations and reflection. But, so he might aver, we cannot get the ideas of uncaused, eternal, and transcendent from our sensations and reflection. Accordingly, Campbell might argue, for example, that while we get an idea of duration from reflection upon our own minds, we do not get an idea of duration without beginning or end. And he might similarly argue that while we get an idea of immanence from our experience, we do not get an idea of transcendence. If all of that is true, the most our experience could yield, in Campbell's view, would be a truncated and incomplete idea of a deity—but that is not the original *IG* in question.

Despite his best efforts, though, there will be difficulties remaining for Campbell on this point. Can we not get the ideas of uncaused, eternal, and transcendent through a simple negation of what we do acquire in sensation and reflection? For example, we experience a caused causer; we add a negation sign to it: now we have an idea of a cause that is *not* caused. We experience the duration of something that began to exist; we add a negation sign: now we have the idea of the duration of something that did *not* begin to exist. We experience something immanent; we add a negation sign: now we have the idea of something that is not immanent but transcendent. And it seems like we could also get the idea of *uncaused* by observing things that have no apparent cause, the idea of *eternal* by amplifying our idea of persistence in both directions, and the idea of *transcendent* by reflection on our position with respect to lesser animals, bugs, and so forth. Where is the problem supposed to be? Unfortunately, it will be difficult for Campbell to give us a satisfactory answer here. Consequently, if it is true that we *could* have constructed or invented the original *IG*—and I see no reason why we could not—then Campbell's revealed-idea argument fails.

Objection 4: Campbell's use of the idea of a revealer introduces a regress problem. Recall that Campbell thinks his revealed-idea argument is needed in the first place because, in his view, traditional natural theology arguments for God's existence rely on an unexplained idea of God; hence Campbell's criticism of Locke's cosmological argument. Accordingly, Campbell thinks we need to account for the acquisition of the original *IG before* we can offer an argument for God's existence. As it turns out, accounting for the acquisition of the original *IG,* he thinks, proves the existence of the revealer, God. Now, assume for the moment that the revealed-idea argument can be defended against all the other objections critics might throw at it. Even then we are right to ask, Does Campbell's revealed-idea argument fall prey to the same criticism he levels against Locke's cosmological argument (and other natural theology arguments for God's existence)?

As we have seen, the basic problem with every other argument for God's existence, in his view, is that they employ *IG* without providing an adequate account of its origination. But applying that very same worry to Campbell's argument, we might ask, How did we originally acquire the idea of a *source-capable-of-revealing-ideas-that-we-cannot-acquire-on-our-own,* introduced at premise R5e in the revealed-idea argument? Let *IR* stand for the *idea* of a source-capable-of-revealing-ideas-that-we-cannot-acquire-on-our-own. Is the original *IR* an idea we could have acquired by means of sensation, reflection, or imagination? It seems to me that Campbell needs to be able to say that we *can* acquire *IR* through one of these means. Yet if sensation and reflection (and, in turn, imagination) are impotent in producing the raw materials out of which we could piece together *IG,* then why would those same faculties be capable of producing the constituent properties of *IR,* especially since the object of *IR* is, by definition, beyond our experience? Precisely how Campbell might respond here is not clear. But suppose he were to say that *IR* was itself a revealed idea. What then? If the original *IR* was revealed to us, then either his revealed-idea argument falls prey to the same worry Campbell has about Locke's cosmological argument, or he needs to explain how we can know that the original *IR* was itself revealed. And to know *that* would require a separate argument that employs the use of the idea of a *source-capable-of-revealing-IR*—call that IR_2. How did we get IR_2? Providing an account for the origination of IR_2 will eventually lead us to make use of an idea of a *source-capable-of-revealing-*IR_2—say, IR_3. How did we get IR_3? Obviously, we are off to the races again, and Campbell is facing a fatal regress problem.

2.5. Conclusion

Campbell's revealed-idea argument is indeed an interesting attempt to demonstrate the existence of God, and it certainly complements his aim to ground his religious system on reasons as opposed to mere enthusiasm. But it appears to collapse under the pressure of the objections raised in this chapter. Accordingly, proponents of this argument, if they wish to defend it, have their work cut out for them. Given how many controversial elements are at play, the revealed-idea argument will perhaps inevitably invite a host of potentially fatal objections. Some of those objections are going to deal with matters I do not bother to mention above. Some critics will likely want to challenge Campbell's idea-empiricism, as well as his rejection of innatism. Others might take issue with the causal adequacy principle implied in premise R11. And so on. Ultimately, the fact that there are so many contentious claims involved in the revealed-idea argument is the very feature that makes it an ungainly apology for theism: it simply occasions too many red flags. Unfortunately for Campbell, that argumentative immodesty is what both makes his argument unique and encumbers it in what may be a tar pit of insurmountable difficulties. A better argument for God's existence would be simpler in nature and court fewer objections. Nonetheless, Campbell's revealed-idea argument does bear witness to a keen intellect, and it represents a fairly novel—albeit unconvincing—contribution to the history of natural theology, which is a feat in its own right.

Chapter 3

From Theism to Christian Theism: On the Arguments from, for, and against Miracles

In addition to explaining the origin of the *idea* of God, the revealed-idea argument demonstrated the *existence* of God, or so Campbell believed. But that, for him, was far from enough. He wanted also to show the truth of *Christian* theism in particular. In fact, at times he seems to have been even more opposed to simple deism than to atheism. Deists were particularly distasteful to him because they borrowed from divine revelation only selectively, wanting, for example, to take the idea of God and leave the rest. Yet equally troubling to Campbell in the grand scheme of things were those Christians who, in defense of their most distinctive religious commitments, offered little more than an emotional appeal. He was unwavering in his view that

> all men who believe and preach Christ, should be able to give a reason of the hope which they entertain, *by adducing the evidences of the gospel—not by telling their [emotional] experience,* which will never convince anybody but an enthusiast. . . . Peter never commanded any man to narrate his own feelings as a reason of the hope which he had in the Messiah. No, the best reason of faith is a well authenticated testimony, of confirmed evidences. Our experience may be a consolation to ourselves . . . but the demonstrations which the Spirit has afforded alone can enable man to say that Jesus is Lord.[1]

Not surprisingly, then, Campbell thought that it was vital to carve a path between the incompleteness of deism on the one hand and watery religious enthusiasm on the other. Accordingly, he tried to develop a systematic argument for his Christian views, one that—in combination with his revealed-idea argument—could go all the way down in making the case for the Christian religion. First and foremost,

Campbell emphasized the historical evidence that certain miracles occurred, in particular that Jesus rose from the dead. In his view, this miracle confirms that the basic tenets of biblical Christianity are divinely revealed, hence true.

By the time Campbell had entered the public arena as an apologist in the early nineteenth century, there was heated debate in America about whether reports of miracles are credible, and people who denied their credibility often drew heavily on David Hume's famous essay "Of Miracles." Naturally, then, in making his case, Campbell replied to Hume.

Campbell's case for Christian theism, particularly as it involves his account of miracles, is the focus of this chapter. I begin by reconstructing his argument *from* miracles for the truth of Christianity (§**3.1**), followed by an analysis of his criteriological argument *for* the miracle of Jesus's resurrection (§**3.2**). While these arguments leave us with a number of difficult questions to answer, my chief concern in this chapter centers on whether Hume's argument against belief in miracles somehow undermines Campbell's central case for Christianity. Accordingly, I turn to a discussion of Hume's argument (§**3.3**), and I reconstruct Campbell's fourfold response to it (§**3.4**). As it turns out, several of Campbell's responses to Hume are borrowed from the work of the Scottish common sense philosopher and theologian George Campbell—the same man whose translations Alexander Campbell saw fit to include in his own edition of the New Testament.[2] So in an effort to reconstruct Alexander Campbell's view, I pay special attention to George Campbell's critique of Hume in *A Dissertation on Miracles*. Ultimately, I contend that although his arguments *from* and *for* miracles may be problematic in other respects, Alexander Campbell provides a competent response to those who might think that Hume somehow singularly defeats Campbell's overall case for Christianity.

3.1. Campbell's Argument from Miracles for Christianity

It is one thing to believe that God exists, but of course it is quite another thing to believe that Christianity is true. The latter involves believing not only that God exists but also that Jesus of Nazareth was resurrected from the dead and that he is the Son of God and savior of mankind. In Campbell's view, we can justifiably advance from simple theistic belief to the more encompassing Christian belief by taking into account how certain miracles identify and authenticate God's revelation to humanity. Naturally, then, miracles play a particularly crucial role in Campbell's overall case for the truth of Christian theism. Although his interpreters have generally failed to pay much attention to his views on miracles, Campbell has a good deal to say about them, and appropriately so.[3] To set the stage for this discussion, we should first get a handle on what he takes a miracle to be and what work he thinks a miracle does in confirming the truth of Christianity.

For Campbell, a miracle is equivalent to what he calls a *supernatural fact.*[4] By *fact,* he means (following Francis Bacon) something done or something said. By *supernatural,* Campbell means something above or beyond the natural realm. And by *nature* or the *natural realm,* he means "the usual course" of events or the "established order of things" in the world. Accordingly, a miracle is something done or something said that results from something "above the reach or power of the established connection of things."[5] In other words, a miraculous occurrence results from something exceeding the productive powers in nature, because it cannot be the effect of any law of nature. So, for example, Campbell thinks that it would be miraculous for a man to walk on water or to come back to life after having died, as both occurrences would be beyond the scope of what the usual course of nature can produce. To the extent that a miraculous occurrence exceeds the productive powers found in nature, it must be brought about by some power that is both beyond the natural realm and capable of producing such an occurrence. According to Campbell, the regular course of nature cannot be violated or suspended by something that is itself subject to, or governed by, the laws of nature. Hence, he says, "none but the Author of nature, or a being not a subject of the laws of nature, can either suspend or control any of her laws or arrangements."[6] In sum, then, Campbell sees a miracle as something done or something said that involves a suspension of the laws of nature caused by an intervening supernatural power. And in his view, there are two basic kinds of miracles: *physical* miracles and *intellectual* miracles, with the latter involving the prophetic foretelling of "some complex future event," the awareness of which extends beyond "any human knowledge of the operations of matter or of mind."[7]

Suppose for the sake of discussion that a miracle were to occur. What function would it serve, in Campbell's view? In brief, he follows John Locke in thinking that a miracle confirms the divine origin, and hence the truth, of the claims made by the person who performs (or is involved in the performance of)[8] the miracle in question.[9] The underlying thought for Campbell as for Locke is that because God's power is greater than the powers found in the natural realm, a miraculous event stands out as a clear indication that supernatural power has been unleashed into the natural world. Effectively, then, a miracle serves as a notification of sorts—or a special sort of flare, so to speak—from God. More specifically, Campbell says that a miracle acts as "a *seal* attached to a proposition," a stamp of the divine origin and approval of the proposition on offer.[10] Elsewhere, for example, he says that "a miracle is a display of supernatural power in attestation of some proposition presented by God to man for his acceptance."[11]

But how exactly does a miracle attest that a proposition is on offer from God? It does this in a roundabout way, Campbell thinks, by certifying that the person who utters the proposition is in possession of divine power, hence in possession of a divine revelation to humanity. Again, he follows Locke fairly closely on this point. Recall that Locke says that in order "to know that any revelation is from God, it is necessary to know that *the messenger that delivers it* is sent from God, and that cannot be known but by some credential given him by God himself."[12] Along the same lines, Campbell thinks that miracles act as "signs manual attached to commissions to *authenticate messengers* from God."[13] Accordingly, miracles "prove the possessor [of miraculous power] to be both a good being and a faithful witness" of God's message.[14] In other words, when someone performs a miracle, he effectively brandishes something akin to an official letter of introduction from God, a letter that thereby verifies its holder as a special envoy of God's revelation to humanity. This letter, in turn, confirms both the truth and the significance of the envoy's message. The miracle confirms that the messenger's deliveries are true precisely because it confirms that those deliveries are from God, and—because God does not lie—we can rest assured that *those* deliveries are true. And because of its startling and remarkable nature, the miracle also signals that there is something important being said and that the messenger deserves "special credit to [his] message."[15] Campbell elaborates: "Suppose any one should arise amongst us in the character of a divine messenger, having some communication from Heaven of transcendent importance to the human race: it would not be sufficient that he solemnly affirm his mission: *he must prove it; he must show the hand and seal of Heaven attached to it.* Nothing like omnipotence or divine power so naturally addresses itself to the human understanding through the senses in evidence of inspiration. He performs physical miracles: this satisfies contemporaries, and they report it to posterity."[16] Thus, in Campbell's view, when someone, *S*, performs a miracle while claiming that *p*, we have sufficient reason to think that (1) *S* speaks for God in claiming that *p*; (2) *p* is true because of 1; and, ultimately, (3) *p* deserves our special attention because of 1 and 2.

With all of that in tow, we are now in a position to appreciate how Campbell develops his case for the truth of Christianity by appealing to the miracles purportedly performed by Jesus (as well as those miracles purportedly performed by the apostles and disciples). In short, he thinks that Jesus is the prime example of someone who, because he "controls, violates or suspends any of the laws of physical nature—curing disease by a word, healing the sick, restoring the maimed, raising the dead, or dispossessing demons—gives evidence that he is sustained by the hand of Omnipotence."[17] And insofar as we can know that Jesus was sustained by God's power when he performed these miracles, we can know that he was the special messenger of God's revelation to humanity and, in turn, that his claims about himself are true and worthy of our special attention.

Let me back up and explain this more fully. In Campbell's view, Christianity is founded on three fundamental claims: (a) that Jesus is the Son of God who died for our sins; (b) that he was buried; (c) and that he was resurrected from the dead.[18] If all of these claims are true, then "the whole system of the Christian religion must be true," according to Campbell.[19] Of course, he thinks that there is no difficulty in acknowledging the historicity of Jesus's crucifixion at Calvary or his burial in the tomb of Joseph of Arimathea. Naturally, then, Campbell recognizes that the more contentious and decisively more significant claims are that Jesus miraculously rose from the dead and that he is the Son of God who died for our sins. Campbell again follows Locke in thinking that if it is true that Jesus was resurrected, then such a paradigmatic miracle confirms that Jesus was indeed a special messenger sent from God and, consequently, that the claim he made about himself (particularly about being the Son of God who died for our sins) is a divinely revealed truth.[20] Not surprisingly, then, Campbell is satisfied to rest his entire case for the truth of Christianity on the historicity of the resurrection in particular. He says, for example, "I am brought forward to this most wonderful of all events, *the resurrection of Jesus Christ,* which is . . . the capital item in the apostolic testimony; and the fact on which the whole religion, and hopes of Christianity, depend and terminate. . . . [T]o prove the whole truth and absolute certainty of the Christian religion is to prove the resurrection of Jesus Christ from the dead."[21] In sum, then, Campbell thinks that if it is true that Jesus was miraculously resurrected from the dead, then we have reason to think that *all three* of the fundamental claims upon which the whole of Christianity is founded are true. (We might also add that because the apostles and disciples performed miracles, then *their* claims that Jesus is the Son of God who died for our sins are also divinely revealed; hence, their claims also confirm the truth of Christianity.)[22] And, of course, Campbell thinks that Jesus miraculously rose from the dead, for reasons we will consider in the following section. Thus, so he concludes, Christianity is true.

We can formalize *Campbell's argument **from** miracles for Christianity* in the following way:

(C1) Christianity is founded upon the following three claims:
[a] Jesus is the Son of God who died for our sins,
[b] Jesus was buried, and
[c] Jesus was resurrected from the dead.

(C2) If these three claims (a, b, and c) are true, then the whole of the Christian religion is true.

(C3) Jesus was executed and buried.

(C4) Jesus performed the miracle of being resurrected from the dead.

(C5) If *S* performs a miracle, then *S* is an authentic messenger of God's revelation to humanity.

(C6) If *S* is an authentic messenger of God's revelation to humanity, then *S*'s claims are true.

(C7) Because Jesus performed the miracle of being resurrected from the dead, he is an authentic messenger of God's revelation to humanity.

(C8) Because Jesus is an authentic messenger of God's revelation to humanity, his claim about being the Son of God who died for our sins is true.

(C9) Thus, the three fundamental claims upon which Christianity is founded are true.

(C10) Therefore, the whole of the Christian religion is true.

We should pause here to note what Campbell's argument above is *not* attempting to show. First, this argument is not an argument for theism per se. As discussed in chapter 2, Campbell is confident that his revealed-idea argument is sufficient (and even necessary) for proving that God exists. Rather, his argument from miracles is meant to provide the levering rationale for advancing from simple theism to Christian theism in particular (this is important for reasons we will see toward the end of the chapter). Second, the argument above is not an argument *for* miracles; rather, it is an argument *from* miracles for the truth of Christianity. What this implies, of course, is that Campbell still needs to offer some account of why he thinks the miracle of Jesus's resurrection actually occurred and hence why premise C4 in particular is true. Obviously, premise C4 is the pivotal linchpin claim in his argument from miracles, and Campbell fittingly goes to some lengths to support it.

But before we examine Campbell's argument *for* the miracle of Jesus's resurrection, we should take note of some of the worries a critic might have with his argument *from* miracles. First off, critics might wonder why we should accept premise C2 as true. Perhaps it is true that Jesus is the Son of God who died for our sins, that he was buried, and that he was resurrected from the dead. But, so the critic might ask, do those claims prove the *whole* of the Christian religion, as Campbell asserts? I suspect that Campbell's response to this sort of question would be reflective of the theological minimalism characteristic of the Stone-Campbell Restoration Movement: believing these three claims is both necessary and sufficient for being a Christian believer. That is, these three claims effectively constitute the whole of what a Christian *must* believe in order to be a Christian. In still other words, these three claims are the essence of the biblical Christian dogma. Accordingly, any additional or supplementary creedal claims or theological doctrines that Christian sects have added to these three claims are *add-ons*. And while those add-ons might be true, they are not essential to what a person must believe in order to be a Christian.

A much more pressing philosophical problem involves premise C6. For the sake of discussion, grant premise C5; that is, grant that if a person actually performs a miracle, then she is indeed an authentic messenger of God's revelation. But even if *that* is true, perhaps the person who is tapped to serve as God's messenger is mistaken in how she relays the divine message. Or worse, perhaps she is deceiving us in the process of delivering the message. Accordingly, because we are in no position to know whether the messenger is relaying God's message accurately, we cannot know whether premise C6 is true—that is, we cannot know whether it is true that *if* S *is an authentic messenger of God's revelation to humanity, then* S*'s claims are true*. And if we cannot know whether this important conditional claim is true, then we lack warrant for affirming premise C6, and Campbell's argument from miracles fails to get off the ground.

Campbell tries to put this sort of worry at bay by borrowing still another move from Locke, who held that no occurrence—no matter how spectacular it may be—actually qualifies as a miracle if it somehow violates the moral law.[23] Similarly, Campbell draws a sharp distinction between what he thinks of as *benevolent* and *malevolent* uses of supernatural power.[24] In his view, if someone employs supernatural power with benevolence, then we can be confident that she is indeed an authentic (hence, reliable) messenger of God's infallible revelation. Alternatively, if someone employs what might otherwise *appear* to be supernatural power but does so in a malevolent way, then we can be sure that her unusual power is not derived of God; hence, it is not truly miraculous in nature; and ultimately, the person unleashing it is not actually an authentic messenger of God's revelation to humanity. Thus, insofar as we can judge the authenticity (hence, the reliability) of the putatively divine messenger by her moral fruit, so to speak, we can indeed affirm premise C6.

Of course, there are still some tough questions facing Campbell's view here. Is his Lockean strategy of responding to the problem above merely a definitional one such that even if some occurrence appears to involve supernatural power, it is not a bona fide, divinely ordained miracle, precisely because it is malevolent? If so, then should we conclude that the power involved was actually supernatural but simply demonic in origin? Or was it merely natural, even though remarkable? And if it is the former—that is, if the power is supernatural but demonic—then why is it not still miraculous, since it involves the non-natural suspension of the usual course of nature? Even more tricky for Campbell is this: How could we ever know what should count as a *benevolent* use of miraculous power *prior* to the delivery of God's revelation through his messengers? This is an especially difficult question for Campbell in particular because he thinks that our sole and original source for moral knowledge is itself divine revelation (a point discussed in chapter 5). Accordingly, a circularity problem looms large for him: we must depend on divine revelation in order to know what is and is not benevolent, but we need to know what is benevolent in order to determine what is miraculous, and hence divinely revealed.

Yet even if Campbell could address this circularity problem satisfactorily, other difficult questions remain: How can we know which of the truly authentic messenger's claims are actually from God? Are all of her claims from the moment of the miraculous occurrence onward (or even prior to that moment) supposed to be regarded as divine revelation? If not, then how do we know when she is speaking for God, and when she is not?

Putting those questions aside for the moment, we can see that Campbell still has the burden of showing that premise C4 is true. What reasons are there for thinking that Jesus (and others) actually performed miracles? Because Campbell clearly regards Jesus's resurrection as the most important miracle of all, we might narrow the question in the following way: Why think that Jesus actually came back to life from the dead? Obviously, if this miracle occurred, then—despite all the other worries one might have about Campbell's argument from miracles—Christianity would have at least something going for it, even if we have difficulty specifying exactly what such a miracle entails by way of supporting the truth of the Christian religion. But did such a miracle really happen, and can we reasonably believe the biblical testimonies concerning it? Campbell certainly recognizes the weight of this question, and he spends a great deal of energy arguing for the historicity of miracles in general and for the resurrection in particular (hence, for premise C4). I turn now to his argument *for* the miracle of Jesus's resurrection.

3.2. Campbell's Criteriological Argument for the Miracle of Resurrection

Historically, Christian apologists have offered at least four different types of arguments for miracles: deductive arguments, probabilistic arguments, abductive or explanatory arguments, and criteriological arguments.[25] Deductive arguments are such that if the premises are true, then the conclusion must be true. Typically, the major premise in a deductive argument for a miracle is that if a miracle report is offered by persons who face great difficulties as a result of their testimonies and if those persons radically change their lives in light of their beliefs, then the miracle report is trustworthy.[26] Probabilistic arguments commonly rely on Bayes's Theorem and are geared toward showing that given some set of facts, it is more probable than not that a miracle occurred.[27] Abductive or explanatory arguments begin with a set of well-established historical facts and try to show that the hypothesis that best explains those facts is that a miracle occurred.[28] Criteriological arguments are aimed at showing that if a miracle report meets some special set of criteria that can be used reliably to establish the historicity of other claims, then the miracle report in question is itself factual. Although at times Campbell can seem to move in the direction of offering an abductive argument for the resurrection,[29] I think we can probably best interpret him as following Charles Leslie in offering a fairly straightforward criteriological argument for the miracle of Jesus's resurrection.[30]

Campbell contends that it is our "every-day practice in the ordinary concerns of life" to determine whether historical claims or other testimonies are true by checking to see whether they meet certain criteria.[31] And only when these criteria are met are we comfortable in believing the claims on offer. That is, we do not simply believe "without scruple" everything reported to us in a testimony, but rather

> [w]e are often glad of the opportunity of examining oral and written testimony [by applying these criteria], and we generally find some way to elicit truth, or detect the fallacy of certain reported facts. These *criteria,* when applied to any reported fact, force us to the conclusion that it is either true or false. Were it not for these *criteria,* by which we are enabled to appreciate the value of testimony, we would, in the ordinary course of society, be liable to constant deceptions, inasmuch as the conscientious speaking of the truth is not the distinguishing virtue of the present age. These *criteria* are various; but wherever there is a perfect consistency and accordance between the fact reported and the testimony, adduced to prove it, conviction of the verity of that fact necessarily follows.[32]

When it comes to miracle reports in particular, the basic idea for Campbell is this: the same criteria that we use to distinguish true testimony from false testimony in our everyday affairs are perfectly adequate for determining true testimony from false testimony when it comes to reports about putatively miraculous occurrences in the past. The trick, then, is to make explicit those criteria that we employ in our everyday practices and ask whether a given miracle report—especially the report of Jesus's resurrection—meets those same criteria. If it does, then we can be confident about the truth of the miracle report on offer. The whole process of looking to these criteria in assessing miracle reports, Campbell thinks, is akin to those everyday tribunals in which we investigate other historical-factual claims, and he is confident that the testimonies concerning Jesus's resurrection are vindicated in this process. He says, for example, that "[i]n whatever court, before whatever judges, by whatever laws or trial you would ascertain the truth or falsehood of Cromwell's protectorate, or the Saxon conquests, of the ascension of the Caesars to imperial power, the victories of Hannibal, the birth, life and death of Cyrus, Alexander, Alfred, or Queen Elizabeth—in the same court, before the same judges, and by the same laws will the resurrection of Jesus be proved."[33]

So what are these special criteria in accordance with which we should try historical claims and testimonies? Campbell consciously follows Charles Leslie in thinking that there are four specific, failsafe criteria that, when jointly met, prove the truth of some historical claim—including the report of a miraculous occurrence. (For ease of reference to this group of criteria and because Campbell borrows them from Leslie, I call these criteria Campbell's *Lesliean criteria.*) We can summarize Campbell's Lesliean criteria in the following way:

- *Sensible fact criterion*: the reported occurrence "must have been what we call sensible facts; such as the eyes of the spectators, and all their other senses might take cognizance of."[34] In other words, the report must involve something done or something said that a witness could have actually perceived through his five senses.
- *Public attestation criterion*: the reported occurrence must have been "exhibited with every imaginable public and popular attestation, and open to the severest scrutiny which their extraordinary character might induce."[35] That is, the reported occurrence must have happened in such a way that would have been publicly known and in such a way that would have made the event one of "remarkable notoriety."[36]
- *Simultaneous commemoration criterion*: certain "monumental and commemorative institutions" must have been "adopted simultaneously" with the reported occurrence.[37] That is, monuments, institutions, or also practices that memorialize the reported occurrence must have been initiated at the time of the reported occurrence.
- *Perpetual commemoration criterion*: those same commemorative monuments, institutions, or also practices that were initiated at the time of the occurrence must have continued down to the present time.

In Campbell's view, if the testimony of some occurrence—including the report of a miraculous occurrence—meets all four of these Lesliean criteria, then we would and should accept that testimony as true. Of course, a report could still be true even if it did not meet all four of these special criteria. But the idea here is that if a report *does* meet all of these criteria, then it cannot be false. Hence Campbell comments, "I repeat, with a confidence that fears no refutation, that no fact accompanied with these four criteria ever was proved to be false. Nay . . . no fact which can abide these criteria CAN be false."[38] Effectively, then, Campbell regards the Lesliean criteria as jointly sufficient, though not necessary, conditions for determining historical truth. Ultimately, Campbell thinks that when it comes to the reports of Jesus's resurrection, these four jointly truth-indicating criteria are indeed satisfactorily met. Therefore, in his view, we can be certain of the truth of those testimonies concerning Jesus's resurrection.

We are now in a position to appreciate *Campbell's criteriological argument **for** the miracle of Jesus's resurrection,* which can be summarized in the following way:

(M1) If the testimony of some occurrence meets the sensible fact criterion, the public attestation criterion, the simultaneous commemoration criterion, *and* the perpetual commemoration criterion, then the testimony is true.
(M2) The testimony of the miracle of Jesus's resurrection meets all four of these Lesliean criteria.
(M3) The testimony of the miracle of Jesus's resurrection is true.

To bring matters full circle, we should note here that if this argument is sound, then we have support for premise C4 of Campbell's argument *from* miracles. And if so, then Campbell has effectively closed the loop in providing a systematic, levering rationale for moving from simple theism to Christian theism in particular.

Now, to be sure, I cannot here survey all of the historical evidence Campbell offers in support of premise M2.[39] However, it is worth noting that he thinks that the various testimonies concerning Jesus's resurrection easily meet the sensible fact criterion because Jesus's putative postmortem appearances were indeed something that witnesses could have perceived through their five senses and, furthermore, the alleged witnesses were the sort of people who would have had particularly reliable capacities for both perceiving these appearances and reporting them accurately.[40] Moreover, he thinks that those same testimonies also easily meet the public attestation criterion: many people, despite their expectations to the contrary, allegedly encountered the resurrected Jesus and, despite the risks of great danger, stood by their testimonies publicly and transformed their lives in accordance with what they reported.[41] Additionally, Campbell thinks that the resurrection accounts meet the simultaneous commemoration criterion and the perpetual commemoration criterion, and as evidence he highlights the Christian practices of baptism and the Eucharist (both of which commemorate the death, burial, and resurrection of Jesus)[42] and the fact that the traditional day of worship shifted from Saturday to Sunday: each of these commemorative practices began at the time of the reported occurrence, and each continues even today.[43] Campbell is especially impressed by these perpetual commemorative practices, and he regards them as a "species of historical evidence of incorruptible integrity, of the highest certainty and authority, and wholly beyond the imputation of fraud or fiction."[44] In his view, for example, it would be just as unlikely for the Saturday-Sunday shift to have occurred (given the falsity of the resurrection accounts) as it would be for Americans to shift the recognition of Independence Day from the Fourth of July to, say, some day in January.

Of course, Campbell's case for premise M2 is hardly beyond criticism. Concerning whether the resurrection accounts meet the sensible fact criterion, critics will note that the reports handed down to us are, at best, indirect in nature—that is, we do not have firsthand reports, only secondhand accounts of those firsthand reports, and even these were recorded many years after the events in question, perhaps long after the original witnesses had died. Secondly, concerning whether the resurrection accounts meet the simultaneous commemoration and perpetual commemoration criteria, critics will wonder whether we actually know *when* these various worship practices actually began and whether they were indeed shared among all Christians. Lastly, concerning Campbell's bold claim that perpetual commemorative practices such as the Eucharist and the Saturday-Sunday shift are of "incorruptible integrity," critics are right to wonder whether we should be so confident. Why should we think that it is impossible or even improbable for an alleged event to be reported and become part of the mythology surrounding some practice or institution even though the event in question never actually happened or did not happen in the way reported? One needs only to be reminded of George Washington and the cherry tree to see the problem here. In any case, I must leave the full evaluation of premise M2 for historians.

Still, even if we are prepared to grant the truth of premise M2, critics may continue to worry about Campbell's criteriological argument in light of premise M1. The most obvious concern here centers on whether the conjunction of the four Lesliean criteria is, in fact, sufficiently truth-indicative in the first place. We might ask, for example, Why does the fact that these criteria are met *guarantee* that the report on offer is true?

Obviously, if there were only even a single case in which a report meets these criteria but nonetheless proves to be false, then Campbell's criteriological argument for the resurrection—at least as it is worded above—would be unsound, because premise M1 would be false (strictly speaking). Of course, to Campbell's credit, it is no easy task to demonstrate the falsity of premise M1 by way of counterexample. Conyers Middleton, for example, reportedly undertook a serious effort to locate a counterexample to Charles Leslie's version of premise M1 but came up empty-handed.[45]

Nevertheless, the possibility that such a counterexample to premise M1 *could* arise inevitably haunts Campbell's criteriological argument. Although he clearly does not think such a counterexample is forthcoming, it would be available to Campbell to word premise M1 more modestly by claiming that if a report meets the Lesliean criteria, then, at the least, we can reasonably regard that report as true. Still, as Timothy McGrew points out, the primary difficulty facing criteriological arguments in general—whether they are worded modestly or not—is that, given their general structure, there is no way for them to factor in "other considerations that might weigh against the historical claim in question."[46] And as McGrew notes, it can be tempting to think that one of those considerations is that "extreme antecedent improbability ought to carry some weight in our evaluation of the credibility of a factual claim."[47] Accordingly, while we might be prepared to grant that Campbell's Lesliean criteria are perhaps sufficient for assessing ordinary historical events, they may very well prove to be insufficient when dealing with cases (such as miracle reports) that appear to involve high degrees of improbability on the front end.

But aside from the concern with the general structure of Campbell's criteriological argument, it remains for Campbell to respond to Hume's especially salient and historically important argument against the rationality of belief in miracles. If Hume's argument is sound, then it is simply unreasonable for us to believe testimonies concerning a miraculous occurrence—even if Campbell's Lesliean criteria are met and even if there were no other difficulties facing his criteriological argument. Accordingly, it would be unreasonable for us to believe either the conclusion at M3 or premise C4, and consequently Campbell's overall case for Christianity would be fatally undermined. So it is especially important for him to respond to Hume.

To say the least, Hume's argument against belief in miracles has been influential among philosophers and theologians since it first appeared, decades before Campbell's time. Indeed, as one commentator puts it, there continues to be a great deal of "genuflecting at Hume's altar" in debates about miracles.[48] In fact, many contemporary theologians and biblical scholars have simply taken Hume's conclusion for granted and have abandoned the sort of case Campbell tries to make for Christianity. For example, many biblical scholars within the so-called Jesus Seminar write off much of the New Testament as unhistorical insofar as it contains reports of miraculous occurrences.[49] The renowned biblical scholar Bart

Ehrman, for instance, betrays his indebtedness to Hume in claiming that "because historians can only establish what probably happened, and a miracle [like the resurrection] is highly improbable, the historian cannot say that it probably occurred."[50] Naturally, then, scholars such as Ehrman would likely view Campbell's appeal to the New Testament witnesses of Jesus's resurrection as deeply misguided. Obviously, if these scholars are correct—and, more importantly, if Hume's argument against belief in miracles is sound—then Campbell's levering rationale for moving from simple theism to Christianity is seriously flawed. So we need to ask whether Hume's famous argument against the belief miracles in fact serves as an undermining defeater for Campbell's overall case for Christianity. To address this question, we should first take a detour to consider Hume's argument.

3.3. Hume's "Of Miracles"

Among the first of his philosophical writings,[51] Hume's "Of Miracles" essay first appeared in 1747 as Section X of his *An Enquiry Concerning Human Understanding.* He opens his essay by praising John Tolliston for providing an argument that is "as concise, and elegant, and strong as any argument can possibly be supposed" against the doctrine of transubstantiation.[52] The real beauty of Tolliston's work, Hume points out, is that it effectively silences the "arrogant bigotry and superstition" associated with that doctrine—and it does so with a single, decisive blow to the head. "I flatter myself," Hume says, "that I have discovered an argument of a like nature, which, if just, will, with the wise and learned, be an everlasting check to all kinds of superstitious delusions, and consequently, will be useful as long as the world endures."[53] The primary delusion Hume has in mind to expose is, of course, the belief in miracles—the very same miracles upon which Campbell mounts his case for Christianity.

Unfortunately, the task of extracting a concise and accurate statement of Hume's main argument in "Of Miracles" is notoriously difficult, if for no other reason than that his essay contains a host of ambiguities that invite a variety of competing interpretations.[54] Nor is it an easy task to pin down exactly what Hume's central aim is in the first place, because several things are going on simultaneously in his essay.[55] Not surprisingly, then, there is very little consensus among scholars about how precisely to reconstruct Hume's argument on miracles. Nonetheless, scholars commonly agree that Hume's central argument is not geared toward showing that it is impossible for miracles to occur.[56] Rather, the argument is typically read as attempting to show that even if miracles were to occur, it would be irrational for us to believe in them on the basis of testimony. With all of this in mind, a little stage setting will be helpful in teasing out his argument for the irrationality of belief in miracles.

Hume begins in good empiricist fashion by reminding us that experience is "our only guide in reasoning concerning matters of fact."[57] That is, our beliefs about the way the world works are empirical beliefs based on experience as opposed to the rational consideration of the various relationships between ideas. Unfortunately, however, experience is "not altogether infallible, but in some cases is apt to lead us into errors."[58] Accordingly, Hume says, the wise man will proportion his beliefs to the evidence available to him in experience.

What exactly does this mean? Consider the following illustration. When we consider all of our experiences of the world, we note that we have observed one event (A-event) followed by another event (B-event). Sometimes, we have experienced an A-event *invariably* conjoined with a B-event: for example, we notice that every time we have tossed a ball into the air (A-event), it has eventually fallen to the ground (B-event). Accordingly, if we are wise and proportion our beliefs to the evidence of our past experience, we will believe with maximal confidence that the next time a ball is tossed up, it will fall back down. In this case, our past experiences of tossed balls offer us what Hume calls a "full proof" that future events will behave in similar ways.

By contrast, we have also experienced circumstances in which one event is *variably* conjoined with another. For example, we have noticed that the start of June in Tennessee (A-event) has typically brought with it warmer temperatures (B-event) than those felt in, say, December. That is, most of the time—say, 90 percent of the time—a week in June is warmer than a week in December in Tennessee. Of course, there have been a few occasions in the past when, for whatever reason, a week in June turned out to be colder than a week in December—but these exceptions are few and far between. Accordingly, if we take all of our past experiences into account, we should indeed expect that a week in June will be warmer than a week in December, but we should not bet the farm on it. In other words, we should recognize that there is some chance that our expectations will be disappointed. And because we should proportion our beliefs to the evidence provided by our past experiences, our belief about Tennessee temperatures in June should be regarded as a matter of probability. Nonetheless, we should incline toward the expectation that June will bring warmer weather, but we should do so with "doubt and hesitation" in keeping with the probability at hand.[59]

While Hume thinks that experiential evidence should guide us in forming judgments, he acknowledges that in many cases we have to rely also on evidence derived from testimony. But he thinks that we would not take testimony to be reliable evidence in any situation had we not already discovered through direct experience that the memories of witnesses are generally pretty decent, that people tend to tell the truth, that they feel a sense of shame when they are caught lying, and so on. In other words, direct experience gives us evidence that testimony is often reliable evidence for forming beliefs. But direct experience is more reliable than testimonial evidence, in Hume's view, if for no other reason than the fact that testimony is based on someone's direct experience. Accordingly, because direct experience is actually prior to testimony, and because the former confirms the reliability of the latter, the quality of the testimonial evidence that we take into account will vary according to the direct experience on which it is originally based.

We can now focus our attention on Hume's view of miracles. In much the same way that Campbell describes a miracle as an occurrence that is beyond the productive powers of the natural order, Hume defines a miracle as a "violation of the laws of nature."[60] What this means is that a miracle is not simply some marvelous and surprising occurrence like, say, an Olympian's running a four-minute mile. Indeed, such an occurrence is exceedingly unusual and even stupefying, but it does not violate a law according to which the natural world operates. However, Hume thinks that the resurrection of a dead man would be more than simply marvelous: *that* would be a bona fide miraculous occurrence because it would violate the "common course of nature."[61]

To get a handle on why the resurrection of a dead man is miraculous, we should have some sense of what Hume takes a law of nature to be. He thinks that a statement of a law of nature is a statement of the invariable regularity involved in the usual course of events in the world. In his view, the laws of nature are established by "firm and unalterable" experience.[62] That is, past experience (for everyone) has always confirmed that the world operated in such and such a way and that the world has never operated contrary to that. Taking note of these past experiences, we can then describe the regularity that we have observed in rule-like statements. So, for example, every time we have seen a man die in the past (A-event), we have also observed that he stays dead (B-event). Given the repeated observation of the invariable conjunction of the A-event with the B-event in question, we can then describe the apparent regularity observed in the natural course of events as follows: when a man dies, he stays dead.[63] Insofar as it is a law of nature that dead men stay dead, a man's coming back to life would be miraculous, because such an occurrence would violate that law.

With all of that in tow, we are now in a position to appreciate the core passage in Hume's famous essay:

> A miracle is a violation of the laws of nature; and as a firm and unalterable experience has established these laws, the proof against a

> miracle, from the very nature of the fact, is as entire as any argument from experience can possibly be imagined. . . . It is no miracle that a man seemingly in good health, should die on a sudden: because such a kind of death, though more unusual than any other, has yet been frequently observed to happen. But it is a miracle, that a dead man should come to life; because that has never been observed, in any age or country. There must, therefore, be a uniform experience against every miraculous event, otherwise the event would not merit that appellation. And as a uniform experience amounts to a proof, there is here a direct and full *proof,* from the nature of the fact, against the existence of any miracle; nor can such a proof be destroyed, or the miracle rendered credible, but by an opposite proof which is superior.
>
> The plain consequence is (and it is a general maxim worthy of our attention), "That no testimony is sufficient to establish a miracle, unless the testimony be of such a kind, that its falsehood would be more miraculous, than the fact, which it endeavors to establish: And even in that case there is a mutual destruction of argument, and the superior only gives us an assurance suitable to that degree of force, which remains, after deducting the inferior."[64]

We can understand Hume here in the following way. Because the laws of nature are established upon firm, unalterable, and uniform experience, and because a wise man proportions his belief to the evidence, the wise man will be utterly confident in his belief that nature will behave according to these laws and that these laws will never be compromised, because, effectively, he has a full proof in hand. Were a miracle to occur, it would constitute a violation of these laws. Now, imagine that someone were to report to us that a miracle took place. What then? Hume contends that we should weigh the evidence on either side of the issue and believe in proportion to the evidence remaining once we subtract the lesser from the greater. The evidence in favor of the miracle *not* occurring is all the firm, unalterable, and uniform experience that establishes the law of nature in the first place. The putative evidence in favor of the miracle having occurred is merely a witness's testimony that it did. But the witness's miracle report inevitably runs contrary to our uniform experience upon which the laws of nature are established. Accordingly, the evidence that the laws of nature were not violated will always be greater than the testimonial evidence that they were—that is, unless the testimony on offer is of such a kind that its falsehood would be more contrary to our experience than the miracle it endeavors to establish would be. But, so Hume assures us, no testimony rises to *that* level. At best it could rise to the level of a counterproof, in which case we might have something of a Mexican standoff. But in that case, if we believe in proportion to the evidence, we should still refrain from believing even the most reliable testimony that a miracle occurred.

Of course, Hume is hardly worried about even such a standoff, and in the second part of his essay, he give four reasons why. First, throughout history, there has never been a miracle "attested by a sufficient number of men, of such unquestioned good-sense, education, and learning, as to secure us against all delusion in themselves; of undoubted integrity, as to place them beyond all suspicion of any design to deceive others; of such credit and reputation in the eyes of mankind, as to have a great deal to lose in case of their being detected."[65] Second, people have a tendency to be drawn to the wonder and surprise involved in reporting a miracle—especially when this is combined with the "spirit of religion"[66]—and this fact undermines the reliability of the witnesses. Third, the putative miracles only ever seem to occur among ignorant and barbarous peoples, and that fact "forms a strong presumption" against the miracle's occurrence. Fourth, for every testimony of a miracle of one religion, there is testimony of a miracle of a competing or incompatible religion; and because these testimonies are effectively in tension with one another, they cancel each other out. In light of these four considerations, then, Hume thinks that the credibility of testimonial evidence for miracles has always been less than impressive. Accordingly, the testimony of miracles has always been outweighed by the impressive evidence (from our uniform experience) that establishes the law of nature in the first place. And because the wise man proportions his belief to the evidence, he would not believe these testimonies. Accordingly, it would be unreasonable for us to not follow suit.

Admittedly, my gloss on Hume's argument here is not terribly sophisticated. While I recognize that there might be other ways of framing the argument Hume may have had in mind when writing his essay, the following summary outline is sufficiently Humean in nature to see how Campbell responds. Moreover, the following summary is sufficiently close to how Hume's essay was read by one of his contemporaries, George Campbell, whose interpretation of the essay was read by Hume and was never corrected.[67] We can summarize *Hume's argument against belief in miracles* in the following way:

(H1) A wise man proportions his belief to the evidence.

(H2) The laws of nature have been established by firm and unalterable experience; that is, past experience has always confirmed the laws of nature and has never been contrary to them.

(H3) Hence, our uniform experience offers full proof that the laws of nature are never violated.

(H4) If a miracle occurs, it is a violation of a law of nature.

(H5) The testimony of a miracle runs contrary to our uniform experience.

(H6) The evidence that the laws of nature are not violated will always be greater than the testimonial evidence that they have been violated, unless the testimony be of such a kind that its falsehood would be more contrary to our experience than the miracle it endeavors to establish would be.

(H7) No testimony of a miracle is of such a kind that its falsehood would be more contrary to our experience than the miracle it endeavors to establish.

(H8) Thus, a wise man would not believe the testimony of a miracle.

(H9) It is unreasonable to believe contrary to how a wise man would believe.

(H10) Thus, it is unreasonable to believe the testimony of a miracle.

If Hume is correct in concluding that it is unreasonable for us to believe the testimony that a miracle occurred, then clearly Campbell's argument *for* the miracle of resurrection is seriously flawed, to the extent that it relies substantially on the testimonial evidence of the biblical writers. In turn, then, premise C4 of Campbell's argument *from* miracles would also be unwarranted, and he would have failed to establish the truth of Christianity on the basis of his appeal to testimony of the resurrection. That Hume's argument caught Campbell's attention is thus unsurprising: it poses the most obvious undermining defeater of his overall case for Christianity. In fact, Campbell regarded Hume's argument as "canonical in all the high schools of infidelity";[68] consequently, he thought that it "deserves a more formal notice."[69] Accordingly, I turn now to Campbell's response to Hume's argument.

3.4. Campbell on Hume's Argument against Belief in Miracles

Campbell thinks that Hume's argument against belief in miracles is deeply and fatally flawed. Before reconstructing his full critique, though, I should note that Campbell borrows heavily from George Campbell's *A Dissertation on Miracles* (1762), which scholars commonly regard as one of the better responses to Hume during his day.[70] (To minimize confusion, I hereafter use George Campbell's full name in every reference to him, and I refer to Alexander Campbell by his surname only.) Campbell repeatedly praises the *Dissertation,* claiming that there is not to be "found in the English language a more complete and masterly refutation of any system of error."[71] He takes it that George Campbell had completely "exploded" Hume's argument, and he thinks that it is "a work of supererogation" to even notice that.[72] In fact, Campbell comments that even Hume felt the crushing weight of George Campbell's critique: "Hume felt himself defeated—completely defeated. He never replied to it. And I have it from living testimony, that when Hume's friends jested him upon the complete defeat of his system, he acknowledged that 'the Scotch theologue had beaten him.'"[73] Whether Campbell's anecdote here is true, I must leave for intellectual historians and Hume scholars to decide. But in any case, Campbell makes it very clear that he stands—and stands confidently—on George Campbell's shoulders in responding to Hume.

I think we can best understand Campbell's response to Hume's argument by organizing it into four different waves of criticism, the first two of which build upon one another and closely mimic the arguments presented in George Campbell's *Dissertation.* First, Campbell suggests that Hume's argument equivocates on the term *experience.* Second, he suggests that premise H5 inevitably invites a difficult dilemma and that Hume's only way out of it is to beg the question against testimony of miracles. Third, he regards premise H3 as unwarranted. And fourth, Campbell indirectly criticizes Hume's argument by suggesting that the question of whether a miraculous occurrence is antecedently highly improbable depends in large part upon the background theory of the one weighing the evidence in the first place.

First Wave: Hume equivocates on the term 'experience.' Campbell thinks that to get a handle on Hume's argument, we first need to be clear on what Hume might mean by the term *experience* in any instance in which it is employed in his argument. Following George Campbell,[74] Campbell thinks that one can mean at least two things when using the term *experience*: one can refer by that term either to direct personal experience or to that experience which is derived of, and compiled from, the testimonies of others. Quoting directly from the *Dissertation,* Campbell defines *personal experience* as that which is "founded in memory, and consists solely of the general maxims and conclusions that each individual has formed from the comparison of the particular facts attested."[75] By contrast, he defines *derived experience* as that which is "founded in testimony, and consists not only of all the experiences of others, which have, through that channel, been communicated to us; but of all the general maxims or conclusion we have formed, from the comparison of particular facts attested."[76]

To get a better view of the distinction between *personal* and *derived* experience, consider the following examples. Every time I have hit my thumb with a hammer in the past, my thumb has been injured. Given all of my memories of this order of events, I put two and two together and come—on the basis of my own personal experience—to the general maxim that *hitting one's thumb with a hammer causes injury.* In this case, my personal experience provides all the evidence I need in order to draw the relevant conclusion. But imagine that I have always lived in a tropical climate, that I have never traveled, and that there is no such thing as refrigeration where I live. How would I ever come to the conclusion *that water becomes solid when the temperature drops below 32°F*—especially since I have never personally witnessed freezing temperatures myself? Obviously, in this case, I would need to supplement my limited personal experiences by making use of the testimonies of others. Imagine, then, that someone from a much colder region informs me about the solidity of frozen water in the winters up north. I now have experience that is derived of testimony from others. That is, while I do not personally or directly experience the solidity of frozen water, I have now acquired some sort of indirect experience of it, as relayed through testimony. Accordingly, I compare the traveler's experiences of water with my own, and I reasonably conclude on the basis of the compiled experience that water becomes solid at below-freezing temperatures.

For Campbell, one of the problems facing Hume's argument is that at premise H2, Hume seems to be talking about experience qua *derived* experience, and at premise H5, he seems to be talking about experience qua *personal* experience. Consequently, if Campbell's line of thinking here is correct, Hume equivocates on a very crucial term in his argument.

The explanation goes like this: recall that Hume says that we have firm, unalterable, and uniform experience that establishes the laws of nature. In other words, we conclude that there are laws of nature in the first place because of the evidence provided by our firm, unalterable, and uniform experiences of the regularities involved in the natural world. But is it I or any other individual who directly and personally entertains all the firm, unalterable, and uniform experience needed to gather the evidence in support of the relevant law? Clearly not, so Campbell thinks. He asks of Hume,

> How do you [Hume qua individual] come into possession of that which you call universal experience? By what evidence do you acquire the assurance that the laws of nature are inviolable? Your *own* observation? Your *own* senses? A narrow horizon, truly, from which to infer the uniformity and the inviolability of the laws of nature! And is this your boasted philosophy, to infer from the evidence of your own senses, for some half-century exercised on an atom of the universe

> . . . the inviolable character of its laws through infinite space and eternal duration? . . . [D]o you call your *own* observations universal experience? Is not universal experience the experience of all men in all places and at all times? It is absurd . . . . [Y]our *own* personal experience is all that you know of this great universe; all the rest is mere belief of the testimony of others.[77]

The basic idea here for Campbell is that when Hume makes reference to the uniform experience that purportedly offers the full proof of the laws of nature, he must be referring to experience qua *derived* experience. That is, Hume must be referring to all of the collective experiences of humanity shared and compiled by means of testimony. In other words, Campbell's view seems to be that when Hume speaks of the uniform experience that always confirms and never disconfirms the laws of nature (as worded in premise H2), he must mean experience qua *derived* experience. Otherwise, if he meant *personal* experience, there would be insufficient evidence—given the limited scope of one's personal experience—for establishing (at least) many of the laws of nature.

Fair enough. But in Campbell's view, the problem emerges when, at premise H5, Hume suggests that the testimonies for a miraculous occurrence run contrary to our uniform experience. Here, so Campbell seems to think, Hume must mean that the miracle report contravenes something more akin to Hume's own *personal* experience. Why? Because, in Campbell's view, if we actually went to the trouble to compile *all* of the experiences derivable from testimony in order to get a sense of what is (or was) universally experienced, then we would also need to take into account the miracle reports as at least a part of our uniform experience. So in order to claim that the testimony of a miracle runs contrary to our uniform experience, Hume must be referring to experience qua personal experience. Consequently, in Campbell's view, Hume shifts the meaning of the term *experience* midstream: at premise H2, he means *derived experience*; and, at premise H5, he means *personal experience.*

Second Wave: Premise H5 invites a difficult dilemma and Hume, in turn, begs the question. In many respects, Campbell's charge of equivocation leads directly into his second objection to Hume's argument. Consider premise H5 again—that the testimony of a miracle runs contrary to our uniform experience. In Campbell's view, Hume invites a difficult dilemma here: interpreted one way, premise H5 is seriously problematic; interpreted another way, premise H5 is plainly false. And, in facing this dilemma, Hume has no other option but to beg the question against the testimony of miracles.

Assume for the moment that when Hume says that *testimony of a miracle runs contrary to our uniform experience,* such a claim means that the testimony of a miracle runs contrary to one's own personal experience. But if by *experience* Hume indeed means personal experience—as it seems he must, in Campbell's view above—then premise H5 invites a serious worry: sure, the testimony of a miracle might indeed be contrary to one's own personal experience, but so would a lot of other testimonies that we are perfectly reasonable to accept. On this point, Campbell says that "if all testimony is to be judged by our *personal* experience, or by our memory, or senses, we shall be reduced in the measure of our information even below the savage himself. It will be impossible for an inhabitant of the torrid zone to be assured that water can become solid as a rock; or for an Icelander to believe in the existence of . . . a Negro. No number of witnesses, however *credible,* could establish such facts in the minds of those who have no recollection of seeing them."[78] The point Campbell is getting at here is that if someone were to reject all of those testimonies that run contrary to her own personal experience, then she would have to toss far too much, and this would leave her admitting far too few testimonial accounts. Accordingly, if someone were to reject all those testimonies that are beyond, or contrary to, the small scope of her own personal experience, she would be incapable of knowing very much about the world: she would effectively occlude the possibility of discerning many of the laws of nature.

To drive this point home, Campbell appeals to Locke's famous king of Siam example, which Hume imports into his own essay in the form of his Indian prince example.[79] Campbell comments that

> Mr. Hume's "splendid, unanswerable and most philosophic argument" . . . when analysed is simply this:—"I cannot believe the testimony of some men, because it is contrary to my own experience and to that of a millionth part of all men, whose experience is, in my judgment, universal experience!" And so deposes the Emperor of Siam:—"I cannot believe one word that an Englishman utters, because he says that in England men and cattle walk upon water congealed into ice, which certainly is a glaring falsehood, because contrary to my experience and to that of all the good people of the torrid zone, which is the universal experience of all mankind in all ages and in all places!"[80]

Obviously, the problem Campbell is getting at here is that if someone were to reject a testimony of a miracle on the grounds that such a testimony is contrary to her own personal experience, then, to be consistent, she would also need to reject any other testimony of any experience beyond the scope of what she has personally encountered. Accordingly, this understanding of premise H5 is clearly too restrictive an account of what it means for something to be a contravention. Understood in this way, then, premise H5 is problematic.

To get around this problem, assume that we take premise H5 to mean that the testimony of a miracle is contrary to uniform experience qua derived experience. In other words, assume that the claim on offer is that the testimony of the miracle is contrary to *all* of the experiences one personally has entertained, as well as all those experiences derived from, and compiled by means of, testimony. But if we interpret premise H5 in this way, a new problem emerges: there now appears to be no principled reason why testimonies that miracles occurred should not count among those testimonies of experience from which we derive the uniform experience in the first place. In other words, if we must make use of testimony to compile the derived uniform experience (against which miracle reports are supposed to run contrary), even testimonies of miracles would also need to be taken into account. This is because, as Campbell says, "derived experience is derived from testimony," and so derived experience "cannot be contrasted with" testimony.[81] Accordingly, it would be incorrect to say that the testimony of a miracle is, necessarily, contrary to our uniform experience. Consequently, Campbell polemically concludes,

> [S]o it comes to pass that Mr. Hume could not believe the testimony of *some men* [those who testify to the occurrence of miracles], because their testimony was contrary to the testimony of *all men*!! But had he heard and examined the testimony of all men before he concluded himself in actual possession of universal experience? No, not a millionth part of the testimony of all men: yet on this veriest fraction of universal experience he presumes to erect a house of refuge for all outlaws of the universe, and calls it the Castle of Universal Experience.[82]

Effectively, Campbell's point here is that we must rely on testimony to compile experiences beyond the small scope of our own personal experiences in an effort to get a handle on what is universally experienced across all ages and places. Part of what that entails is that we cannot simply reject miracle reports as necessarily inadmissible: they, too, are among the experiences that we would need to compile in our effort to know what is universally or uniformly experienced in the first place. Accordingly, given this interpretation of what the term *experience* means (experience qua derived experience), premise H5 is false: miracle reports are not necessarily contraventions. Consequently, if Hume insists on claiming that testimonies of miracles are contrary to our uniform experience, then he is simply begging the question against miracle reports.

Ultimately, in Campbell's view, the project of assessing Hume's argument as it pertains to testimony of Jesus's resurrection leads us to one basic question:

> *Shall we admit the testimony of the apostles, upon the application of principles founded on observation, and as certain as is our experience of human affairs; or shall we reject that testimony upon the application of principles that are altogether beyond the range of observation, and as doubtful and imperfect in their nature as is our experience of the counsels of Heaven?* The former is founded on EXPERIENCE, the latter upon ASSUMPTION; and here I make my stand, and say, ["]Attack it who may—that our faith in Christianity is most certainly based upon *experience*—and [Hume's] infidelity upon *assumption*—upon ASSUMPTION throughout.["][83]

Here, I think Campbell clearly means to be following George Campbell, when he says,

> Now since . . . the far greater part of this experience, which comprises every age and every country, must be derived to us by testimony; that the experience may be *firm, uniform,* and *unalterable,* there must be no contrary testimony whatever. Yet, by [Hume's] own hypothesis, the miracles he would thus confute are supported by testimony. At the same time, to give strength to his argument, he is under a necessity of supposing, that there is no exception from the testimonies against them. Thus he falls into the paralogism which is called *begging the question.* What he gives with one hand, he takes with the other.[84]

It may be worth noting here that Campbell's second wave of criticism stems in part from his underlying conviction that our reliance on testimony is, in an important sense, *prior* to our reliance on experience.[85] Accordingly, pitting testimony against experience is problematic, in his view, because the former inevitably informs us as to that which constitutes our collective uniform experience. By way of contrast, recall that Hume thinks we would not regard testimony as reliable evidence in any given situation had we not already discovered through experience that the memories of witnesses are generally pretty decent, that people tend to tell the truth, that they feel a sense of shame when they are caught lying, and so forth. In other words, we learn to accept testimony on the basis of direct, personal experience. For Hume, experience is always more reliable than testimony because testimony is always based on someone's direct personal experience. But contra Hume, Campbell seems to think that our reliance on testimony actually *precedes* our personal experience that later confirms the reliability of testimony.[86] He suggests that both the propensity to tell the truth and the propensity to accept testimony as true (unless there is some positive reason to think that it is false) are not somehow learned by experience in the way that Hume suggests but are actually innate functions of the human mind. For example, Campbell uses the term *credulity* to describe "the native bias to receive truth upon testimony." He continues: "I say, credulity is as natural to man as breathing. This is a wise provision in the constitution of the human mind, that it must, and with the utmost ease, does assent to testimony; for without it, there could be no improvability in man."[87] If Campbell is correct about this, then Hume is wrong to suppose that the reliance on testimony is something that we learn from personal experience. Accordingly, Hume is wrong to privilege personal experience—and especially derived experience—over and above testimony for miracles.

Third Wave: Premise H3 is unwarranted. Recall that premise H3 of Hume's argument claims that *our uniform experience offers full proof that the laws of nature are never violated.* Campbell seems to think that we would lack justification for making such a claim. Although he nowhere develops this view in any detail, Campbell says that "silence is not contradictory testimony. The testimony of two men can prove in a court of law an affirmative proposition—the testimony of ten thousand cannot prove a negative; still less can their *silence* prove any thing."[88] I think we can interpret Campbell's view here in the following way: No amount of experience—whether personal or derived from testimony—provides evidence that something does *not* or *never* occurs (in this case, the violation of a law of nature). At most, our collective, derived experience testifies that such an event *has not yet* occurred. But—to make use of a clunky turn of phrase—we do not actually observe *nevers* or *not-occurrings*. For, when we observe the world around us, we experience things happening; we do not actually observe things *not*-happening or things *never*-occuring.[89]

Peter van Inwagen captures what Campbell may have been trying to get at when he discusses Thomas Jefferson's unwillingness to believe a Yankee parson's testimony that stones fall from the sky. Allegedly, Jefferson refused to believe the testimony in question on the grounds that (a) he had personally observed on numerous occasions that stones do *not* fall from the sky; and (b) he had observed Yankee parsons lying in the past. With reference to the first reason, van Inwagen explains Jefferson's error in the following way:

> Experience may have testified to some persons at some points in history that the earth is at the center of the universe or that maggots are spontaneously generated in dung, but [contrary to what Jefferson thought] it had never testified to anyone that stones do *not* fall from the sky. . . . Although experience may have testified that if stones ever fall from the sky, their doing so is a very uncommon event, it has not testified that stones *never* fall from the sky.
>
> It is very hard indeed to find a sense in which experience testifies in any direct or immediate sense that events of some sort never happen—or in which stories of events of some sort are contrary to experience. If direct, immediate experience testifies to anything (truly or falsely) its testimony seems to be essentially "positive": it testifies that events of certain sort *do* happen.[90]

If van Inwagen is correct about this point, then it seems that experience—whether personal or compiled—does not actually prove negative claims such as "violations of laws of nature *never* occur" and "the laws of nature are *never* violated." And if that is correct, then premise H3 is at least questionable and at worst unwarranted. Recall that Hume says that a resurrection from the dead "has never been observed, in any age or country." But in Campbell's view, the simple fact that even ten thousand people throughout space and time have never observed a resurrection is not tantamount to an observation that resurrections *never* occur. Rather, these ten thousand people are merely silent on the topic of resurrection; their silence does not constitute a full proof.[91]

Fourth Wave: Background theories matter. Animating Hume's argument against the rationality of belief in miracles is the view that it is, antecedently, highly improbable that testimonies of miraculous occurrences such as Jesus's resurrection are actually true, given the laws of nature that we seem to observe. But in many respects, whether we regard the testimony of a miracle as highly unlikely in the first place hinges on one's background theory about the laws of nature. Richard Swinburne, for example, worries that Hume's argument does not sufficiently take into account the manner in which one's background theory about the laws of nature affects how one assesses the historical evidence (including testimony, memories, and physical traces) for a miraculous occurrence.[92] Consider two different background theories (*BT*) that we might hold about the laws of nature:

- BT_1 = the laws of nature are ultimate, depend on nothing for their existence, and have no exceptions.

- BT_2 = the laws of nature are sustained by a God who can be expected to intervene occasionally in the natural order of things.

If we hold BT_1, then testimony of something like Jesus's resurrection may indeed seem highly unlikely on the front end. Accordingly, one might suspect that Campbell's Lesliean criteria are inadequate for the task at hand. However, if we hold BT_2, then testimony of the resurrection will seem considerably less unlikely than it would if we hold BT_1. Accordingly, we might be considerably less suspicious of Campbell's criteriological argument. So, at the end of the day, whether we regard Jesus's resurrection to be antecedently highly improbable will ultimately depend, at least in part, upon our background theory about the laws of nature.

So the question now becomes this: Should we accept BT_1 or BT_2? If we have a decent, independent reasons for accepting BT_2—and Campbell, like Swinburne, thinks that we do—then it seems that there would be much less reason for us to view testimony of miracles with deep suspicion. In other words, if we already have reason to think that God exists and that the laws of nature are in some sense controlled by him, then the occurrence of a miracle is by no means antecedently highly improbable.[93]

I think we can read Campbell as gesturing somewhat in Swinburne's direction in his exchange with Humphrey Marshal about the role of testimony in proving the resurrection of Jesus. Apparently, Marshal, a deist, takes resurrection testimony to be insurmountably implausible because such an occurrence is, in the first place, "unnatural, irrational, incredible, and impossible."[94] But in reply to Marshal, Campbell wonders why Jesus's resurrection would seem so antecedently highly unlikely to Marshal, especially since Marshal himself actually believes that God exists and that he created the world. Campbell says to Marshal,

> Yet you profess to be a Deist—one who believes that there is an Omnipotent Creator—one who believes in the . . . fact of giving birth to the first man without a mother! The greatest miracle in the Bible you [already] believe upon the testimony of your senses, exercised upon the things which are seen! That the cold and inanimate earth, in her virgin state, brought forth a rational and sentient being, you believe, for . . . you boast that you are a Deist or Theist! If, then, it was not unnatural, irrational, nor impossible for the cold and inanimate earth, in a virgin state, to bring forth a son . . . with what pretension to reason can you say that it is irrational, unnatural, and impossible for the married earth to bring forth what has been committed to here; or that God

> cannot raise from the dust a dead man, when he raised a living race out of inanimate dust, as you believe?[95]

Borrowing a move from Swinburne, we might read Campbell's point here in the following way. One might hold to theistic background theory about the laws of nature, or one might hold a nontheistic background theory. On the theistic background theory, God exists and is the creator of the natural world and, accordingly, has the power to suspend the laws of nature. On the nontheistic background theory, the natural world is all that exists and the laws of nature are inviolable. Now, if one's operative background theory is the nontheistic one, then one might inevitably think it antecedently highly improbable that testimonies of miracles are true. However, if one's operative background theory is the theistic one, then it will certainly seem much less antecedently improbable that the God who is capable of raising humanity from dust also raised Jesus from the dead. So part of what is at stake is the operative background theory. Campbell clearly thinks that the theistic background theory is well supported in light of his revealed-idea argument for the existence of God. To the extent that the theistic background theory is well supported, then Marshal (and hence Hume) is mistaken in supposing, on the front end, that it is antecedently highly improbable that testimonies of miracles are true. Admittedly, given this view, miracles could not be used to provide an argument for theism, because one could not conclude that, probably, there has been a miracle unless he already believes in God. But recall that Campbell thinks he already has good reason to believe that God exists, and his appeal to miracles is employed as a levering argument aimed at advancing one from mere theism to Christian theism in particular.

3.5. Conclusion

If Campbell is on target in his four responses to Hume's argument against belief in miracle reports, then his overall case for Christianity is not somehow decisively defeated by Hume's effort to throw a single fatal blow. Accordingly, if Hume's argument is indeed flawed and does not undermine Campbell's case, then we must consider the strength of Campbell's argument *from* miracles, as well as his argument *for* miracles, on their own merits. Those arguments may indeed fall prey to other concerns one might have, but Hume's argument is not what singularly undermines them. As we have seen, in his effort to carve a middle path between deism and religious enthusiasm, Campbell argues that miracles—particularly the resurrection of Jesus—provide the basis upon which one can mount a case for the truth of Christian theism in particular. The first leg of this case for Christianity is his argument from miracles. There, Campbell argues that if Jesus really was raised from the dead, then he was indeed a special envoy of God's revelation and hence his claims about being the Son of God who died for our sins are true. Of course, Campbell thinks that the antecedent of this conditional is true, and he provides his criteriological argument for the miracle of resurrection of Jesus in support.

Yet even if Campbell's four-pronged response to Hume manages to put the argument against belief in miracles at bay, Campbell still needs to address other worries that critics might have when considering his overall case for Christianity. As we have seen, some rather tricky questions linger in the background: How could we know whether God's messenger is mistaken or deceptive in relaying God's revelation? Which of the messenger's claims are revealed, and which are not? Lastly, when we consider Campbell's criteriological argument for the miracle of resurrection, we must determine whether the Lesliean criteria are actually met and whether meeting these four criteria really indicates the truth of the testimony in question. With these questions remaining, Campbell passes the baton; those who wish to take it from him need to provide decent enough answers or locate better arguments altogether.

Chapter 4

On the Problem of Evil and the Problem of Divine Hiddenness

Unlike many Christians over the years, Campbell took seriously the philosophical challenges posed by atheists and religious skeptics; he did not think a Christian could simply dismiss or ignore them. Neither did he think that they are easily addressed. It did not surprise him when in 1826, for example, he received a letter from a young skeptic. The letter's author ("Mr. D" in the published version) wanted to become a Christian to fulfill his mother's deathbed wish, but he could not bring himself to believe in the Christian God, given the evil in the world and the biblical doctrine of eternal damnation.[1] In the first of six replies, Campbell empathized with Mr. D, writing at one point, "I know there are many 'seeking religion,' who find [only] a sort of religion that does not wear well; a whole suit of it will become thread-bare in a few months."[2] The suit starts to wither and unravel, so he ventured, when formidable arguments are brought against it. For Campbell, though, the problem was not Christianity itself but the Christians who misrepresented it. They were often ill equipped to defend it properly and hence made it look flimsy. "Weak minds, like gun powder, are easily blown up," Campbell told Mr. D,[3] and some of the weakest religious minds were "like phosphorous" in that they "take fire without a single spark."[4]

Throughout his career, Campbell tried to offer the help that was needed. He addressed, directly and indirectly, several of the most difficult problems posed to Christian belief, problems that generate arguments for atheism. The most salient of these problems is the problem of evil, as it is called, so Campbell's response to it deserves a particularly close look. Oddly, though, it has not received much attention from the scholars who have discussed his philosophical work in any detail.[5] What is more, the most notable runner-up to the problem of evil is the so-called problem of divine hiddenness, and no one to my knowledge has considered Campbell's remarks on it. This shortage of discussion is understandable enough, in part because

Campbell's responses to these problems are often buried in and scattered throughout his writings on other topics (such as hell, providence, universalism, and the role of the will in forming beliefs), and some work is required to piece together what his responses were. But the work needs to be done, especially given how important Campbell must have thought it was to address these two problems.

This chapter is devoted to reconstructing his responses to them. At the least, the responses I present here are properly Campbellite, even if Campbell did not fully or consciously formulate them. Within his body of written work are the resources with which to develop these responses. I begin with an explanation of what one of the relevant arguments for atheism is, the so-called *logical* argument from evil, and then discuss how Campbell defends theism against it (§**4.1**). Then I examine the so-called *evidential* argument from evil and Campbell's response to it (§**4.2**). The chapter concludes with a reconstruction of Campbell's response to the problem of divine hiddenness (§**4.3**). I contend that Campbell offers a version of the free will defense against the logical version of the argument from evil and that he offers the resources for something akin to a skeptical theist response to the evidential version of the argument from evil. When it comes to the worries about the apparent hiddenness of God—and hence the argument from divine hiddenness—Campbell suggests that the real problem at hand is (among other things) the epistemic orientation of the nonbeliever, not the available evidence for God's existence.

4.1. The Logical Problem of Evil and Campbell's Free Will Defense

It is standard practice these days for philosophers to begin their discussions of the atheological argument from evil by first noting that there are at least two distinct versions of it.[6] The *logical* version of the argument from evil holds that God's existence is logically incompatible with the existence of any amount of evil in the world. The more modest, *evidential* formulation of the argument from evil claims only that the existence of gratuitous or pointless evil provides strong evidence that God does not exist. Although Campbell nowhere acknowledges the distinction between the logical and evidential versions of this argument—and even if it might seem somewhat anachronistic to read a nineteenth-century thinker in light of this relatively recent distinction—he nonetheless provides the resources for responding to both, or so I argue below. I turn now to a consideration of the traditional problem of evil and the logical argument from evil.

In his famous *Dialogues Concerning Natural Religion,* David Hume offers a succinct and well-rehearsed statement of the problem associated with maintaining theistic belief in light of the undeniable reality of evil in the world. After the characters in the dialogue entertain a lengthy discussion about the various forms of suffering and calamity in the world, Philo says, "Epicurus' old questions are yet unanswered. Is [God] willing to prevent evil, but not able? then is he impotent. Is he able, but not willing? then is he malevolent. Is he both able and willing? whence then is evil?"[7] In a passage that in many respects echoes Philo, Campbell imagines the problem in the following way:

> A pretty world this, to come from a *rational first cause*! Talk not of wisdom while you see so much folly in the universe! Only see the waste of water and the waste of land; only look . . . how many half-begun operations, and how many unfinished enterprises there are. Look at the deformities and the irregularities, and the mal-adaptions everywhere. Talk not of *goodness* . . . don't you see poisons lurking in your fields and gardens—pestilence and death stealing upon you in the invisible miasmata? Talk not of *justice*: see the good man punished for his virtue, and the wicked rewarded for his vice, etc., etc. So the idea of God is laughed out of the world."[8]

The central problem recognized by both Campbell and Hume stems from the combination of the fact that God is supposed to be omnipotent, omniscient, and omnibenevolent and the fact that, nonetheless, evil exists in the world. Yet, if God actually exists—and if he really is what theists take him to be—then it seems as though the world would be much different than it is. The obvious challenge for theists, then, is to explain why the world is so beset by evils that God, if he exists, should have been able and willing to leave out of the picture, so to speak. This is the very sort of problem Mr. D poses to Campbell when he writes that "as the Deity was the first cause of all things, he was responsible for all things, especially for *evil*, as he possessed a greater power to prevent it than the immediate cause."[9] If we take the liberty of extending Mr. D's reasoning here just a bit, we might say that if the deity is indeed the ultimate cause of evil, then either he is not omnipotent or he is not omnibenevolent—in either case, he is not what we have traditionally thought of as God. So either God simply does not exist or the deity is not what we thought he was, in which case he is unworthy of worship and unworthy of being called *God* in the first place.

This challenge to explain God's omnibenevolence and omnipotence in light of the reality of evil, in turn, provides the elements of a positive case for atheism. Although there are many ways in which one might formulate it, a fairly simple analysis of the *logical argument from evil* runs as follows:[10]

(L1) For something to be God, it must be omniscient, omnipotent, and omnibenevolent.

(L2) If something is unaware of all evils in the world, it is not omniscient.

(L3) If something is unable to prevent all evils in the world, it is not omnipotent.

(L4) If something is unwilling to prevent all evils in the world, it is not omnibenevolent.

(L5) So, if evil exists in the world, God does not exist.[11]

(L6) Evil exists in the world.

(L7) Thus, God does not exist.

In reference to this argument, Campbell clearly affirms premise L1 to the extent that he believes that when we are talking about God, we are indeed talking about an all-knowing, all-powerful, and maximally good being. And in his view, premise L2 is true insofar as "the Omniscient One" is fully aware of all the present and future evils in the world. More specifically, Campbell says that "before any creature was made, the result . . . on the present plan of things, was as perfectly well known to the Creator as it will be in any future period, and also that any other possible result on any other plan, was just as well known."[12] In other words, prior to the initial creative act, God would have known all the possible outcomes of (or within) the world he might create—including any evils that might arise. Additionally, Campbell clearly affirms premise L6, as he nowhere tries to downplay or disguise the reality of evil in the world.[13]

Campbell's response to the logical argument from evil is probably best interpreted as a rejection of premise L4—and, in turn, a rejection of premises L3 and L5. In short, he argues that, *precisely because of his omnibenevolence,* God chose to create humans who are free to act wrongly. And, in Campbell's view, it is logically impossible for God to both create free human agents and prevent them from introducing evil into the world when they act wrongly. Yet the fact that God is logically restricted from preventing the evil introduced by the misuse of human freedom in no way diminishes his omnipotence, so Campbell contends. Accordingly, if his account is correct, then premises L3, L4, and L5 are each problematic, and the logical argument from evil is unsound.

Effectively, Campbell's response to the logical argument from evil proceeds by way of denying the claim that an omnibenevolent being would be willing to prevent *all* evil from occurring. Although his take on this point is somewhat more convoluted and roundabout than an interpreter might wish, I take his view to be something like the following. As an omnibenevolent creator, God's fundamental goal in the initial creative act was to bring about a world populated with creatures capable of achieving the highest happiness, or the best end-state possible. Campbell thinks that this state of highest happiness consists of (at least) two things: recognizing God as the supreme "governor" of the universe; and becoming morally praiseworthy by obeying the moral laws he legislates.[14] Now, in order for creatures to have the capacity to genuinely obey God's laws—and, hence, in order for them to properly respect God as governor—they must have the capacity to *disobey* the moral law and nonetheless choose to follow it. That is, those creatures must have free will. For if these creatures were simply unable to disobey the moral laws, they would be little more than preprogrammed automata, and as such, they would not be neither praiseworthy nor blameworthy for any of their actions.

In explaining this last point, Campbell imagines a race of "infallible creatures," where by *infallible* he clearly means *unable to disobey the moral law.* Supposing there were such creatures, he says:

> What then? None of them *could* have become Satan [in the sense of disobeying God's moral laws]. But what next? None of them could have been capable of moral good. For it is essential to moral good that the agent act freely according to the last dictate, or the best dictate of his understanding. Moisture is not more essential to vegetation than this liberty of acting according to the views or feelings of the agent is to moral good. Please consider, that if a rational being was created incapable of disobeying [the moral law], he must, *on that very account,* be incapable of obeying. He then acts like a mill wheel, in the motions of which there is no choice; no virtue, no vice, no moral good, no moral evil. A little reflection is all that is wanting to see that a race of beings created incapable of disobeying (*i.e. infallible,*) are as incapable of moral good or moral evil; of virtue or vice; of rewards or punishments; of happiness or misery, as the stones of the field.[15]

The implication of Campbell's view here is that free will is a necessary condition for the possibility of (a) any genuine obedience to the governor-God, (b) any actual moral goodness in following the moral law, and hence (c) the highest happiness for which an omnibenevolent creator would aim. Recognizing all of this, then, the omnibenevolent God created humans with free will. However, in giving humans free will, God thereby endowed humans with the capacity to disobey the moral law by acting wrongly—and hence with the capacity to introduce some measure of evil into the world. The one necessarily accompanies the other. Accordingly, Campbell adds that, "if God had given birth to a system which in its very nature excluded the *possibility* of evil, it would have also excluded the possibility of his being a governor. A creator he might have been, but a governor he could not have been; and unless exhibited as a governor, no rational creature ever could have known him in that way essential to happiness."[16] Campbell's view here seems to be that God could not express himself as an omnibenevolent governor without first establishing a moral government in which there are citizens who are truly governed by, and hence capable of genuinely obeying (and disobeying), his moral laws.[17] This means that God's moral government effectively requires that those governed have free will, which necessarily ushers in the *possibility* of evil. And only within such a moral government is the highest happiness possible. Of course, there could have been a different world in which there were no such moral government, but it would not have been as good in the grand scheme of things as the world in which such a government could exist.

Thus, in Campbell's view, it is precisely God's omnibenevolence that led him to create a world populated with genuinely free creatures. And this act necessarily ushered in the possibility of evils arising from the misuse of that freedom—evils that God is simply unable to prevent, by virtue of the fact that they stem from the freedom that his benevolence led him to create in the first place. Campbell says, for example,

> The universe issued from the goodness of God. Not to display his power and wisdom, but to give vent to his benignity, God created the heavens and the earth, and peopled them with all variety of being. Infinite wisdom and almighty power did but execute the designs of eternal love. *Goodness is the impulsive attribute* which prompted all that the counsel and band of the Lord have executed. The current of the universe all runs on the side of benevolence. "Abundant in goodness and truth," *all God's designs are for the diffusion of bliss on the largest possible scale.* Evil there is; but, under the benevolent administration of the Father of mercies, there will be as much good, with as little evil, as almighty power, guided by infinite wisdom, can achieve.[18]

So, contrary to premise L4, Campbell argues that God's benevolence led him not only to be unwilling to prevent all evils but actually to want to create the conditions for the possibility of evil that necessarily accompany human freedom. The only alternatives available to God would have been either to create no world at all or to create a world populated with only nonfree creatures who are incapable of doing evil. Admittedly, choosing either of those options would have allowed God to prevent all evils because either option would have occluded the conditions for the possibility of evil. But neither of those options would have allowed for the highest happiness or best end-state involved in humans' respecting God as governor and obeying the moral laws he legislates—an end-state that an omnibenevolent God would indeed desire, or so Campbell thinks. Accordingly, Campbell's view ultimately boils down to this: a world populated with free human agents and the resultant *possibility* of evil in it is, all things considered, better than a world without free agents in the picture (or no world at all). And if that is true, then premise L4 is, strictly speaking, false.

Of course, there are numerous ways in which critics might wish to challenge Campbell's account here. Is it actually true that there is no other way for God to achieve the highest happiness or best end-state without giving humans the freedom to act wrongly? And is the highest happiness or best end-state really wrapped up in recognizing God as governor and obeying his moral laws? Why think that God would have any need or desire to be recognized as governor by his inferiors? And so on.

Admittedly, these are difficult questions for Campbell to answer, especially within the methodological constraints of natural theology. But, with that said, I do not think Campbell actually needs to demonstrate that his account above is correct in every respect in order to provide a serious response to the logical argument from evil. That is, Campbell need not specify what God's *actual* reasons are for allowing evil to occur. (To show that would be for Campbell to offer a theodicy.)[19] All Campbell needs to commit himself to is the *possibility* that the good achieved by endowing humans with free will outweighs the evil introduced by the misuse of that free will. Accordingly, he would need to have shown only that it is *possible* that God might be unwilling to prevent all evil because it is possible that, if God did eliminate the conditions for moral evil, then the best end-state would not be on the cards, so to speak. And if Campbell's account provides even a possible explanation as to why an omnibenevolent God would be unwilling to prevent all evil, then the atheist cannot assert that the reality of evil and the existence of God are logically incompatible. Hence, the logical argument from evil fails to demonstrate the nonexistence of God.

But even if we interpret Campbell as offering merely a *defense* against the logical problem of evil (as opposed to offering a full-blown theodicy), there are still some worries his account will occasion. The most obvious question is this: Why was it not within the power of an *all-powerful* God to have done more? Is it not a strike against God's omnipotence that he was unable to give humans freedom without also preventing evil from occurring? At this juncture, J. L. Mackie's query regarding free will defenses is particularly apropos:

> If God has made men such that in their free choices they sometimes prefer what is good and sometimes what is evil, why could he not have made men such that they always freely choose the good? If there is no logical impossibility in a man's freely choosing the good on one, or on several, occasions, there cannot be a logical impossibility in his freely choosing the good on every occasion. God was not, then, faced with a choice between making innocent automata and making beings who, in acting freely, would sometimes go wrong: there was open to him the obviously better possibility of making beings who would act freely *but always go right.* Clearly, his failure to avail himself of this possibility is inconsistent with his being both omnipotent and wholly good.[20]

To see Mackie's point here in high relief, it might be helpful to consider the following illustration. Imagine the immense array of possible worlds (*PW*$_1$ through *PW*$_n$) that an omniscient God could have surveyed prior to the initial creative act. For example, in *PW*$_1$, there are free creatures, 80 percent of whom freely act rightly most of time, 10 percent of whom freely act rightly all of the time, and 10 percent of whom always freely act wrongly. In *PW*$_2$, all free creatures freely act wrongly at least some of the time. In *PW*$_3$, every other free creature freely acts rightly all of the time, and everyone else freely acts wrongly at least some of the time. And so on. (Obviously, there are an untold number of these possible worlds.) Now, among this array of possible worlds, would there not be at least one world in which every free creature always *freely* acts rightly? As Mackie notes, there is nothing logically impossible about a free creature freely acting rightly on every single occasion. And if that is correct, then there is at least one possible world in which *every* free creature freely chooses to act rightly on every occasion. To simplify matters, let *goody-goody world* stand for the possible world in which every free creature always freely chooses to act rightly. Given his omniscience, there is no reason why God would not have surveyed *that* possible world prior to the initial creative act. So, the challenge on offer from Mackie is this: If an omniscient, omnibenevolent, and omnipotent God exists, why did he not actualize goody-goody world? Because it was clearly not actualized, Mackie concludes that either God is not omnipotent or he is not omnibenevolent—and, in either case, he is not God, traditionally understood.

It is available for Campbell to reply to this sort of criticism by arguing that even if goody-goody world is one of the many possible worlds God would have *surveyed* prior to the initial creative act, he could not have actualized that particular world all at once by himself in the initial creative act. Campbell clearly thinks that there are some things that even omnipotence cannot do—and actualizing goody-goody world would clearly have to be one of those things.

Of course, claiming that *there are some things that omnipotence cannot do* might initially sound strange to us, because our inclination might be to suppose that an omnipotent being has *absolutely* unlimited power. But for Campbell, this view of omnipotence is shortsighted. The basic idea for him is that no one—not even an omnipotent being—would be able to do that which is logically impossible for him to do. Campbell says, for example, "There are some things impossible to Omnipotence. Hills cannot be made without vallies [*sic*]; shadows, without substances; nor rational beings, without free agency."[21] In short, omnipotence would be unable to create a hill without thereby creating a valley, because the existence of the former necessarily accompanies the existence of the latter. There could be no such thing as a hill-sans-valley, as such a thing is effectively on par with a square-circle: neither can be conceived. And not even omnipotence has the power to wade out past the confines of logical possibility. Yet the fact that God is unable to do the logically impossible act in no way counts as a strike against his omnipotence, for when it comes to doing the logically impossible act, there is actually *nothing* there to do.[22] Consequently, in Campbell's view, we ought to think of omnipotence as the power to do anything that is logically possible.

But, of course, we need to double back and ask, Why would it be logically impossible for an omnipotent God to actualize goody-goody world—especially since, as Mackie notes, goody-goody world is a logically possible world that God would have surveyed prior to the initial creative act? Campbell clearly thinks that one of the logical limits facing an omnipotent being is this: just as omnipotence cannot create a hill-sans-valley, omnipotence cannot create genuinely free humans who lack the capacity for sometimes acting wrongly. At least part of what it means to be free, in Campbell's view, is to be able to choose whether to act rightly or wrongly. And having the capacity to act wrongly is to have the capacity to introduce some measure of evil into the world. Accordingly, when an omnipotent God creates free humans, he cannot also avoid creating the conditions for the possibility of at least some evil arising in the world; doing *both* would be akin to creating a hill-sans-valley or a square-circle. Of course, it is logically possible that all free human agents, in due course, freely choose to act rightly on every single occasion in such a way that would indeed bring goody-goody world to fruition. But—and here is the rub—it is logically impossible for God *alone* to actualize goody-goody world in the *initial* creative act, because doing so would require him to both (a) create genuinely free creatures and (b) ensure that those creatures will never misuse their freedom.

But not even an omnipotent God can bring about the *combination* of (a) and (b) at the same time, because his doing the former entails the inability of his doing the latter. As Campbell puts it, "It is not possible in mechanics, nor in morals, nor in religion, to have a rule which will prevent error so long as those who use it are free and fallible agents."[23] Consequently, we are left with what may seem like a counter-intuitive predicament: it is logically impossible for God in the initial creative act to ensure that the world he is creating is the logically possible, goody-goody world.[24] At best, God could sow the seeds of goody-goody world, so to speak, by creating free human agents in the initial creative act. In turn, he could then earnestly desire that the free agents he created would take it from there to bring goody-goody world to fruition. But it would be logically impossible for God alone to force the full bloom of goody-goody world into existence all at once in the initial creative act.

So, ultimately, if what I have interpreted as Campbell's view is correct, then premises L4, L3, and L5 of the logical argument from evil are problematic, in which case the argument fails. Consequently, if Campbell's account is correct, then the undeniable reality of evil in the world does not somehow demonstrate the nonexistence of God.

I should note at the close of this section that what I have interpreted as Campbell's response to the logical argument from evil in many respects anticipates the formulation of the free will defense made popular in recent decades by Alvin Plantinga, who summarizes his view as follows:

> A world containing creatures who are significantly free (and freely perform more good than evil actions) is more valuable, all else being equal, than a world containing no free creatures at all. Now God can create free creatures, but He can't *cause* or *determine* them to do only what is right. For if He does so, then they aren't significantly free after all; they do not do what is right *freely.* To create creatures capable of moral good, therefore, He must create creatures capable of moral evil; and He can't give these creatures the freedom to perform evil and at the same time prevent them from doing so. As it turned out, sadly enough, some of the free creatures God created went wrong in the exercise of their freedom; this is the source of moral evil. The fact that free creatures sometimes go wrong, however, counts neither against God's omnipotence nor against His goodness; for He could have forestalled the occurrence of moral evil only by removing the possibility of moral good.[25]

4.2. The Evidential Argument from Evil and Campbell's Skeptical Theist Response

Thanks in part to responses like the one seen above—and thanks perhaps most notably to Plantinga's now-famous formulation of the free will defense[26]—many philosophers these days are prepared to concede that *logical* versions of the argument from evil are unsound,[27] hence pose no real threat to theism.[28] That is, many contemporary philosophers seem willing to concede that the existence of evil *simpliciter* is indeed compatible with the existence of an omnipotent and omnibenevolent God. Not surprisingly, then, many atheists have put their eggs in other baskets, and attention is increasingly focused on a more modest formulation of the argument from evil typically referred to as the *evidential* argument from evil.[29] According to this line of reasoning, the problem is not that evil *simpliciter* is somehow incompatible with the existence of God, but rather that there are certain kinds of evil in the world that, because they apparently serve no greater purpose, provide compelling evidence that God does not exist.

Proponents of the evidential argument from evil typically proceed with the observation that *it sure seems to us* that there are certain instances of evil in the world that serve no morally justifying purpose. That is, it appears to us that there are certain evils that are neither required for some greater compensating good (like, say, free will) nor preventive of some equally bad or worse evil. In other words, it appears to us that there are certain evils in the world that an all-powerful and all-knowing God could have prevented without thereby forfeiting some greater good or thereby permitting some equally bad or worse evil. Call those evils *gratuitous* or *pointless evils.* To present us with an example of what appears to be a pointless evil, William Rowe has us imagine a young fawn's being severely "burned in a fire caused by lightning, and suffering terribly for five days before death ends its life."[30] Examples of this sort are particularly problematic, as Rowe explains, because they do not seem to involve free will at any level, and so we are have no recourse to the free will defense seen above to explain why evils of this sort would be permitted by God.[31] Accordingly, the fawn's suffering appears to us to serve no justifying purpose in the grand scheme of things; it is apparently pointless. To make matters worse on this front, other examples like Rowe's fawn are fairly easy to come by.

The problem that these apparently pointless evils pose is simple: if God actually exists, he could have prevented pointless evils precisely because they are utterly pointless, and preventing these evils would not have involved giving up on some greater good or permitting some equally bad or worse evil. And it seems as though God would and should want to prevent any such evils. Consider Rowe's fawn for the moment. It sure seems that God could have prevented this instance of suffering without having to strip the world of free human agents; nor would God have had to permit some worse evil if he had just prevented (or at least quickly ended) the fawn's suffering. Consequently, theists are left with a particularly tricky question: Why did an omniscient, omnibenevolent, and omnipotent God not prevent all of these apparently pointless evils? That he apparently did not, then, provides evidence that God probably does not exist—or so some argue.

Following Rowe, we can summarize the *evidential argument from evil* in the following way:[32]

(E1) If God exists, there would be no pointless evils in the world.
(E2) But, probably, there are pointless evils in the world.
(E3) Therefore, probably, God does not exist.

Before teasing out a Campbellite response to this kind of argument, we should first spend the time to get a handle on premise E1. Note that this premise is not saying that there would be a complete absence of all evils in the world if God exists, but only that there would be an absence of those evils that do not serve some greater purpose either by facilitating a greater good or by preventing some equally bad or worse evil. Accordingly, premise E1 is fully consistent with Campbell's free will defense against the logical argument from evil, for, in Campbell's view, God could and would prevent all evils that are logically possible for him to prevent. (Recall that Campbell thinks that "there will be as much good, with as little evil, as almighty power, guided by infinite wisdom, can achieve.")[33] However, in Campbell's view, there will perhaps remain some evils that God simply cannot prevent—those evils that stem from the misuse of human freedom. But strictly speaking, *those* evils would not be pointless in the relevant sense: they are nonpointless to the extent that they result from the necessary conditions of creating the greater good of a world populated with free human agents. Thus, there *is* a reason why those nonpointless evils exist: God cannot prevent them while also providing the conditions for the possibility of the greatest end-state in creation. But according to Campbell, God would indeed prevent all other evils—that is, God *would* prevent pointless evils. Consequently, Campbell seems committed to premise E1.[34]

That leaves us then with premise E2. What reasons do we have for thinking that, probably, there are genuinely pointless evils in the world? The most obvious reason for thinking this is that certain evils, like Rowe's fawn, *appear to us* to be pointless. Rowe admits that this observation alone does not constitute a knockdown, drag-out proof that the evils in question are, in fact, pointless. However, the fact that they appear to us to be pointless does give us decent enough grounds for believing that certain evils are probably pointless. And nearly everyone can agree that certain evils *appear to us* to be pointless.[35] So, at the very least, it seems that we are well warranted in concluding that, probably, there are some pointless evils in the world. And if that is correct, then the theist has a serious problem on her hands.

The question we need to ask at this juncture is whether Rowe is correct in thinking that the fact that certain evils *appear to us* to be pointless provides us with adequate grounds for concluding that the evils in question are probably bona fide pointless evils. Many philosophers—so-called skeptical theists most notably[36]—challenge the evidential argument from evil by arguing that we simply cannot know whether those evils that appear to us to be pointless are, in fact, pointless in the grand scheme of things. Accordingly, we cannot know whether premise E2 is true, and we would therefore be mistaken to affirm it.

One way of framing the skeptical theist's view here goes as follows. Presumably, Rowe and other proponents of the evidential argument from evil think that the fawn's suffering is a prime example of pointless evil because we neither see nor can we even fathom what greater good is brought about, or what worse evil is avoided by, allowing this particular instance of evil. That is, we cannot detect the possible reason that would justify God for allowing the evil in question. Accordingly, we infer from the fact that *we cannot think of a reason* God could have for allowing the evil in question to the conclusion that, *probably, there is not one*; thus, probably, the evil in question is pointless. Following Stephen Wykstra's lead,[37] call the inference involved here the *noseeum inference* (that is, "We no see'm, so they probably ain't there!"). Skeptical theists typically respond to the evidential argument from evil by claiming that the noseeum inference used to support premise E2 is faulty.

Why is this? Consider an analogy. Because of her limited understanding of pedagogy and her lack of experience with a particular teacher, a student might not be able to detect the reasons why, say, her philosophy teacher is so obscure about certain things during class. Nonetheless, the student would be mistaken to infer from the fact that she is unable to detect her teacher's reasons to the conclusion that he has no good reasons in the first place. That kind of inference would be unreliable, because the teacher may have some excellent pedagogical reasons for his obscurity—and those reasons might very well extend beyond the student's grasp at the moment.[38] Furthermore, good pedagogical practice might actually require that the teacher neither disclose his reasons for being obscure nor make an effort to quell the discomfort caused by his intentional obscurity. Accordingly, that the student cannot detect her teacher's reasons does not justify her in concluding that, probably, there are none.[39] In much the same way that the student stands in relation to her teacher's reasons for his obscurity, humans stand in relation to the range of reasons God may have for allowing certain evils, if God exists. Why should we humans expect to have access to the *full* range of reasons an omniscient God (if he exists) may have access to when deciding whether to permit some evil?[40] Perhaps God sees that some worse evil would be ushered in or that some greater good would be precluded if he prevented the fawn's suffering. And perhaps God's reasons here—that is, facts about the good and evils of which he is fully aware—are simply beyond our ken, and perhaps it would be ill-advised for God to make an effort to disclose them to us. Accordingly, because it is unreasonable for us to think that we *do* have access to the full range of reasons that God may have for permitting some evil (if he exists), then we have no way of knowing whether our inability to detect God's reasons for allowing some evil gives us any decent indication that, probably, there are none in the first place. So we are simply unable to determine whether any instance of evil is actually (or even probably) pointless. Hence, we cannot know whether premise E2 is true, and we lack warrant for affirming it. Accordingly, the evidential argument from evil fails to get off the ground.

Although Campbell nowhere attempts to develop this sort of position in great detail, I think we can interpret him as offering the resources for something of a skeptical theist response to the evidential argument from evil. Campbell certainly has no problem admitting that some evils can appear to us at times to be utterly pointless. But in his view, the fact that certain features of the world *appear* pointless to us says more about *us*—that we have a limited perspective on reality and that we are impatient creatures—than it does about the nature of the evils present in the world. Were we to have an omniscient perspective, we would be able to see whether there are, in fact, any good reasons for not preventing certain evils or for not making things any different than they are. But we clearly enjoy no such perch. And Campbell clearly thinks that if an omniscient God exists, he may have access to reasons that are well beyond our reach—just as a teacher might have his reasons that the student cannot detect and need not have access to.[41]

Imagine, Campbell says, that someone were to ask why God did not just skip past all the undesirable phases of the world's history and introduce "the best possible order of things first."

> Such cavilers remind me of the child who asks, whether from curiosity or petulance: Why does not the ripe ear of corn come up from the seed deposited in the earth? Why does not the full ripe ear first present itself to our eye? Would not a kind and benevolent being have done this rather than have kept us waiting for many months, for the tedious process of germinating, growing, shooting, blossoming? etc., etc. Could not an almighty, and benevolent being, have produced the ripe ear without waiting for a sprout, stalk, leaves, blossoms, and all

> the other preparations of nature to form an ear of corn? We are, even in the common concerns of life, but poor judges of propriety; and it is extreme arrogance for us to arraign Omniscience at the tribunal of our reason when we cannot tell the reason why the blossom precedes the fruit.[42]

The relevant point here is that, just as an omniscient God may well have his reasons for making corn grow in a certain way (and reasons we cannot access), he may also have reasons for allowing those evils that we would indeed want left out of the picture.[43] Thus, it is unreasonable for us to think that we have access to the full range of God's possible reasons for allowing those evils. Nonetheless, Campbell warns that "there is an error into which we are all apt to fall, in attempting to scan the moral government of the world."[44] Because we are impatient, we grow troubled with the "state of suspense upon any subject which interests us."[45] But "rather than remain in suspense," we succumb to the temptation to overestimate our "very incorrect or partial views of things," and we start drawing conclusions about the status of certain evils we encounter.[46] Unfortunately for us, though, "our views are always partial at best, but much more so when we have not put ourselves to the trouble to analyze with patience, the whole data" that would be available to God, were he to exist.[47] In turn, our impatience drives us to the dubious conclusion that, because we cannot detect the reasons why things are the way they are, there are (probably) no good reasons. In other words, our impatience and lack of humility motivates our noseeum inference. Eventually, this leads us to indict God as either morally culpable or simply nonexistent.

Commenting further on this same sort of point above, Campbell offers the following analogy:

> When I hear persons caviling at the present state of things [including what appear to be pointlessly evil states of affairs in the world], and objecting to matters which they do not understand, I figure to myself, a person stationed in a small room, say ten feet square, before which is passing continually a map ten thousand square miles in extent; ten feet of which only, at a time, can be seen through an opening in one side. In this small room he sits and peruses this map, for seventy years. For many weeks at a time he sees nothing but immense oceans of water; then apparently boundless forests; then prodigious chains of mountains; then deserts, flats, wastes, and wildernesses. Here and there a succession of beautiful country passes before his eyes. After contemplating this map for seventy years, he exclaims, "What an

> irrational, ill-conducted, and incongruous-looking thing is this! I have seen forests, deserts, and oceans, interspersed here and there with some small specks of beautiful country. I must conclude that the Creator of this planet was either unwise or not benevolent." But, suppose, that on a sudden, the walls of his cottage fell down, and his vision was enlarged and strengthened so as to comprehend, in one glance, the whole sweep of ten thousand square miles; what a wonderful revolution would he undergo! Infinite wisdom and design now appear, where before he saw nothing but confusion and deformity. . . . *We* have but a small part of the picture before us.[48]

Campbell's point here can be interpreted in the following way. Just as the man in the small room does not have access to the full landscape behind the wall, we do not have access to the full range of reasons that God (if he exists) may have for allowing certain evils. The fundamental mistake we make is that, just like the man in the room, we take ourselves to have access to the full range of reasons we would need in order to determine whether there are, in fact, good reasons for God to allow certain evils. Consequently, when we find ourselves unable to detect the reasons why certain evils would be allowed, we conclude that those evils are probably utterly pointless: we make the noseeum inference. But the noseeum inference is unreliable in this case because, like the man in the room, we are being unreasonable in thinking that we have access to the reasons God may have, if he exists. And if that is the case, then the noseeum inference here would be faulty; we would not be able to determine whether an evil is, in fact, pointless. Thus, with the skeptical theists, Campbell could claim that *we cannot know* whether premise E2 is true; hence, it lacks warrant, and the evidential argument from evil fails to get off the ground.

To be sure, there are several worries one might have about skeptical theism in general and, hence, about what I have interpreted as Campbell's response to the evidential argument from evil. I cannot discuss each of those worries here.[49] However, one of the most pressing and difficult questions for any skeptical theist, including Campbell, is this: If we cannot reliably determine whether some *apparently* pointless evil is, in fact, pointless, then are we not left in the dark when it comes to deciding how to act in a host of troubling scenarios?[50]

To illustrate the problem here, imagine that a wildfire is quickly approaching my neighborhood. Imagine further that if I do not quickly intervene, the fire will consume my neighbor's sleeping baby. Let *B* stand for the impending evil of the baby's suffering and death by fire. It certainly *appears to me* that *B*, were it to occur, would be pointless. But how could I know that for sure? Consistent with the skeptical theist's response to premise E2 above, it seems that Campbell would be committed to saying that I am unable to determine whether God might have good reasons for allowing *B*. Perhaps God sees fit to allow *B* because, for reasons unknowable by me, *B* is necessary to bring about some greater good or to prevent some worse evil. And if *B* is, in fact, *not* pointless, then it might be morally problematic for me to intervene to prevent *B* from occurring. Thus, since I have no way of determining whether *B* is *actually* (or even probably) pointless, it seems that I would also have no reliable way of determining whether I should intervene to save the baby's life from the encroaching wildfire. In other words, my skepticism about the status of *B*'s gratuitousness leaves me in the dark when it comes to deciding whether to prevent *B*.

To be sure, I can only speculate about what Campbell might say here, although I think it is available for him to reply in the following way. Admittedly, we might not be able to know whether *B* is, in fact, pointless; hence our skepticism about premise E2 of the evidential argument from evil. But as it concerns *my* duty to the neighbor's baby, the ensuing skepticism about whether *B* is pointless is neither here nor there. In Campbell's view, the way we should proceed in determining how to act is not always (or even primarily) by trying to calculate how much good a particular course of action will promote or how much pointless evil it will prevent. That is, in Campbell's view, the appropriate procedure for making moral decisions does not always revolve around an attempt to determine which actions best square with one's speculation about what God's reasons may or may not be for allowing some evil to occur. Rather, in his view, the appropriate way for us to determine how we should act in a given situation is by recognizing God as governor, by discerning his laws (as given in his revelation), and by obeying them. In other words, our moral deliberations should begin with an attempt to determine what God's laws are, how they apply to the situation, and what they require of us in the given circumstance. Regarding the decision involving *B*, Campbell might say that it would be reasonable for me to conclude—by acknowledging God's revealed command to love my neighbor as myself—that I do have perfectly adequate reason to intervene to prevent *B* from occurring.[51] Accordingly, it would be right for me to intervene to prevent *B*, even if God were to see fit to allow *B* in the grand scheme of things. My duty is to obey God's law as it is presented to me—not to try to determine what God's reasons may be for allowing some evil to occur.[52]

Of course, some critics will no doubt find this sort of reply unconvincing at best, especially if they are inclined to reject the whole prospect of divine revelation in the first place.[53] But, in any case, whether this Campbellite reply to the moral objection to skeptical theism is acceptable at the end of the day, I must leave here for readers to decide.

4.3. Campbell on the Problem of Divine Hiddenness

Bertrand Russell—one of the most notable atheist philosophers of the twentieth century—was once asked what he would say for himself if it turned out that he was wrong about his atheism and he had to face God after he died. He replied, "Why, I should say, 'God, you gave us insufficient evidence.'"[54] Russell's characteristically clever quip here captures much of the spirit behind what has become in recent decades one of the most widely discussed arguments for atheism—the so-called argument from divine hiddenness. While the argument from divine hiddenness is similar to the argument from evil in several important ways, the former is increasingly viewed as distinct and as giving the latter a run for its money in posing a threat to theism.[55]

Consider for a moment what we might think of as *God's hiddenness* relative to humans. That is, consider what some people take to be the shortage—or even the lack—of obvious and overwhelming evidence that God exists. Campbell clearly believed that this apparent hiddenness problem poses a serious challenge for theists, especially in light of the fact that God (were he to exist) could have provided much more (and much stronger) evidence of his existence if he had wanted to. In his effort to anticipate how an atheist's challenge to Christians on this point might run, Campbell says,

> I will, without hesitation, admit that the evidences of the truth of Christianity might have been easily augmented if it had pleased the founder of it, or had it been compatible with the whole plan of things. . . . God might speak in all the languages of the world in the same instant of time, and inform all nations, *viva voce*, that the contents of the New Testament were worthy of universal acceptation. . . . ["]Why, tell me, ye Christians. . . . Why was not the evidence greater . . . than it is? Your systems will not enable you to answer this question I am sure. Ask your Doctors, and they cannot tell you. Ask your systems, and they have forgotten it. Yet it is a fact that the evidences are adjusted upon a certain scale and amount to a certain maximum beyond which they do not go.["][56]

Campbell's imagined challenge on behalf of the atheist helps bring the following kind of questions into sharper focus: Why is God's existence *not* more obvious than it can appear to some people to be? That is, if the Christian God actually exists, then why is there not more and better evidence to that effect? If he exists and is actually omnipotent, surely he would be able to offer immense and compelling evidence of his existence. And if God were really omnibenevolent and perfectly loving, would he not want to make sure that we know about him by providing us with adequate evidence?

Seizing upon these very sorts of questions, some philosophers in recent years have argued that the apparent weakness or shortage of evidence for God's existence provides the makings of a positive case for atheism.[57] In short, some argue that a truly omnibenevolent (and hence perfectly loving) God would indeed offer a great deal of evidence for his existence[58]—so much evidence, in fact, that *not* believing in his existence would be patently irrational. But, so the argument goes, there is no such measure of evidence for God's existence. After all, some individuals indeed *rationally* refrain from believing in God. So God must not exist.

With some adjustments on the recent work of J. L. Schellenberg,[59] we can formalize the *argument from divine hiddenness* in the following way:

(Dh1) If there is a God, he is (among other things) omnibenevolent.

(Dh2) If an omnibenevolent God exists, he provides enough evidence of his existence to make rational nonbelief impossible. In other words, if an omnibenevolent God exists, he makes sure that the evidence is so strong that one would be irrational to not believe that God exists. (Let the term *superevidence* stand for this measure of evidence that an omnibenevolent God would provide.)

(Dh3) If there is superevidence of God's existence, then there is no one who rationally refrains from believing in God.

(Dh4) Some people rationally refrain from belief in God's existence.

(Dh5) So, there is no such superevidence of God's existence.

(Dh6) So, an omnibenevolent God does not exist.

(Dh7) Thus, God does not exist.

Before considering Campbell's response to this sort of argument, we should get a handle on the rationale behind premise Dh2. The thought here is fairly simple: Because God is good and loving, he would clearly want his creatures to be able to obtain good things. And because God is *omni*benevolent and perfectly loving, he would want people to be able to reach the best possible good, namely, a proper relationship with him. But, for one to partake in a relationship with God, one must first *believe* in God's existence. And for one to believe in God's existence, one must have some sort of evidence that God exists, since belief is not simply a matter of voluntary control—that is, one cannot simply cause herself to believe something willy-nilly. Accordingly, an omnibenevolent God would provide enough evidence of his existence to render nonbelief something that would occur only if a person somehow failed to use her rational faculties properly. In other words, the measure of evidence an omnibenevolent God would provide would be so ample (and of a certain quality) that it would be one's own fault for not believing in God's existence. In still other words, an omnibenevolent God would provide what I am calling *superevidence* of his existence, as defined in premise Dh2.

I submit that we can read Campbell as offering a twofold strategy for responding to the argument from divine hiddenness. Specifically, he apparently rejects both premise Dh2 and premise Dh4. For reasons that will become clear later on, this approach may appear to be a problematic combination of responses. For the moment, though, consider each part separately.

Premise Dh2 is the conditional claim that if an omnibenevolent God exists, he provides superevidence of his existence. Campbell clearly thinks that this conditional claim is false. Now, in order to falsify this claim, one would need to show that an omnibenevolent God might have a positive reason for *not* providing such superevidence of his existence. What reason might (or does) God have? In Campbell's view, an omnibenevolent God would want to avoid obliterating the moral significance of believing in his existence. This may require (and, Campbell thinks, does require) that the quality and extent of the evidence God provides of his existence be limited to some measure less than full-blown superevidence so that our free human choices can be involved at some level in the process of coming to belief in God's existence. Specifically, Campbell thinks that if God were to offer greater "evidences" than we actually have, then

> all excellency in faith would have been *destroyed*. . . . While a small proportion of the evidence [that we actually have] is sufficient for some, it is all necessary for others; and those who do not believe upon the whole of it and have one objection remaining when the whole is heard and examined, that which would remove this one objection would destroy every virtue and excellency properly belonging to faith. *Faith built upon evidence greater than the whole amount divinely vouchsafed, would have nothing moral about it*; it would be as unavoidable as the motions of a mill wheel under a powerful head of water, or as the waving tops of pines beneath a whirlwind.[60]

The idea here for Campbell seems to be that if God were to provide superevidence as opposed to the amount of evidence for his existence that we actually have available to us, then belief in God's existence would be effectively thrust upon all humans who rationally consider the matter. That is, if God were to provide superevidence, then the evidence would be so strong and overwhelming that no one could rationally refrain from believing in him. Accordingly, our free choices would in no way affect whether we believe in God's existence, hence, believing in his existence would lack any real moral significance.[61] But, so Campbell suggests, a world in which our free choices have some sort of effect on whether we believe in God's existence (hence a world in which belief in God has moral significance) is, in the grand scheme of things, better than a world in which our belief in God's existence is unavoidable. Of course, he thinks that God is certainly able to go the extra mile and provide those signs and wonders that would compel all nonbelievers into belief. For example, God could simply "*cure* such infidels" of their unbelief.[62] But Campbell thinks that "it is incompatible with the principles of [God's] moral government [as an omnibenevolent governor] to display omnipotence this way."[63] Thus, Campbell's view is that if an omnibenevolent God exists, he would actually want to *withhold* a certain amount of evidence of his existence—the difference between superevidence and the amount of evidence we actually have—in order to preserve the moral significance of believing in God's existence. And if that is correct, then premise Dh2 is false: it is simply not the case that if an omnibenevolent God exists, he necessarily provides superevidence of his existence (as opposed to the amount of evidence we have).

This account leaves Campbell endorsing what may seem like a strange view here. What all of the above implies is that because an omnibenevolent God (were he to exist) would not necessarily provide superevidence of his existence, it may be possible for some individuals to *rationally* refrain from believing in God; such a looming possibility may be a necessary by-product of an omnibenevolent God's plan to make a better world than there would otherwise be by preserving the conditions for the moral significance of belief in God's existence. At the least, the possibility of rational nonbelief cannot be ruled out. And if Campbell is correct about all of this, then premise Dh2 is false, and the argument from divine hiddenness is unsound.

Of course, there are some important questions remaining for Campbell's view here. Why should we think that some measure of divine hiddenness is required so that free choice can be involved at some level in the process of coming to belief in God's existence? Would God not be resourceful enough to make himself less obscure while at the same time doing so in a way that would avoid obliterating the moral significance of believing in his existence? And, furthermore, why should we think that preserving the moral significance of believing in God's existence would outweigh the other potential goods God might have in mind? Unfortunately, Campbell does not attempt to address these questions head on, so his interpreters still have some work to do in developing his position fully.

In any case, Campbell's rejection of premise Dh2 might be especially difficult to support if we interpret him as offering us God's *actual* reason for not providing the full measure of superevidence. But perhaps we need not read his view in that way. Instead, we might interpret his view more modestly as saying only that there are *possible* reasons an omnibenevolent God might have for providing something less than the full-blown superevidence. And if preserving the moral significance of belief in God's existence is even a possible reason why an omnibenevolent God might withhold the full measure of superevidence, then it would be incorrect to say that if an omnibenevolent God exists, he (necessarily) provides enough evidence of his existence to make rational nonbelief impossible.

At this juncture, the proponent of the argument from divine hiddenness might respond by conceding that Campbell's account offers us at least a possible reason God might not provide superevidence such that, strictly speaking, premise Dh2 is false. But, so she might ask, what if we simply revise the argument by substituting a more modest claim in the place of premise Dh2? Perhaps all a proponent of the argument needs to say is this: if an omnibenevolent God exists, it is reasonable for us to expect that he would provide superevidence. Obviously, mutatis mutandis, such a revision would yield only a probabilistic conclusion for the argument from divine hiddenness. But because this reformulation involves a weaker version of premise Dh2, it is less threatened by the strategy deployed immediately above.

I suspect that Campbell's reply here would ultimately come down to this: aside from what God specifically reveals to us about himself, we have no reliable way of determining what is and is not reasonable for us to expect of an omnibenevolent God vis-à-vis his provision of evidence of his existence. That is, aside from what God reveals to us about himself, we have no way of determining the precise amount of evidence of his existence that he would want to provide (or would be justified in providing). Accordingly, so Campbell might continue, those thinkers who antecedently bar any appeal to divine revelation would lack a sufficient basis for their claims about what we could reasonably expect God to do in this case. (Recall that, as discussed in chapter 2, Campbell thinks that sans revelation we would lack even the *idea* of God in the first place.) So, at best, those who exclude all appeals to revelation would, in Campbell's view, lack warrant for even the more modest claim about what is reasonable for us to expect of God with respect to his provision of evidence of his existence. Ultimately, then, Campbell might be interpreted as claiming that premise Dh2 is either patently false or, at its best, unwarranted.

Turning to Campbell's second response to the argument from divine hiddenness, we see that he seems to be of the mind that premise Dh4 is false because God actually *does* provide superevidence. (In case the reader suspects that Campbell wants to have his cake and eat it too here, be aware that I return to this point below.) There are several places in Campbell's writings where he suggests—contrary to what his rejection of premise Dh2 implies—that no one can *rationally* refrain from believing in Christianity, hence no one can *rationally* refrain from believing in God's existence in the first place. For example, he explicitly states that "no man philosophically or rationally can object to the Christian religion" and that "if a person act rationally, upon principles of reason, they *must* assent to the truth and certainty of the Christian religion."[64] And there are other such passages where Campbell suggests that the evidence in support of Christianity is so overwhelming that one would indeed be irrational to refrain from belief.[65] Obviously, if Campbell is right about all of this, then premise Dh4 is false, and the argument from divine hiddenness is unsound.

But clearly, denying premise Dh4 leaves some difficult problems for Campbell's view. Perhaps the most obvious problem is that it is exceedingly difficult to make good on the bold claim that, because God actually does provide superevidence, rational nonbelief is impossible. Even if we leave aside the question about what that putative superevidence is supposed to be, we must still confront this question: Are all nonbelievers really irrational in some way when it comes to their nonbelief in God's existence? Of course, there probably are some nonbelievers who are irrational in their nonbelief in God's existence. Some atheists, for instance, seem to manifest poor inferential skills when it comes to assessing religious matters, for whatever reason. But in all fairness, saying with a straight face that *all* nonbelievers whatsoever are irrational in their nonbelief is difficult, because some nonbelievers seem to bear all the markings of rationality in their nonbelief: they are perfectly open-minded and even eager about the possibility of God's existence, they are judicious and thorough in assessing the available evidence, and they are sincere and intelligent in seeking the truth of the matter. Nonetheless, some of these people do not believe in God's existence, even after much consideration. And it is hard to see how *those* individuals fail to be rational in their nonbelief. Consequently, if Campbell is indeed claiming that no one can *rationally* refrain from belief in God's existence, then his view here presents us with a difficult and bitter pill to swallow in light of what appears to be empirical evidence to the contrary.

A second and related problem is this: if God actually does provide superevidence—that is, if God offers evidence sufficient to render rational nonbelief impossible—then what, in Campbell's view, accounts for the fact that there are so many apparently rational people who do not believe in God's existence? In other words, if superevidence of God's existence is really available to everyone, then why do so many smart, honest, and sincere people fail to believe in God? Campbell's response to this question is certainly not to say that all nonbelievers are irrational in every respect. In fact, he admits that many religious skeptics are "honest men and good citizens" and that they generally employ their rational faculties quite well.[66] But he does seem to think that nonbelievers nonetheless fail to reason properly when it comes to the evidence of God's existence and, furthermore, that they deceive themselves when they conclude that they have reasoned properly about it.[67] Granting Campbell's view here for the moment, we should ask, What causes these otherwise honest, decent, and rational people to get off the proper track on this particular issue?

In short, Campbell thinks that these individuals make certain choices in their lives that in due course either blind them to the available evidence of God's existence or somehow prejudice their assessment of that evidence.[68] His view here seems to go as follows. Campbell clearly thinks that the process of forming beliefs requires that we have evidence of some sort. Hence, he says that "no man can believe without evidence"; that is, we cannot simply cause ourselves to believe something on the basis of volition or will alone.[69] However, Campbell thinks that the will nonetheless plays an *indirect* role in the process of forming beliefs.[70] In his view, the will controls whether and to what extent we allow ourselves to employ the faculties of recollection, reflection, imagination, reasoning, and judging, as well as whether and how we weigh the testimony of other people.[71] For example, he thinks that whereas we exercise the faculty of imagination when we abstract a quality from one simple idea and combine it with the quality of another to form a complex idea, what initiates this whole process in the first place is the will.[72] In much the same way, the very process of inquiry is initiated by the will, and the will, in turn, affects how that inquiry is undertaken at several steps along the way.[73] Furthermore, he asserts that "the understanding is not independent of the will, nor the will of the understanding" and that the will has "immense power" over the understanding.[74] As it turns out, the will is indeed influenced by our passions, prejudices, and the various interests we may have. Accordingly, because the will affects both *whether* we engage the evidence for God's existence and the *manner* in which we engage or understand that evidence, our inquiries into the existence of God are influenced on some level by any passions, prejudices, and interests we may have.

In sum, then, one's inquiries concerning the evidence of God's existence are affected by her will and, hence, her moral character—at least on some level.[75] What this all implies for Campbell is that an important part of the process of recognizing and assessing the available evidence of God's existence falls squarely on the shoulders of the one who might be looking at it. And how one's volition inclines her to be oriented to the evidence in front of her, in turn, affects what she actually "sees" in an epistemic sense. Call one's orientation to the evidence for some target proposition her *epistemic orientation*. When someone with a certain epistemic orientation surveys all the available evidence of God's existence, she might—with Bertrand Russell—find it lacking and insufficient. But, in Campbell's view, the problem is wrapped up in how her will affects her epistemic orientation and how that orientation, in turn, affects her assessment of the evidence; the problem is *not* that the evidence is lacking.

To illustrate this point about epistemic orientation, it may be helpful to consider Ludwig Wittgenstein's famous discussion of the ambiguous duck-rabbit image below.[76]

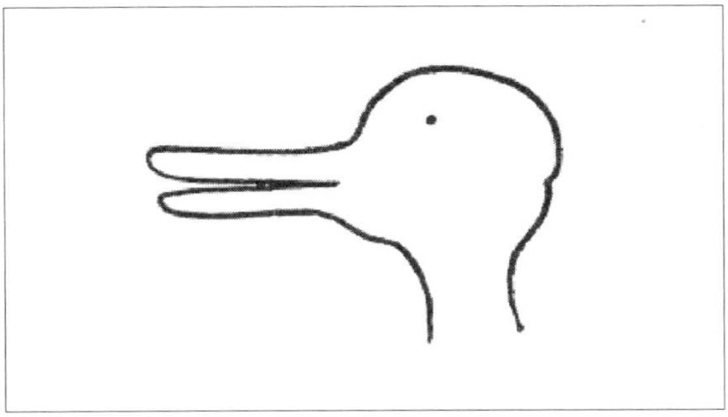

Notice that a shift of attention—initiated by the will—reorients us in a way that affects the meaning of all the elements of the image. If we keep our heads straight and focus our attention on the duck's bill opening to the left, we clearly see a duck. However, if we choose to pivot the tips of our heads ninety degrees left and toward the floor, and if we focus our attention on the eye looking up and to the right, we see a rabbit. But despite how we choose to orient ourselves, the image remains the same; it is our orientation to the image that makes the difference in what we observe. In much the same way, according to Campbell, God provides superevidence of his existence as the image before us. But if we make certain kinds of choices in our lives, our epistemic orientation with respect to that superevidence may lead us to regard it as insufficient for belief in God's existence.

Thus, for Campbell, the process of deciding whether we believe in God's existence involves our epistemic orientation to the evidence available, and this orientation is affected by certain choices we voluntarily make and have made in the past. Specifically, in his view, sin takes its toll on our rational capacities, at least in certain respects. As he puts it, "[T]he loss of holiness, in consequence of which the soul is biased by passions, prejudices, and natural disrelish for spiritual things, must necessarily diminish the clearness and ability of the mind, in the investigation of truth."[77] Elsewhere, Campbell comments that "[just] as the natural eye may be dimmed and jaundiced by a disturbed digestion . . . so may the mental sight be so vitiated by a diseased heart."[78] Accordingly, certain moral failures can steer the cognitive commitments of the atheist. He says, for example, that "the *moral* atheist precedes the *speculative* atheist" and that atheism should be "always regarded as a disease of the heart."[79] (In some sense, we might read Campbell's view here as a reflection on beatitude: blessed are the pure in heart, for they shall see God.) Still elsewhere, while commenting on the available evidence for Christianity, Campbell says that if one rejects belief in the resurrection "against the accumulated weight of evidences, from all sources . . . must I not suppose that *some passion, or prejudice, beclouds your reason*?"[80] In sum, then, Campbell thinks that God provides super-evidence of his existence; however, sinfulness can cause one to have a faulty epistemic orientation to that evidence, and such an orientation can impinge upon one's assessment of whether God actually exists. Effectively, then, the cognitive residue of sin impairs one's rational faculties, at least with respect to certain issues.

So how, in Campbell's view, does one avoid the beclouding of reason with respect to religious matters? Imagine, he says, that a man is speaking to us at a great distance. If we want to hear what is being said, we need to get within a certain audible distance of him before that can happen. Similarly, in Campbell's view, for us to achieve the proper epistemic orientation to the evidence of God's existence and his revelation, we must put ourselves within the range of what Campbell calls the *understanding distance.*[81] Yet doing this requires of us a certain kind of moral effort—an effort of the will. Campbell pictures this understanding distance as a circle, at the center of which stands God. In order for us to cross over the circumference of this circle and enter into the understanding distance, we must cultivate and practice epistemic and moral humility. Campbell explains by saying,

> Humility of mind, or what is in effect the same, contempt for all earth-born pre-eminence, prepares the mind for the reception of this light; or, what is virtually the same, opens the ear to hear the voice of God. Amidst the din of all the arguments from the flesh, the world, and Satan, a person is so deaf that he cannot hear the still small voice of God's philanthropy. But, receding from pride, covetousness, and false ambition; from the love of the world; and in coming within the circle, the circumference of which is unfeigned humility, and the centre of which is God himself—the voice of God is distinctly heard and clearly understood. All within this circle are taught of God; all without it are under the influence of the wicked one. "God resisteth the proud, but he giveth grace to the humble."[82]

The relevant point Campbell is making here is this: there are some free and morally significant choices involved in orienting ourselves to the evidence of God's existence. And unless we orient ourselves appropriately, we can expect neither to enter within the understanding distance nor to see that there is ample evidence of God's existence. Accordingly, Campbell thinks some nonbelievers are "too ignorant to be addressed by reason—too wise in their own conceits to learn any thing, and their conscience so perfectly seared as to have become insusceptible of conviction."[83] The basic problem is a lack of rationality brought on by shoddy epistemic orientation caused by a moral disorder affecting the will. In this case, arguments and evidence will fail to compel; only a change of heart will allow the mind to work properly as it should.[84]

If the foregoing account is correct, then Campbell has explained why apparently rational people end up not believing in God's existence, despite the fact that God provides superevidence—that is, evidence sufficient to render rational nonbelief impossible. With this account in hand, Campbell might stick to his guns and reject premise Dh4 as false.

But, of course, his view will still invite some tough questions. First, are we really supposed to think that there is no one who rationally refrains from belief in God, despite the fact that there appears to be empirical evidence to the contrary? And second, are we really supposed to conclude that all persons who refrain from believing in God do so only because of some irrationality introduced by some sin or moral failing in their lives? To the extent that Campbell answers these questions affirmatively, controversy will remain. With respect to the first question, some critics will wonder whether Campbell's answer abandons his empiricism. With respect to the second question, some critics will no doubt regard Campbell's answer to be somewhat ad hoc and possibly even offensive.

But even aside from those issues, one last tricky question remains for Campbell's view: Can he consistently reject *both* premise Dh2 *and* premise Dh4 in the way that he does? Recall that Campbell denies premise Dh2 by saying that God has a good reason for not offering superevidence: he wants to protect free will and the moral significance of belief in God. However, in denying premise Dh4, Campbell implies that God *actually does* provide superevidence. Clearly God cannot both provide superevidence and *not* provide superevidence. Consequently, Campbell's twofold strategy for responding to the argument from divine hiddenness is inconsistent—or so one might argue.

There are at least three possible solutions to this potential inconsistency problem available to Campbell. First, Campbell could refrain from denying premise Dh2 and simply reject premise Dh4. Second, he could refrain from denying premise Dh4 and just reject premise Dh2. My suspicion is that one of these two solutions is probably Campbell's simplest way out of the problem, and taking the second route may invite fewer objections.

A third possible solution to the looming inconsistency problem here may require some interpretative acrobatics. For example, we might interpret Campbell as claiming that premise Dh4 is false and that premise Dh2 is merely unwarranted. In other words, regarding premise Dh2, we might read Campbell as meaning to say only that for all we know, an omnibenevolent God *might have* good reasons for not providing superevidence and that *perhaps* God's reason here is that he needed to protect free will so that believing in God is morally significant. If there is some such reason that God might have, then we cannot conclude with impunity that if God exists, he necessarily provides superevidence such that rational nonbelief is impossible. Perhaps it is true that if God exists he would necessarily provide superevidence—and perhaps it is not. But *we* cannot know what God *must necessarily* do here. Accordingly, we would not have any way of knowing whether premise Dh2 is true, and we would lack warrant for affirming it.

With that in tow, Campbell could then bite the bullet and argue that premise Dh4 is simply false. The view would be that, as a matter of fact, God *does* provide superevidence—whether or not it was *necessary* for him to do so. Accordingly, Campbell would not be committed to the contradictory set of claims that God does provide superevidence and God does not provide superevidence. On this interpretation, he would be committed to saying only that we cannot know one way or the other what God *must* provide by way of evidence, but that he does, in fact, provide superevidence. Consequently, given this sort of interpretation, Campbell would be off the hook, at least with respect to the inconsistency objection.

Nonetheless, a remaining difficulty with this compromise interpretation of Campbell's argument is the fact that, at a certain point, interpreters have to confront the text wherein he fairly clearly suggests that God's *actual* reason for not providing superevidence is that he wants to protect free will so that believing in God can remain morally significant. Accordingly, so it seems, Campbell thinks premise Dh2 is not merely unwarranted but *false*. Consequently, at some point, either Campbell or his interpreters will have to let go of something to avoid the inconsistency problem mentioned above.

4.4. Conclusion

Scholars have largely overlooked Campbell's views when it comes to the problem of evil and the problem of divine hiddenness. Yet he does provide some interesting, though perhaps imperfect, resources for responding to the arguments from evil and the argument from divine hiddenness. While Campbell's free will defense against the logical problem of evil may seem to be on target for the most part, his responses to both the evidential formulation of the argument from evil and the argument from divine hiddenness are not exactly airtight and are in need of further development. Regarding his response to the evidential argument from evil, it remains for Campbell's interpreters to explain how he can respond to the moral objection to skeptical theism mentioned above, among the other sorts of objections critics might reasonably pose. (Given that the debates over skeptical theism are still very much in play, I think Campbell can be forgiven for not anticipating all of the questions he would need to answer.) It also remains for Campbell's interpreters to resolve some of the difficulties involved in his twofold response to the argument from divine hiddenness. As I argue immediately above, I do not think Campbell can have his cake and eat it too in trying to defeat this argument by rejecting *both* premise Dh2 and premise Dh4 as false, so I have tried to massage his view accordingly. Whether his responses to those challenges can be further developed in such a way that puts the remaining questions to rest, I leave for readers to decide.

Chapter 5

On Revelation, Divine Commands, and Morality

One of the central and recurring themes in Campbell's philosophy of religion is the importance of divine revelation. In fact, his reliance on divine revelation is what most distinguished him from the deists and natural religionists of his day. He argued that divine revelation is what gives us the very idea of God in the first place, and, so he thought, explaining the *revealed* origin of that idea helps demonstrate God's existence. Furthermore, he held that we need God's revelation through Jesus and through the authors of the Bible if we are to mount an adequate case for moving from simple theism to Christian theism in particular. But Campbell also thought that we need divine revelation in order to discover what is right, what is wrong, what is good, and what is bad.

As he saw it, moral philosophy is about five basic things: the origin, nature, relations, obligations, and destiny of mankind.[1] And for Campbell, we need divine revelation in order to get the truth about these five things. More generally, he believed that "there is no separating true morality from true religion: they stand in the relation of cause and effect."[2] In other words, he had something to say about one of the most salient issues in moral philosophy, namely, how religion bears on morality. Campbell's views on that issue are the focus of this chapter.

Many scholars over the years have discussed Campbell's views on morality. Typically, though, they have focused on his practical (or, applied) ethics, particularly the stances he took on issues involving slavery, war, capital punishment, and moral education.[3] Almost no attention has been given to his moral epistemology (his views about how we come to discover moral truths) or his metaethics (his views about the metaphysical grounding of morality). This chapter is an attempt to fill the gap. I begin by reconstructing Campbell's moral epistemology (§**5.1**). Because Campbell argues that we can originally discover moral truths only by means of faith in the testimony of the biblical writers, he needs to explain—among other things—what we should do concerning those issues about which the Bible says little or nothing. To show how he might do this, I imagine his response to what I call the *problem of biblical silence* (§**5.2**). In addressing Campbell's metaethics, I think we can ascribe to him a divine command theory of right conduct (§**5.3**). Finally, I consider one of the most pressing objections to Campbell's divine command theory—an objection stemming from Plato's *Euthyphro*—and I consider two responses he could offer to it (§**5.4**).

5.1. Campbell's Moral Epistemology

One of the tasks of moral philosophy is to explain how we can come to have an awareness of, or have knowledge about, what is good and evil and what our duties and obligations are. It is easy enough to see why this kind of task is important. Obviously, we need to be able to discover moral truths—assuming there are such things—in order to know whether a particular course of action is morally required, permissible, or forbidden. And were we to have some clear sense of how to discover moral truths in the first place, then we would be one step closer to gaining the insight we need to conduct our lives as we should.

So how, in Campbell's view, can we discover moral truths? He thinks that, unfortunately, moral philosophers throughout history have failed miserably when it comes to answering this sort of question. They have failed, so Campbell thinks, because they have been searching for an answer in all the wrong places, so to speak. Because they have viewed moral philosophy as an inductive science of sorts, they have presumed that by making observations, examining facts, and conducting experiments, we can discover true moral propositions and principles "from the mere light of nature."[4] But, in Campbell's view, these moral philosophers have mistakenly assumed that humans actually possess all the appropriate cognitive equipment (or have the full range of experience) that we need in order to discover moral truths on our own. Hence, they have mistakenly overlooked the role that divine revelation and religious faith play in this discovery process. Thus, for Campbell, these moral philosophers have failed to successfully explain how we can originally discover moral truths, and thus their moral theories have been fundamentally misguided in other respects as well.

In light of these supposed failures, Campbell concludes that "upon the whole, the provisions of moral philosophy [heretofore] are not adequate to the wants of humanity."[5] As a result, "we are thus placed under a . . . constraint to look [elsewhere] for a clearer and more intelligible standard of duty."[6] Fortunately for us, so Campbell thinks, we are not left to our own devices when it comes to morality. He contends that a "complete and perfect knowledge of the subject, were it made dependent upon our *own* exertions, would require an intimate and perfect acquaintance with the universe. . . . We are not, however, made dependent for the science of our duty upon our ability to acquire a knowledge that is wholly unattainable. The divine precept happily comes to our relief, and rescues man from a difficulty absolutely insurmountable."[7] So, ultimately, Campbell thinks that we can initially acquire moral truths only by coming into contact with the divine revelation of the moral law.

We should pause here to take note of the roundabout way in which Campbell develops this position. He thinks that the desire for knowledge is a universal "energizing principle" among humans; it is the "*soul of the soul* of man," he says.[8] (When Campbell uses the term *knowledge* here, he seems to mean nothing more than true belief.) But of all the things humans naturally desire to know, how to lead a good or "happy" life ranks at the very top. Hence, moral philosophy—or what Campbell sometimes refers to as the *science of happiness*—is especially important to us. In order to attain genuine happiness, he thinks, we need to employ all of our powers and capacities in a way that accords with the rules of morality and in a way that is "in harmony with all our relations and obligations to the creation of which we are a part."[9] But in order to do that, we must first discover what the rules of morality are. And in order to discover the rules of morality, we need to have some sense of where we should start looking for them, so to speak. Thus, for Campbell, the first and most basic question we have to address when thinking about how to be happy (hence, when it comes to doing moral philosophy) is an epistemological one: how can we discover what the rules of morality are? Stated differently, how can we come to have true beliefs about good and evil, right and wrong, duty and obligation?

Of course, one might be tempted to think that the answer to this question is simply *tradition*: as infants, we learn moral truths from, say, our parents or teachers, and their instruction, in turn, sculpts our moral consciences. But for Campbell, such a flat-footed response does not squarely address the real question at hand: we need to understand how humans (and hence the tradition itself) *originally* acquired moral truths in the first place. (From there, of course, it might be easy enough to explain how those truths are transmitted to succeeding generations.) If we were to know how the first person to possess moral truths acquired them, then we would know how we can best discern moral truths in the present. So, in Campbell's view, we need to determine how the first human to possess moral truths discerned them, in order to gain a robust answer to what he seems to regard as the first question of moral philosophy. Hence, he says, "I ask not what are his powers of retaining [moral] knowledge, nor what are his powers of applying or of enjoying knowledge; but what are his powers of acquiring it?"[10] Presumably, we might *retain* moral truths by means of the memory or by passing them down through tradition, and we might *apply* moral truths in our lives by means of reasoning or a well-honed moral conscience. But even if those accounts are correct, we would still need to know how humans originally *acquired* basic moral truths. And, so Campbell seems to think, the best way for us to determine that is by answering the following question: By means of which *faculty* did humans originally discover moral truths?

According to Campbell, there are only four possible candidates to consider: the faculties of instinct, sense, reason, and faith. The basic gist of his argument is that because humans do not possess moral instinct and because they could not have discovered moral truths—at least in the first instance—through either sensory perception or human reasoning, then, by elimination, humans must have originally discovered moral truths through the faculty of faith. Now, to be sure, it can seem a little odd to think of faith as a faculty. But Campbell seems to think of faith as a faculty only in the sense that it is the power with which we believe something on the basis of the testimony of others. Specifically, he thinks of faith as that faculty through which we believe in the testimony of those through whom God has revealed himself to humanity. And ultimately, Campbell thinks that the only faculty through which humans could have originally discerned moral truths is the faculty of believing in the testimony of the biblical writers to whom God revealed the moral law. Presumably, once humans initially acquired these moral truths, they were able to pass those truths down through tradition; once those truths were contained in the tradition, humans were then able to discern them through, say, reason. However, humanity must have first discovered these moral truths through faith in the testimony of God's messengers.

Given that Campbell's argument proceeds by way of elimination, we should pause here to take note of why he thinks humans could *not* have originally discovered moral truths by means of instinct, sense, or reason. And to get a handle on all of that, we should also ascertain what he means by the terms *instinct, sense,* and *reason.*

By *instinct* Campbell means "that innate or natural rule of life . . . written upon and incorporated with[in] the nature of every animal; by which it is enabled to govern itself."[11] Effectively, instinct is to an animal what, say, software is to a computer. Just as software instructs the computer to behave in such and such a way when certain prompts are given, instinct informs the animal on what its ends are and, thus, how it should act in any given situation. Accordingly, when an animal has instinct, it already possesses everything it needs in order to live as it should. Thus, in Campbell's view, when an animal possesses a robust instinct, it gains "nothing by experience or observation: hence the swallow builds her nest, the beaver his dam, the bee its cell, and the ant her cities and storehouses."[12] Now, whereas certain non-human animals may appear to possess instinct—and hence the "rule of life" appropriate to them[13]—humans do not, in Campbell's view. He says, for example, that "man has little or no instinct; and, in this point, is more neglected by his Creator than any other creature."[14] Consistent with his Lockean tendencies, Campbell thinks that humans are born as moral blank slates: we do not, in his view, somehow come into the world preprogrammed with those ideas and beliefs we need in order to live ethical and happy lives. His reason for thinking this is simple enough: left with *only* our own moral instincts to guide us, humans would quickly "perish from the earth," and this fact, he thinks, provides "an evident proof that [humans were] not made to be led by it."[15] Of course, it is difficult to know how we might test Campbell's assertion here. How could we know whether or when a person was being guided exclusively by his instincts? And if we assume that a person's reliance upon her moral instinct alone would quickly led to her demise, are we not begging the question against the view that we have moral instinct? In any case, if it is true that humans lack moral instinct in the first place, then instinct could not have been the faculty by which humans originally discovered moral truths.

By *sense* Campbell means "those external organs, usually denominated the five senses, through which we become acquainted with the sensible properties of all objects around us."[16] Why does he think that our sensory faculties could not have been the means through which humans originally acquired true moral beliefs? Unfortunately, Campbell does not offer much here by way of explanation or argument. However, he seems to gesture in the direction of saying that we can rule out the sensory faculties for the following sort of reason: the capacity for discovering moral truths is unique to humans; but if the sensory faculties are the means by which moral truths are discovered, then the capacity for discerning moral truths would not be unique to humans; thus, the sensory faculties are not the means by which humans originally discovered moral truths. Now, *if* this is indeed Campbell's case for ruling out the sensory faculties as the means by which humans could have originally discovered moral truths, then his case is not at all convincing. Why should we expect in the first place that physical and intellectual capacities would be distributed in such a way that would guarantee that the capacity for discerning moral truths is unique to humans? Taking a different approach, perhaps Campbell would want to rule out the sensory faculties (as the means by which we originally discovered moral truths) because he thinks that they do nothing more than allow us to perceive material objects, and moral truths are not themselves the sort of things we can actually taste, see, hear, touch, or smell. In any case, Campbell's position here is not clear, so let us leave this to the side for the moment.

By *reason* Campbell means "a power bestowed on man, of comparing things, and propositions concerning things, and of deducing propositions from them . . . a faculty of discriminating one name, or thing, or attribute from another, and of forming just conceptions of it."[17] Despite reason's many functions, Campbell thinks that it lacks *creative* power and that this deficiency is significant. Just as the eye needs light in order to see, so too does the faculty of reason need input from something else—say, tradition or revelation—in order to have anything to reason *about*. Without these inputs, the faculty of reason "would be useless to man in all the great points which the inductive and true philosophy . . . humbly acknowledges she cannot teach."[18] Of course, in response to Campbell's view here, critics are right to wonder why the faculty of reason needs input from tradition or revelation in order to function. We might ask, Could reason not function in the relevant way with the input it receives from, say, sensory perception? Again, sadly, Campbell does not offer much here by way of argument. However, one might want to argue on his behalf that even with input from sensory perception, reason would be unable to discover moral truths, precisely because sensory perception itself does not give us access to any moral propositions about which the faculty of reason could then reason. In any case, Campbell thinks that reason is not the faculty by which humans could have originally discovered moral truth.

Because the faculties of instinct, sense, and reason are all impotent when it comes to the original acquisition of moral truths, we are left with only the faculty of faith, or so Campbell thinks. He describes faith as "the ennobling faculty of man. . . . This puts him in possession of the experience of all other men by believing their testimony. Instinct, sense and reason, however enlarged in their operations, are confined to a single individual of the race, and that within a very narrow circle, a mere atom of creation and but for a moment of time; while faith encompasses the area of universal experience, and appropriates to its possession the acquisitions of all men in all ages of time."[19] The basic idea for Campbell is that faith is the only faculty through which humans can come into contact with, or believe in, the testimonies of those to whom God has directly revealed himself. And if we assume that God has revealed the moral law to certain messengers, then the only way that the rest of humanity could have originally discovered the truth about the moral law was through faith in the testimonies of those through whom God had directly revealed it. The moral law itself, in Campbell's view, was something that God had to reveal. For example, Campbell says, "To reveal such mysteries . . . is not the province . . . of the mere light of nature or of reason; but the peculiar and worthy object of a communication supernatural and divine."[20] Thus, faith, in his view, is that faculty through which humanity as a whole discovers God's communication of the moral law. Specifically, faith is the faculty through which we believe the moral truths contained in the "sublime and awful volume—the Bible."[21]

Effectively, then, Campbell's view is that God's revelation is the ultimate *source* of the moral law, and faith in the testimony of those to whom God has revealed it was the *means* by which humans originally discovered the truth about the moral law. And, so Campbell thinks, were it not for the divine revelation of the moral law that humans received by faith, we would have had no way of originally discerning moral truths: humans are utterly dependent upon God's revelation. What this implies, in his view, is that moral philosophers have deluded themselves in thinking that humans can come to discover moral truths without the aid of divine revelation and faith. Accordingly, he says that "if the physical sciences—natural philosophy in all its branches—be true sciences, because founded on their own facts, observations and inductions, that science usually called moral philosophy is not a true science, because [it was] not founded on its own facts, observations and inductions, but on assumptions and plagiarisms from tradition and divine revelation: borrowing, instead of originating and demonstrating, all its fundamental principles."[22] When Campbell says here that moral philosophy, throughout history, has borrowed its fundamental principles, he is saying that moral philosophy has relied unknowingly upon the moral propositions and principles passed down through various traditions that, insofar as they are true, are ultimately traceable back to God's revelation of the moral law. These traditions (undoubtedly, in his view) have twisted and confused the moral law over time, but nonetheless have provided the material from which moral philosophers have drawn their "assumptions and plagiarisms." And these traditions—contaminated as they may be—are ultimately derived from God's initial revelation to Abraham, according to Campbell. For example, he goes so far as to claim,

> Tradition, then, and not induction, originated in the minds of the Socratic school all the light of the origin, moral obligations and destiny of man, which this school and the Grecian and the Roman world from it enjoyed. The history of the whole matter is this:—The Romans borrowed from the Greeks, the Greeks stole from the Egyptians and Phenicians [*sic*], while they borrowed from the Chaldeans and Assyrians, who stole from the Abrahamic family all their notions of the spirituality, eternity and unity of God, the primitive state of man, his fall, sacrifice, priests, altars, immortality of the soul, a future state, eternal judgment and ultimate retribution of all men according to their works.[23]

Ultimately, then, Campbell thinks that humans can in the first instance come to discover moral truths only by gaining access to God's revelation of the moral law through faith in the testimony of the biblical writers. We can summarize Campbell's *argument about how we originally discover moral truth* in the following way:

(T1) The only possible faculties by which humans could have originally discovered moral truths are
[a] instinct,
[b] sense,
[c] reason, and
[d] faith.

(T2) Humans could not have originally discovered moral truths by means of instinct, because humans do not possess instinct.

(T3) Humans could not have originally discovered moral truths by means of sense.

(T4) Humans could not have originally discovered moral truths by means of reason.

(T5) By elimination, then, faith is the only faculty through which humans could have originally discovered moral truths.

When it comes to assessing this argument, I think there is simply no way around admitting that Campbell is in serious trouble. First, elimination arguments of this sort are notoriously susceptible to the charge that the list of possible options from which the elimination proceeds is not itself exhaustive, and Campbell's argument here is no exception. Consider premise T1. Why would we suppose at the outset that the only possible faculties by which we could have originally discovered moral truths are the faculties of instinct, sense, reason, and faith? Campbell seems quite confident that his list covers all the possible bases. He says, for example, "Some philosophers, indeed, are not so generous" in their list of possible faculties.[24] Yet he boldly asserts that "none . . . give him [humans] more; and we are willing that he should appear with all his armor on—with all his intellectual apparatus in full requisition, that we may demonstrate that he was made to be led, preeminently and supremely, by a power that despoils speculative philosophy of all its proud assumptions, and gives to tradition, in its broadest and fullest sense, a very elevated standing among the sources of intelligence accessible to man."[25] At any rate, Campbell clearly recognizes the need to provide an exhaustive list of the possible faculties in order to get his elimination argument off the ground. Of course, many a slip between cup and lip. And critics are right to press him with the following question: are there not additional possible candidates—that is, other possible faculties—that Campbell would need to rule out to make his case by elimination?

For example, some philosophers, such as Joseph Butler, have suggested that we can discern moral truths by means of the *conscience.*[26] Others, such as David Hume, have suggested that we become aware of good and evil by means of a *moral sentiment,* an emotional sensitivity of sorts that expresses itself in terms of approval or disapproval states.[27] Unfortunately, despite the fact that Campbell was clearly familiar with both Butler and Hume's work, he does not even consider these possible candidates when formulating his elimination argument above. Admittedly, he does discuss conscience in another essay. There, he describes conscience as "the power or faculty of discerning and judging the thought, motives, intents and purposes of our hearts and lives, as to their acceptability or inacceptability [*sic*] according to which we are approved or disapproved by the infallible Judge and Arbiter of human destiny."[28] However, Campbell thinks that while conscience may be the faculty by which we can *apply* the moral law in our lives, it is not a faculty by which we *acquire* moral truths or first derive "a conviction of our duty."[29] Accordingly, conscience still needs the input of God's revelation to inform it as to what our duties and obligation are in the first place.[30] Sadly, though, Campbell does not sufficiently explain *why* conscience—or a Humean moral sentiment—is not itself a faculty through which we could have originally discovered moral truth; he merely asserts that it is not. In any case, the general problem facing Campbell's argument above is that premise T1 does not actually provide an exhaustive list of all the possible faculties by which we may have originally discerned moral truth. Because that is the case, premise T1 is false, and Campbell's argument by elimination fails to get off the ground.

But, second, even if grant premise T1 for the sake of discussion, there are still some serious concerns we might have with his argument, particularly with premise T4. Grant for the moment that humans do not have a moral instinct. Grant also that humans could not originally discover moral truth by means of sensory perception. But why should we suppose that we cannot originally discern moral truths by means of reason? Is reason not the faculty by which we consider the strength of the various arguments surrounding a particular course of action? And is moral reasoning—that is, the consideration of reasons, evidence, arguments, objections, and replies—not the means by which we normally come to discern what is right and wrong in a given situation? Unfortunately, Campbell nowhere explains why reason is supposed to be utterly impotent in the initial discovery of moral truths.

Thus, at the end of the day, Campbell's elimination argument relies upon (at least) two exceedingly questionable premises: premise T1 appears to be false, and he provides us with little to no warrant for affirming premise T4, even if it is true.

And obviously, if either premise T1 or T4 is problematic, then the conclusion at T5 is unwarranted, and his elimination argument falls flat on its face. Of course, part of the problem involved in assessing Campbell's argument is that he does not say enough about why any faculty other than faith is supposed to be utterly impotent in the original discovery of moral truth. I suspect that Campbell wants to say this because of his more fundamental conviction that because morality somehow stems from God's will, and because we cannot know God's will unless he actually reveals it to us, we cannot originally discover moral truths without looking to the messengers of God's revelation to humanity. But even if Campbell's basic metaphysical conviction is correct (that morality stems from God's will), it does not directly follow that we could have no means of originally discerning God's moral law unless he specifically revealed it to us through special messengers like the biblical writers. In other words, even if the moral law stems from God's will, it does not follow that the only faculty through which we originally discover moral truth is faith in the testimony of the biblical writers. Perhaps God designed us in such a way that allows us to discover his moral law by means of reason, conscience, imagination, or something akin to Hume's moral sentiment.

5.2. The Problem of Biblical Silence and the Law of Expediency

For the purposes of further examining Campbell's view about the relationship between religion and morality, grant that the conclusion at T5 is true for the time being. That is, grant that we can originally discover moral truths only by believing in the testimony of those to whom God has specifically revealed them, namely, the biblical writers. At this juncture, a different problem emerges for Campbell. What are we to do in the face of what I call the *problem of biblical silence*? In other words, what should we do when the Bible is unclear, ambiguous, indeterminate, or completely mute with respect to a particular course of action or a particular issue? How can we know how to proceed, for example, with respect to genetic engineering, embryonic stem cell research, prenatal spina bifida repair surgeries, recreational use of marijuana, and a host of other issues that are not directly (or, in some cases, even indirectly) discussed in the Bible?

For Campbell, the response to these sorts of questions—and hence to the problem of biblical silence—would build off an important hermeneutical principle characteristic of the Restoration tradition: where the Bible speaks, we speak; where the Bible is silent, we are silent. Call this normative principle the *no-speak principle* for short. To be precise, the no-speak principle conveys Campbell's attitude specifically about those beliefs or doctrines that the church should regard as essential for church membership: if the Bible says that some belief, *p*, is essential, then so should the church; if the Bible does not say *p* is essential, then neither should the church regard *p* as a term of communion. As Harold Lunger explains, "Alexander Campbell began his career in this country 'under the conviction that nothing that was not as old as the New Testament should be made an article of faith, a rule of practice, or a term of communion amongst Christians.' That is to say, he was a primitivist who went back to the New Testament for the normative patterns of Christian faith and practice."[31] In fact, many early Restorationists emphasized the maxim outlined in Thomas Campbell's *Declaration and Address,* according to which "nothing ought to be inculcated upon Christians as articles of faith; nor required of them as terms of communion, but what is expressly taught and enjoined upon them in the word of God."[32] For Alexander Campbell, this meant that the no-speak principle should guide the church in deciding how to deal with creedal statements and theological doctrines not explicitly expressed in the biblical texts: with respect to those extra-biblical doctrines, the church should simply remain silent. He says, for example,

> Concerning these and all such doctrines [those not specifically outlined in the Bible], and all the speculations to which they have given rise, *we have the privilege neither to affirm nor deny—neither to believe nor doubt; because God has not proposed them to us in his word, and there is no command to believe them.* If they are deduced from the Scriptures, we have them in the facts and declarations of God's Spirit: if they are not deduced from the Bible, we are free from all the difficulties and strifes [*sic*] which they have engendered and created.[33]

Although Campbell endorses the no-speak principle specifically for the purpose of deciding which doctrines the church should regard as essential, the same principle also gives him a resource for responding to the problem of biblical silence. The thought here goes as follows: In cases where the Bible offers a clear and determinate statement of God's revelation of the moral law, we are in a position to say what is good and evil and what our moral duties and obligations are. But with respect to those actions and states of affairs about which the Bible is indeed silent, we are not in a position to say what is morally right or wrong or what is morally good and evil. So, for example, if the Bible clearly states that God commands us to perform a particular action, then we can say that we are morally obligated to perform that action. Similarly, if the Bible clearly states that God allows (but does not require) a particular action, then we can say that performing that action is morally optional. And further, if the Bible clearly states that God condemns a particular action, then we can say that that action is wrong and we are morally forbidden to perform it. That is, where the biblical texts speak, we can in turn speak about what is right and wrong and what is good and bad in those cases. But what about in cases where the Bible is silent? Let *N* stand for a particular course of action about which the Bible says absolutely nothing. Assuming the no-speak principle—that is, if we should remain silent where the Bible is silent—we simply cannot say what the moral status of *N* is, precisely because God has not revealed it. Accordingly, in these cases, we should practice a sort of epistemic humility and suspend judgment about the moral status of *N*. That is, with respect to courses of action about which the biblical revelation of God's moral law is in fact silent, we should remain silent as well, at least as far as our *moral* judgments are concerned.

Of course, the problem here is that we commonly find ourselves in a position of needing to know whether we should engage in *N*, despite the fact that the Bible is silent about *N*. Accordingly, there appear to be many cases in which suspending moral judgment about *N* is out of the question for us, given what is at stake in the situation at hand. In Campbell's view, though, just because we cannot determine the *moral* status of *N* does not entail that we have to (or even should) suspend *all* judgments pertaining to *N*. He suggests that we can still make nonmoral, prudential judgments about *N*. That is, he suggests that we can still make judgments about whether engaging in *N* would be *expedient*. These judgments are indeed judgments about whether and how we should act, but, for Campbell, they are not judgments about the *moral* status of the action in question. In other words, these judgments are not about what the moral law requires but about what the *law of expediency* requires. On this point, Campbell elaborates by saying that

> there are many things left to the law of expediency, concerning which no [divine] precepts are found in the apostolic writings. . . . They are then, in one sentence, those things, or forms of action, which it was impossible or unnecessary to reduce to special precepts; consequently they are not faith, piety, nor morality; because whatever is of the faith, of the worship, or of the morality of Christianity, was both possible and necessary to be promulgated; and is expressly and fully propounded in the sacred Scriptures. The law of expediency, then, has no place in determining the article of faith, acts of worship, nor principles of morality.[34]

Accordingly, while we might formulate—and, in turn, act on the basis of—our prudential or expediency judgments about *N*, we should not regard those judgments as being reflective of the moral law since, given the no-speak principle, we are in no position to say what the moral status of *N* actually is.

We should pause here to get a better handle on all of this. Campbell's view seems to go as follows. Because, *ex hypothesi,* the Bible is silent with respect to *N,* we cannot say whether engaging in *N* is morally right or wrong: it may be, or it may not be. However, even if *N* is morally permissible (which is something that we cannot determine), that fact alone does not mean that engaging in *N* would the smart thing to do (which is something that we *can* determine). That is, even if engaging in *N* is morally permissible, engaging in *N* might be a poor means for achieving some given end-in-sight. Consequently, so Campbell seems to suggest, the question of whether we should engage in *N* ought to be decided on the basis of something akin to means-end rationality—that is, by determining whether engaging in *N* is expedient. Accordingly, if *N* is *in*expedient for us, then even if *N* is morally permissible, it is nonetheless a course of action from which we should refrain.

It may be worth noting here that these expediency or prudential ought-claims are roughly on the order of what Immanuel Kant describes as hypothetical imperatives.[35] This sort of imperative can be explained by way of the following illustration. Imagine that you want to earn a college degree. To get that degree, though, you have to go to class. Thus, given your goals, you ought to go to class. So, the imperative of going to class here is hypothetical in nature: *if* you want to achieve a certain end (getting the degree), then you ought to employ certain means (going to class). For Campbell, the expedient course of action is a hypothetically imperative one—but it is not categorically or morally imperative. Accordingly, Campbell says, "The law of expediency, then, has no place in determining the article of faith, acts of worship, nor principles of morality. All these require a '*thus saith the Lord*' in express statements, and the sacred writings have clearly defined and decided them. But in other matters that may be called the circumstantials . . . the people of God are left to their own discretion and to the facilities and exigencies of society."[36]

So, to bring the matter full circle, we can summarize what appears to be a Campbellite response to the problem of biblical silence in the following way:

- If and when the Bible is silent with respect to a particular course of action, *N,* we cannot say whether *N* is morally right or wrong, and we should suspend moral judgment about *N.*
- However, we can determine whether engaging in *N* would be expedient, and this determination allows us to formulate a prudential judgment about whether to engage in *N.*

To be sure, this Campbellite response to the problem of biblical silence is not without its problems, as at least two difficult questions remain: In cases where the Bible is genuinely silent, is that silence a permissive or prohibitive one? And what gets to count as biblical silence in the first place?

Regarding the first question, Campbell's view seems to be open to conflicting interpretations. On the one hand, he seems to imply that biblical silence about *N* entails skepticism about the moral status of *N*. That is, he seems to suggest that because the Bible says nothing about *N*, we cannot know whether *N* is right or wrong, and thus we should suspend moral judgments about *N*. But if biblical silence about *N* entails our moral skepticism about *N*, then even if engaging in *N* would be expedient for us, the most appropriate thing for us to do would be to disregard any expediency-judgments about *N* and remain in suspense about whether we should engage in *N*. For even if *N* is expedient for us, it may be immoral nonetheless. Consequently, insofar as we cannot know whether engaging in *N* is immoral, we should refrain from *N*, even if it would be expedient. Accordingly, if we are appropriately cautious, biblical silence is best regarded as a prohibitive silence.

On the other hand, recall that Campbell explicitly asserts that *all* moral principles "require a '*thus saith the Lord*' in express statements." We might reasonably interpret this to mean that for every moral principle (from which we derive specific moral rules), there is a corresponding divine statement in the Bible. Consequently, if the Bible is silent about *N*, then *N* does not actually involve a genuinely *moral* matter at all—otherwise the Bible would not be utterly silent about it. But note: this means that moral skepticism does not ensue with respect to *N*. That is, it is not the case that we cannot know whether engaging in *N* is moral: given biblical silence in this case, *we know that the question of whether to engage in N is not a moral one at all.* And if this question is not a moral one, then we are wholly free to determine whether to engage in *N* on the basis of our expediency-judgments. Accordingly, given this sort of interpretation, biblical silence is permissive in nature.

No matter how we choose to interpret him on this point, Campbell's view will invite some serious worries. On the one hand, if we read him as saying that biblical silence about *N* entails our moral skepticism about *N*, then Campbell's view would indeed inject a significant dose of skepticism into our moral lives, and we are right back to the question we started with at the outset of this section: what should we do in those cases about which the Bible says absolutely nothing? Unfortunately, his appeal to expediency-judgments would appear to be perfectly unhelpful: when the Bible is silent, we should suspend moral judgment, err on the side of caution, and do nothing, given that we cannot know what the moral status of *N* is. But this sort of skepticism threatens to cripple us as moral agents. On the other hand, if we interpret Campbell as suggesting that biblical silence is permissive in nature, then there would be a variety of actions that—despite the fact that they appear to us to have some sort of moral status—are not genuinely moral matters after all but merely prudential matters. But are we really supposed to think that just because the Bible is silent with respect to, say, genetic engineering, there are actually no robustly moral dimensions to the issue in question?

The second difficult question that Campbell's view invites is more practical in nature. What gets to count as biblical silence in the first place? Should we say that the Bible is silent on the issue of, say, abortion simply because that particular action is nowhere explicitly discussed in the Bible? Or does the fact that Jeremiah 1:5 and Psalm 139:13–16 contain references to life inside the womb provide enough biblical data for us to say that the Bible is not, in fact, *silent* about it? Does the fact that the Bible addresses the issue of usury and the treatment of strangers mean that the Bible is not silent on, say, whether we have financial obligations to the distant needy? The difficulty involved in these questions is this: whether and to what extent the Bible actually addresses some *particular* courses of action or states of affairs is not always clear. Accordingly, there is a lack of clarity on when, if ever, Campbell's no-speak principle would and should come into play.

5.3. Campbell and Divine Command Theory

As discussed above, Campbell thinks that humans can initially discover the truth about right and wrong, good and evil, duty and obligation only by means of faith in the testimony of the biblical writers through whom God has revealed the moral law. Thus, for Campbell, were we to lack access to God's revelation of the moral law, we would have no way of originally discovering moral truths. So far in this chapter, I have discussed only Campbell's moral epistemology; we do not yet have in plain view his account of the metaphysical grounding of morality. So to gain a full understanding of Campbell's view about the relationship between religion and morality, we still need to examine his metaethics. That is, we still need to examine his views about what actually makes a particular course of action right or wrong such that the moral law would require or prohibit it in the first place. For even if we know that God reveals the moral law to us through the Bible—and even if we know that humans cannot originally discover moral truths except through faith in the testimonies of the biblical writers—we do not yet have in sight Campbell's metaethical explanation for what makes an action obligatory, permissible, or wrong in the first place. So, at this juncture, we need to ask of Campbell, What is it that makes a right action *right*, and what makes a wrong action *wrong*?

One of the traditional theistic responses to this sort of question comes in the form of what philosophers typically call *divine command theory.* According to this theory, morality depends entirely on God's commands (or, alternatively, on his will or his preferences), and God's commanding (or willing or preferring) is what functions as the right-making (or wrong-making) mechanism, so to speak. In other words, for some theists, the answer to the question asked of Campbell above is this: God's commands are what make some actions right and some actions wrong. More specifically, in this view, an action is morally obligatory if and only if God commands that we perform it; an action is wrong or immoral if and only if God commands that we not perform it; and an action is morally optional if and only if God neither commands us to perform it nor commands that we refrain from performing it.

Now, some philosophers want to construe divine command theory more widely as not only a theory of *right conduct*—that is, a theory about what makes an action obligatory, wrong, or optional—but also a theory of *value*—that is, a theory about what makes something good, bad, or value-neutral.[37] According to this wider view of divine command theory, something is good if and only if God commands us to bring it about or preserve it. Something is bad if and only if God commands us to refrain from bringing it about or preserving it. And something is value-neutral if and only if God neither commands that we bring it about or preserve it nor commands that we refrain from doing so. At any rate, we might think of divine command theory a theory of right conduct or also a theory of value.

Regarding his account for the metaphysical ground of morality, I think Campbell is probably best interpreted as being committed to a simple divine command theory of right conduct. For reasons that will become clear in the following section, I do not think Campbell should be read as endorsing a divine command theory of value. To see all of this, we should back up and get a sense of how he thinks moral responsibilities arise in the first place.

Campbell thinks that moral responsibilities emerge only in the course of a social relationship between two agents. Specifically, he says that "the doctrine of responsibility is the doctrine of moral relations between an inferior and a superior—between a dependent and an independent being; as well as between such co-ordinates as enter into any social compact implying or involving obligations to each other."[38] Although he seems to suggests here that some specific sorts of obligations emerge as a product of contractual agreement between two roughly coequal agents, unfortunately he says almost nothing else about that, so I will not pursue it any further. In general, though, when discussing the origin of moral responsibility, Campbell tends to emphasize the relation between superior and inferior agents, as well as the governing authority that emanates from this hierarchical social relation. Effectively, in his view, moral responsibilities issue from the authority that a superior agent has over its inferior.

In his effort to explain this point, Campbell draws a parallel between the physical order and the moral order. When we survey the natural world, he says, we continually observe what appears to be the manifestation of a universal law according to which "the minors must be subject to the majors; that the inferior masses shall depend on the superior for all that gives them life and comfort."[39] For example, when we observe our solar system, we see that the smaller heavenly bodies are somehow influenced and governed by the larger bodies insofar as the former are dependent upon the latter for "their respective gravities, their central positions and perpetual quiescence."[40] Were this hierarchical arrangement somehow disrupted, Campbell says, "confusion and destruction would instantly ensue," and not one atom in the universe would remain "unscathed."[41] He seems to think that observations of this sort are particularly telling because they somehow give us insight into the nature of the moral order as well. Just as the inferior stands in relation to the superior in the physical universe, so too does the inferior stand in relation to the superior in the moral universe. He says, for example, "One great mind, nature's spiritual and eternal sun, constitutes the mighty center around which, in their respective orbits, all pure minds, primary or secondary—angelic or human—revolve."[42] Were this hierarchical social arrangement somehow upset, havoc would be wrought upon the moral order.

The upshot of this explanatory analogy between the physical order and the moral order seems to be this: the most significant and basic moral obligations that humans incur stem from the simple fact that humans stand in an absolutely subservient relation to an ontologically superior agent, namely, God. Because God is so vastly superior to humans—and because we are inevitably dependent on him for our very existence—he has not only complete power to compel our obedience but also legitimate governing authority to command our obedience. And, in Campbell's view, God has indeed issued such binding commands, and those commands constitute the moral law that we must obey; hence, the emergence of our most basic moral responsibilities. For example, Campbell regards the Ten Commandments as "the summary outline of all our duties to God and to our fellow-man."[43] What makes these commands morally obligatory for us, so Campbell thinks, is the simple fact that they were issued by the supreme governor and lawgiver of the universe, the one who has complete moral authority over us precisely because he is superior to us in every conceivable sense.

Accordingly, Campbell says that God's governing authority is "the authority that *sanctions* the purely moral code."[44] He continues, "The authority that sanctions [the precepts of the moral law] is asserted and clearly stated in the sublime preamble, 'I AM THE LORD THY GOD': '*therefore*.' This is a nonesuch *therefore*. It has no parallel in all the tomes of earth. Without the recognition of its preamble or premises, neither religion nor morality can be studied, taught or learned."[45] Admittedly, this passage is somewhat opaque. But I think we can interpret Campbell here as saying that given God's governing authority over us, his commands are perfectly sufficient to render an action morally obligatory or prohibited. And to the degree that God's governing authority has no parallel, his commands are *exclusively* sufficient to render an action morally obligatory or prohibited.

To illustrate Campbell's view, imagine that God were to say, "I am the Lord thy God: therefore, *thou shalt not murder*." What makes obeying the rule in question binding for Campbell is not the fact that murder diminishes human flourishing (or some other such fact) but solely the fact that it was commanded by a God who has absolute governing authority over us. Accordingly, the only premise involved in arguing that *thou shalt not murder* is that the one issuing the rule has governing lordship over us precisely because he is God: this relation of superiority establishes his authority to demand certain things of us and, in turn, to obligate us. From that sole premise, so Campbell seems to suggest, whatever God commands is thereby morally obligatory for us, precisely because we are under his governing authority. Elsewhere, for example, Campbell comments that the "sacred objects of that heaven-born morality" are objects that "*flowed from the lips* of the Great Teacher."[46] Still elsewhere, he says that

> [t]he God of the Bible is the Lawgiver of the Universe, and he has . . . fully revealed his will touching all the duties arising from all the relation in which man stands to man. . . . God is the author of all human relations. He has created the relation of husband and wife, parent and child, master and servant, magistrate and subject. He has also *prescribed the duties* of husbands and wives, of parents and children, of masters and servants, of governors and governed, towards each other. Our moral righteousness, as well as our piety, is to be approved or condemned by his statutes and precepts.[47]

Given Campbell's views above, I think we can reasonably attribute to him some version of a divine command theory of right conduct: what makes an action right (or wrong) is the fact that God commands (or forbids) it.

Now, unfortunately, Campbell complicates things a bit. He says in his 1820 debate with John Walker that there are actually two basic types of moral duties—what he calls (following James Beattie)[48] *moral-positive duties* and what he calls *moral-natural duties.* On the one hand, moral-positive duties are those obligations that stem solely from the fact that God has commanded us to do something. As Campbell says, they "depend entirely for their moral obligation upon some express precept of the Deity," and "the obligation is altogether in the command."[49] Left to our own unaided devices, we are neither able to discover that we have these moral-positive duties nor able to discover what those duties are nor able to discern the reasons why they would be imposed upon us by God. Hence, we have to depend entirely upon God's revelation of his commands to discover what the moral-positive duties are and that we have these duties in the first place—ours is simply to obey the commands given. For example, Campbell describes Adam's duty to abstain from eating the proverbial apple as a moral-positive duty: "Adam in Eden, could not, by the exercise of any faculty he possessed, see any thing in the nature of the forbidden fruit, prohibiting him from the use of it, and rendering it sinful for him to touch it. *The positive precept of the Almighty alone, rendered it a sin for him to eat it, and a duty for him to abstain from it.* So of all other positive institutions, both in the Old Testament and the New."[50]

On the other hand, Campbell describes moral-natural duties as those duties whose "obligation is not only in the [divine] command, but also *in the nature of things.*"[51] Although he does not develop this view in any detail, he might mean that moral-natural duties are somehow metaphysically grounded in facts about human nature or the order of the universe or that they are reflective of necessarily true moral propositions. In any case, he explains that these moral-natural duties are "more or less discernable" by "the light of nature" alone.[52] For example, he says that "Adam in paradise, without a law [or a revelation from God], knew that it was right to love his wife, to cherish and protect her as himself. And now, though fallen, men perceive such virtues as truth, honesty, and common justice, to be, in the nature of things, necessary and right.[53]

Given that Campbell mentions these two sorts of moral duties, it might seem that his full account for the metaphysical ground of morality is somewhat more complicated than previously explained. He asserts in passing, for instance, that moral-positive duties "are right because they are commanded [by God]" and that moral-natural duties "are commanded [by God] because they are right."[54] Thus, Campbell's view about the metaphysical ground of morality would seem to be a combination of a divine command theory of right conduct on the one hand and something akin to natural law theory on the other hand. For Campbell seems to be hinting here that God's commands are sufficient *but not necessary* to cause an action to be obligatory and that some moral obligations are embedded in the nature of things or are grounded in necessary moral truths that are discoverable through reason alone. Call this sort of explanation of the metaphysical grounding of the rules of morality a *combination theory.*

Nonetheless, treating Campbell as an unqualified divine command theorist still seems best. For one thing, a combination theory is a problematic metaethical view in its own right, and given its complexity, it may invite even more objections than an unqualified divine command theory would in the first place. Moreover, the combination theory is a particularly problematic view for Campbell because it does not square as well with his moral epistemology discussed above as does an unqualified divine command theory. Recall that he goes to some length to argue that the *only* means by which we can originally discover moral truth is through faith in the testimony of those who reveal God's commands. Accordingly, the sole source for these truths is the biblical revelation, and that alone. He specifically says,

> None but the Author of human nature could have suggested such a moral code as the Christian Scriptures have promulged to the world. The reason is obvious. A perfect and infallible knowledge of the whole constitution of man, as an animal, intellectual and moral being—of all his relations to that whole universe of which he is a part, is essentially prerequisite. . . . *Now such a knowledge of the human constitution, and of the whole universe, no mere man, however gifted by nature, or cultivated by art, has ever possessed.* Therefore, a perfect moral code out of the Bible is not to be expected or found in all the learning and science of the world.[55]

If Campbell were to endorse a combination theory (as opposed to an unqualified divine command theory), then it seems that there would be an increased probability of his being committed to saying that there are some moral truths that we need not depend on God's revelation to discover, which is something he explicitly and repeatedly denies. Admittedly, endorsing a combination theory does not altogether rule out such a moral epistemology. But a combination theory fits less neatly with Campbell's moral epistemology than does an unqualified divine command theory.

In light of these considerations, then, we probably *need* to be able to interpret him as endorsing an unqualified divine command theory of right conduct, given the text. And, happily, we can. Because Campbell made his remarks about the distinction between moral-positive and moral-natural duties in passing, it is open to us to treat them as something of a slip on his part. Furthermore, given that his remarks were made some twenty years before he developed his moral epistemology, we certainly have the option of viewing his remarks as a slip made in the process of developing his final position. Thus, at the end of the day, I think we can best interpret Campbell as endorsing an unqualified divine command theory of right conduct as his account for what metaphysically grounds morality.

5.4. The Euthyphro Dilemma

One of the most pressing arguments against divine command theory stems in part from a conversation that occurs in Plato's famous dialogue *Euthyphro*. In that dialogue, the characters Socrates and Euthyphro are trying to pin down an appropriate definition of piety. After considering a variety of definitions, Euthyphro finally proposes that piety can be understood as *what the gods love* and that impiety can be understood as *what the gods hate*. Socrates responds to his interlocutor by posing a tricky question that philosophers commonly refer to as *Euthyphro's Dilemma*: Do the gods love the pious action because it is pious, or is the pious action pious because it is loved by the gods?[56] Although Socrates's question here specifically concerns the relation between piety and what the gods love, we can alter the question just a bit to raise a similar question for Campbell about the relation between moral obligations and God's commands: Does God command an action *because it is morally obligatory*, or is an action obligatory *because God commands it*? Effectively, this question is asking Campbell to choose one of the following two options:

(1) The fact that an action is morally obligatory is what makes God command it; or
(2) God's commanding an action is what makes it obligatory.[57]

Clearly, given his commitment to a divine command theory of right conduct, Campbell's would choose the second option—that God's commanding an action is what makes it obligatory.

Fair enough. But the problem now is that if option 2 is true, then God's commands are apparently utterly arbitrary, given that God has no particular reason for issuing his commands in the way that he does. Why? If option 2 is true, then the simple fact that God commands an action is what actually makes it morally obligatory in the first place. What this means, though, is that there is nothing independent of, or logically prior to, God's commanding an action that makes the action in question obligatory. Thus, before God commands it, the action in question is neither right nor wrong. Accordingly, prior to issuing the command, God has nothing to appeal to in order to inform his decision about what to command—that is, there are no reasons why he should command for or against the action in question.

Consider the following example for the purposes of illustration. Imagine that God has not yet commanded us to love our neighbors but that he is preparing to do so. Given option 2, prior to God's command, it is neither right nor wrong for us to love our neighbors. On the basis of what reason, then, could God base his command that we love our neighbors? Were option 2 true, there would appear to be no such reasons. He could just as easily command us to hate our neighbors—after all, there would be no reason why he should not. And, assuming option 2 is true, were God to command us to hate our neighbors, then it would be obligatory for us to do so.

But now let us alter the illustration just a bit to drive the point home. Imagine that God *did* have a reason for commanding us to love our neighbors. Suppose God's reason was that he knew that there is something about loving one's neighbors that makes it right. Perhaps God knew that loving one's neighbor helps to increase human happiness in the world. Or perhaps God knew that the proposition *people should love their neighbors* is necessarily true. But in either case, if there were such a reason upon which God could base his command, then option 2 would be false: there would be something independent of God's command that renders the act of loving one's neighbors obligatory. Effectively, then, we would be rejecting option 2—and hence rejecting divine command theory—if we were to suppose that God has good reasons for his commands.

Ultimately, then, it can seem that, if Campbell affirms option 2, then he is committed to saying that God's commands are utterly arbitrary.[58] And this arbitrariness poses some very difficult problems for him. For one thing, given option 2, the rules of morality would themselves be arbitrary, and that can seem like an unacceptable view of morality in its own right. But even if Campbell were willing to bite that bullet here, another problem would soon emerge for him. Insofar as Campbell would be committed to saying that God's commands are utterly arbitrary given option 2, Campbell would thereby appear to be committed to saying that God himself is not fully rational, because God does not have good reasons for all of his actions. And saying *that* about God is a problem—especially for theists such as Campbell—because, as a maximally knowledgeable and wise being, God is supposed to be fully rational. And since God is supposed to be fully rational, he could not make utterly arbitrary commands. So, even for theists such as Campbell, option 2 is problematic, or so it can seem.[59]

Effectively, then, this second concern over arbitrariness gives way to a serious argument against divine command theory. And if that argument is sound, then

Campbell's appeal to divine command theory as a way of accounting for the metaphysical ground for morality is deeply problematic. It will be helpful to pause here to summarize the *argument from arbitrariness against divine command theory.*

(A1) If divine command theory is true, then God's commanding an action is what makes it obligatory.
(A2) If God's commanding an action is what makes it obligatory, then prior to his commanding any action there are no reasons upon which his commands could be based.
(A3) If there are no reasons upon which God's commands could be based, then God's commands are arbitrary.
(A4) Thus, if divine command theory is true, then God's commands are arbitrary.
(A5) If God's commands are arbitrary, then God is not fully rational.
(A6) By definition, God is supposed to be fully rational.
(A7) Thus, since God is fully rational, God's commands are not arbitrary.
(A8) Thus, since God's commands are not arbitrary, divine command theory is false.

The most obvious way for Campbell to sidestep this argument from arbitrariness altogether is to double back to the original dilemma and go with option 1—the fact that an action is morally obligatory is what makes God command it in the first place. But if Campbell chooses this first option, then he has to reject the main thrust of his divine command theory of right conduct: it is not the case that God's commanding an action is what makes it obligatory. But if Campbell rejects divine command theory in order to avoid the argument from arbitrariness, then he is left empty-handed when he goes to answer the question asked at the outset of the previous section: what is the metaphysical ground of the moral law in the first place? Furthermore, if Campbell rejects his divine command theory of right conduct, then he has left himself with no basis on which to say that religion is the source of morality or that "morals . . . are wholly supernatural and divine."[60] So, clearly, Campbell faces a difficult dilemma here. On the one hand, if he accepts divine command theory, then he apparently commits himself to saying that God's commands are arbitrary and, hence, to saying that God is not fully rational. That conclusion squarely conflicts with Campbell's view of God. On the other hand, if he rejects divine command theory to sidestep the argument from arbitrariness, then he appears to be unable to provide an account for the metaphysical ground of morality or to provide an account for how morality depends upon God.

There are at least two possible moves that Campbell could make at this juncture. First, he could streamline his divine command theory so that it avoids the arbitrariness objection in the first place. This can be done, in part, by divorcing his divine command theory of right conduct from a divine command theory of value. Accordingly, Campbell could emphasize the fact that God is necessarily and intrinsically good and, in turn, emphasize that God's commands must be consistent with his nature as an intrinsically good being. Second, Campbell could abandon his divine command theory of right conduct and admit that there are certain moral propositions that are necessarily true and independent of God's commands. However, given this view, morality is still dependent upon God because he created human nature such that these necessary moral truths apply to humans.[61] I now turn to a brief discussion of each of these strategies.

Strategy 1: Campbell could streamline his divine command theory. One way of responding to the argument from arbitrariness on Campbell's behalf is by denying premise A2—that is, by denying the claim that if Campbell's divine command theory is true, then, prior to God's commanding any action, there are no reasons upon which his commands could be based. How might we do this? We could begin by drawing attention to the fact that if God exists, he is an omnibenevolent being. Part of what it means to say that God is an omnibenevolent being, so one might contend, is that he is *necessarily* and *intrinsically* good; if something were not necessarily and intrinsically good, it would not be God. God is necessarily good in the sense that it is impossible for him to *not* be good. And he is intrinsically good in the sense that he is good in and of himself—that is, he does not somehow borrow his goodness, so to speak, from anything external to himself. If it is correct to say that God is necessarily and intrinsically good, then it is open for Campbell to argue that God's necessary and intrinsic goodness acts as a sort of limiting constraint on the kinds of commands that God could actually issue in the first place. That is, God's commands would have to be consistent with, or reflective of, his nature as an intrinsically good being. (Were he to command something that was inconsistent with his intrinsically good nature, then he would not be *necessarily* good.) This means that, ultimately, God's commands would necessarily be based on his reflection on his own nature as an intrinsically good being; hence, his commands are not arbitrary, because they are based on his perfect reasoning about his own divine nature.

We may be able to read Campbell as gesturing in this very sort of direction when he claims that the source of human duty resides in divine reason itself. He says, for example, "The reason of God is the supreme law of the spiritual universe.—*And his oracles are but expressions of that reason.* His word, or his law, is, therefore, Divinely rational. It is holy, just, and good."[62] Perhaps what Campbell is getting at here is that because God is a necessarily and intrinsically good being and because his commands are necessarily in accord with his reasoning upon his own divine nature as an intrinsically good being, his commands are themselves nonarbitrary, insofar as they are commands to perform those actions that promote what is consistent with, or reflective of, his own nature.

Now, recall that premise A2 says that prior to God's commanding some action, there are no reasons for or against that action upon which he could base his commands. Accordingly, prior to commanding us to love our neighbor, God could have no reason for issuing such a command. But I think it is available for Campbell to reply in the following way: God actually does have a reason for commanding us to love our neighbors, for that action promotes things that are consistent with, and reflective of, his own nature as an intrinsically good being. God's nature is effectively the paradigm or form of goodness itself to which all other things can be compared. And because he is *necessarily* good, God cannot issue commands that promote what is inconsistent with his own divine nature. Consequently, so Campbell might argue, the reason upon which any of God's commands is based is that the action commanded would promote or preserve something reflective of God's own good nature. And although God has a reason upon which to base his command, that reason does not stem from any facts external to God's own nature.

Perhaps another illustration will be helpful here. Imagine that God is considering whether to command us to commit adultery. According to Campbell's divine command theory of right conduct, *if* God actually were to command us to commit adultery, then cheating on one's spouse would, indeed, be morally obligatory. However, according to the view we are considering, God cannot actually command us to commit adultery, because the act of cheating on one's spouse brings about harm (and violates trust, and so forth). But why is bringing about harm a bad thing, and why is it such that God cannot command that we bring it about? In short, given the theory of value under consideration, bringing about harm is bad precisely *because it is inconsistent with God's nature* as an intrinsically good being. And because God is *necessarily* good, he cannot command an action that promotes something inconsistent with his intrinsically good nature. Accordingly, then, what makes harming one's spouse *bad* is that it is inconsistent with God's nature. But what makes the act of adultery *wrong* or *immoral* is that God commands us to refrain from it—and he does so precisely because adultery brings about bad states of affairs that are inconsistent with his nature.

To be sure, this kind of response to the argument from arbitrariness has two separate components: a *theory of value,* which is rooted in God's nature as an omnibenevolent being; and a *theory of right conduct,* which is rooted in the act of God's commanding an action. Call this theory of value a *divine **nature** theory of value.* On this theory of value, as we have already seen, God himself is intrinsically good. Accordingly, something is *extrinsically* good if and only if it is consistent with, or reflective of, God's nature as an intrinsically good being. And something is bad if and only if it is inconsistent with his divine nature. Note that this divine nature theory of value does not say that something's value is contingent upon whether God commands that it be brought about or preserved. Rather, something's value is contingent on whether it is consistent with, or reflective of, God's divine nature. In contrast, given the divine command theory of right conduct, whether an action is right or wrong depends upon whether God commands it. That said, at least as I am imagining Campbell's defense against the argument from arbitrariness, his divine command theory of right conduct would need to be parasitic upon something like a divine nature theory of value: an action is obligatory because God commands it, but God necessarily commands that action because it promotes something reflective of his intrinsically good nature.

An example will be helpful here to further illustrate this distinction between Campbell's theory of right conduct and his theory of value, as well as the dependence of the former on the latter. Consider a case of child abuse. The harm that a child endures when his drunken mother abuses him is certainly *bad,* and it is bad because it is inconsistent with God's intrinsically good nature. However, the act of refraining from child abuse is obligatory because God necessarily commands us to refrain from that action, precisely because it promotes states of affairs that are incompatible with his nature. Accordingly, God's commands are perfectly nonarbitrary because they are based on his reasoning about his own nature as a necessarily and intrinsically good being.

With all of this in tow, then, we can see how Campbell might be able to deny premise A2 of the argument from arbitrariness. If premise A2 is false, then the rest of that argument fails to get off the ground. Accordingly, if we understand Campbell's divine command theory as a merely a theory of right conduct—and if we supplement it with the divine nature theory of value sketched above—then we can read him as providing a cogent account for what grounds morality. In particular, Campbell's divine command theory of right conduct would explain the metaphysical grounding for right and wrong, duty and obligation.

Strategy 2: Campbell could reject divine command theory but maintain that God created human nature such that moral truths apply. Another way that one might want to respond to the argument from arbitrariness on Campbell's behalf is by simply accepting defeat and walking away from a divine command theory of right conduct. Accordingly, Campbell could say that, in fact, God commands certain actions *because* they are obligatory. In so doing, Campbell's view would need to come to terms with the fact that something independent of God's commands (or even his nature) is what makes an action obligatory in the first place. But can a theist such as Campbell make this move—especially since he believes morality is dependent on God? Does this move not simply take religion out of the picture when it comes to morality?

Perhaps Campbell could argue for something like the following.[63] Although God's commanding an action is not what causes it to be obligatory, morality is still dependent on God insofar as he created *us* in such a way that the rules of morality apply to our lives. Out of all the possible things God could have created, he created us such that we have a certain nature, and he created the world in which we live to operate in certain kinds of ways. Accordingly, God created us in such a way that we are harmed by certain actions and benefited by others. So, for example, humans were designed in such a way that we suffer when we are punched in the nose or when someone steals our property. But we (and the world in which we live) could have been made much differently; we could have been made indestructible or the world could have been designed such that theft would not negatively affect our interests in any way. However, God created us specifically (and placed us in a certain kind of environment) such that certain moral truths apply. Mark Timmons offers a helpful analogy in making this sort of point.

> Suppose that I want to build a machine of some sort but that there are various ways in which I might design the machine's motor. I might construct it so that it runs on gasoline, or I might make it so that it runs on vegetable oil, or on beer, or whatever. The worth of the machine is its running well. If I make the one that runs on gasoline, I should fill its tank with gas. But, if I make the one that runs on vegetable oil, I should fill its tank accordingly. The idea is that whether I should fill the machine with one fluid or another depends on two factors: (1) facts about various sorts of motors and (2) my decision about what sort of motor to create.
>
> The suggestion, then, is that for various sorts of possible creatures subject to moral requirements, there are basic moral principles whose truth or correctness does not depend on God's commands (just as facts about various motors and what they will run on is not up to me). However, since God has control over the kind of creature he will create, he does exert control over which set of principles is to be followed (just as it is up to me to decide what kind of motor to build.)[64]

So whereas, for example, the fact that God's command is not what makes loving one's neighbors obligatory, the fact that he created us such that loving one's neighbors affects us in certain sorts of ways is what makes the moral truth that *it is a duty to love one's neighbors* apply to us. And the fact that this moral truth applies to us is owing to the fact that we were created by God in such and such a way. Thus, in an important sense, morality is dependent upon God: he created us in such a way that certain moral rules apply to us. However, in another sense, morality is entirely independent of God: he did not make certain actions right or wrong by virtue of his commands.

Campbell might appear to hint in the direction of this sort of account about the relation between God and morality. For example, he agrees with one writer (James Simpson)[65] that God created humans and the world in such a way that both operate happily when the rules of morality are followed. Campbell says,

> Our most profound moralists . . . have been constrained to announce it as a result of their most studious and deep researches into the physical constitution of the world, that "*it is actually arranged on the principle of favoring virtue and punishing vice,*" just as evidently as it is "*adapted to all the faculties of man, as an intelligent, moral, and religious being.*" "Whenever," says one of our best writers on the constitution of man—"whenever the dictates of the moral sentiments . . . are opposed by the solicitations of the animal propensities, the latter must yield; otherwise, by the constitution of external nature, evil will inevitably ensue." This is what we mean by alleging that nature is constituted in harmony with the supremacy of the moral feelings, guided by intellect. Hence the happiness not merely of the individual himself, but of the whole human race, by the insuperable arrangement of the Creator, are made consequent upon the obedience of a cultivated and enlightened moral nature, to a moral code.[66]

Nevertheless, this passage by no means makes it clear that Campbell somehow thinks that God's commands are *not* what makes actions obligatory or that God's commands are *not* what grounds the moral code. Consequently, reading him in that way would be a bit of a stretch, especially given everything that he says that suggests he is a divine command theorist.

In any case, even if this second strategy would offer Campbell a way of sidestepping the argument from arbitrariness, it would come at the cost of his rejecting his divine command theory of right conduct. Accordingly, Campbell would still need to provide an account for what actually makes an action right or wrong in the first place. Moreover, this second strategy is particularly problematic for Campbell because any non-divine command theory of right conduct would, as mentioned above, seem to stand in some tension with his moral epistemology according to which we can originally discern moral truths only by means of faith in the testimony of those through whom God has revealed the moral law. Consequently, at the end of the day, it seems to me that the best move for Campbell to make when responding to the argument from arbitrariness is the first strategy outlined above.

5.5. Conclusion

Campbell clearly thinks that there is an intimate relationship between religion and morality. In fact, in his view, the latter is wholly dependent upon the former. As we have seen, he thinks the only way we can originally discover moral truth is by means of faith in the testimony of the biblical writers. I do not think, however, that his elimination argument concerning how we originally discover moral truth is sound, as it falls prey to the charge that his list of the possible faculties by which might we discern moral truth is not exhaustive. Furthermore, he fails to support the linchpin claim that we cannot originally discover moral truth through the use of reason. It remains for Campbell to argue why he thinks reason is so impotent. Otherwise, his elimination argument that we originally discern moral truth solely through faith is perfectly unconvincing. But even if we grant that this argument is sound, Campbell's view invites the worries related to the problem of biblical silence, and he effectively bites the bullet in endorsing his no-speak principle. It remains for Campbell's interpreters to explain whether biblical silence is permissive—such that we have recourse to prudential judgments based on the law of expediency—or whether biblical silence is prohibitive. It also remains for Campbell's interpreters to say something about what should count as biblical silence in the first place. When it comes to explaining the metaphysical ground of the rules of morality, I think it is best to read Campbell as a simple divine command theorist, at least when it comes to his theory of right conduct. Such a theory of right conduct, when combined with a theory of value rooted in the nature of God as an intrinsically and necessarily good being, can be successfully defended against the argument from arbitrariness.

Epilogue

Alexander Campbell did something significant. As one of the main figureheads of a religious movement that would eventually attract millions of followers, he stepped up to the task of giving a serious philosophical case for many of the views around which his religious movement sought to promote unity. Although many religious leaders in his day did not attempt to tackle the challenges to faith that atheists and religious skeptics could pose, Campbell welcomed these challenges and trenchantly engaged them, modeling a life of intellectual courage and serious thought. Along the way, he drew upon and responded to many important figures in the history of modern philosophy—from Bacon and Locke to Hume and the Scottish common sense philosophers—in his effort to offer an apology that could stave off the intellectual scurvy of religious enthusiasm and provide a spine for antebellum American Christians.

Yet, as I show in chapter 2, not every feature of Campbell's philosophy of religion should be seen as a repurposed import. While his revealed-idea argument for God's existence may seem to resemble Descartes's trademark argument in many ways, it nonetheless remains a novel contribution to natural theology. Contra Locke and Hume (who thought the idea of God is derived of ideas acquired through sense perception), Campbell believed that we simply cannot explain the origin of the idea of God without allowing that it was divinely presented to humanity, though not as an innate idea, as Descartes believed. And given his emphasis on the revealed origin of the idea of God, Campbell stood in stark contrast not only with many of his philosophical forerunners but also with succeeding generations of nineteenth- and early twentieth-century American philosophers, many of whom—the pragmatists most notably—viewed religion as little more than the natural outgrowth of human efforts to address their own fears, desires, and practical needs. And indeed Campbell thought that recognizing the supernatural cause of the original idea of God helps demonstrate the reality of the object of that idea: the fact that the idea was revealed shows that there is a divine *revealer.* In turn, he thought that getting clear on the revealed origin of the idea of God can help us put our finger on the reason why previous arguments for God's existence failed: their proponents unknowingly relied on an idea that is borrowed from beyond the methodological constraints of natural theology.

Although some of Campbell's interpreters have suggested that he was somehow opposed to natural theology in general, given the logical structure of his revealed-idea argument in particular, their interpretations fail to appreciate the nuance of his thinking—after all, his case for theism did not rely on a putatively revealed premise. However, Campbell's efforts in natural theology—particularly his revealed-idea argument—were indeed aimed at making the case for revealed theology. In his eyes, though, the former inevitably serves as the handmaiden to the latter, even if the former retains epistemic priority. Unfortunately for Campbell, his revealed-idea argument suffers from numerous problems. He shortchanged the possibility that we can derive the idea of God by constructing it from the materials available to us in sensation and reflection or, otherwise, by perceiving the object of that idea directly. And, further, his argument invites a pernicious and perhaps insuperable regress problem. Accordingly, while Campbell's revealed-idea argument is rightly regarded as a novel, it falls flat. Fortunately for theists, the case for God's existence need not—and, I think, does not—rely on anything akin to the revealed-idea argument.

But the intellectual fight for Campbell was not just over theism simpliciter but also over Christian theism in particular, and that battle caused him to follow Locke in emphasizing the role of miracles and the rationality of believing in them on the basis of testimony. While less unique than his argument for theism, as discussed in chapter 3, Campbell's argument *from* miracles was geared toward showing that the miracle of resurrection confirms the divinely revealed nature of Jesus's claims about himself and that, more generally, miracles help to confirm the reliability of the biblical writers by authenticating them as divine spokespersons. To give teeth to his argument from miracles, Campbell also recognized that he needed to make a case for the historicity of the resurrection in particular, and (following Charles Leslie) he offered his criteriological argument *for* the resurrection. In turn, he stood on the shoulders of George Campbell to defend his overall case for Christianity against Hume's famous attack on the credibility of miracle reports. But while Campbell's four-pronged response to Hume was able to neutralize that assault, his overall case for the truth of Christian theism still raises some difficult questions. Campbell's argument from miracles pivoted heavily on the Lockean premise that if someone performs a miracle, then that person is an authentic messenger of God's revelation and, hence, that person's claims are true. But even if we know that someone is an authentic messenger of God's revelation because he has performed a miracle, it is hard to say why we can be sure that that messenger is reliably relaying God's revelation. Accordingly, Campbell's case for Christian theism is missing a small but crucial piece of the overall puzzle. On other fronts, Campbell's criteriological argument for the miracle of resurrection invites some tough questions, particularly these: Are the Lesliean criteria with which he evaluated the testimony of the resurrection actually met? And—equally important—are those criteria, even if met, sufficiently truth indicative in the way Campbell thought they were? As more and more work is done in the area of what has been recently labeled *ramified* natural theology, these questions will need to be addressed by those who might want to draw upon Campbell to make a levering case from theism to Christian theism.

Not only was it important to Campbell to make the positive case for theism and Christian theism, but he thought it crucial that Christians consider and be able to respond to the objections aimed against their views. As discussed in chapter 4, he provided some competent resources with which to respond to the problems of evil and divine hiddenness and the arguments for atheism that they generate. In response to the logical argument from evil, Campbell stressed free will and the impossibility of God's giving humans free will while, at the same time, preventing them from misusing it to introduce evil into the world. In response to the evidential argument from evil, he stressed the inscrutability of God's reasons, an inscrutability that leaves us unable to determine whether a particular instance of evil is gratuitous. And in response to the argument from divine hiddenness, he emphasized how sin can negatively affect one's epistemic orientation such that, even though the evidence for God's existence is sufficient, one can fail to recognize it. While Campbell's response to the logical argument from evil is hardly unique in the history of theological reflections on the topic, it moves more or less in the right direction, especially when interpreted as a defense and not as a theodicy. More impressive to me is his protoskeptical theism, as it anticipated some of the basic moves that many theistic philosophers have made in recent years in responding to the evidential argument from evil. Of course, a remaining challenge for those who want to make use of Campbell's skeptical move is to show how skeptical theism can withstand the various objections against it, especially the objection that skeptical theism threatens to cripple our ordinary moral practice. Regarding his response to the argument from divine hiddenness, I think it says a good deal about Campbell's seriousness as a thinker that he anticipated and took seriously the challenge posed by divine hiddenness long before that issue had received much explicit attention from philosophers of religion. His twofold response to that argument, though—with its emphasis on the faulty epistemic orientation of the nonbeliever—needs more work, especially if it is to rest on the claim that all nonbelievers are irrational in their nonbelief.

Campbell's work in philosophy of religion also included his views about the relation between religion and morality. As discussed in chapter 5, Campbell believed that humans cannot originally acquire moral truths unless we have faith in the testimony of those to whom the moral law was divinely revealed in the first place. Campbell's elimination argument for this view is unconvincing, and in general I do not see much promise in his moral epistemology moving forward. Why was Campbell so pessimistic when it comes to our ability to discover moral truths by means of reason or some faculty other than that which he defines as the faculty of faith? This remains something of a curiosity because, in general, Campbell was fairly optimistic about the reasoning process when properly undertaken. Unfortunately, I think Campbell simply overreached here and his moral epistemology, as a whole, suffered because of it. At any rate, Campbell tried to provide some useful resources for responding to one of the more obvious challenges to his moral epistemology—what I have labeled the problem of biblical silence—by arguing that the law of expediency becomes salient when the biblical texts leave an issue unaddressed. A challenge for his interpreters moving forward is this: What should we count as biblical silence in the first place? And in light of Campbell's no-speak principle, when that biblical silence obtains, is it permissive or is it prohibitive? Unfortunately, moving in either direction here invites additional worries for Campbell, so this dilemma is a difficult one.

Regarding Campbell's account for the metaphysical grounding of morality, I have ascribed to him a simple divine command theory of right conduct. Although this theory of right conduct can perhaps be defended against the argument from arbitrariness (when it is properly tweaked and amended with a divine nature theory of value), a lot more work needs to be done by those who affirm Campbell's version of divine command theory. Specifically, the challenge is to not only deflect the objections leveled against it but also offer some compelling reasons to accept this theory of right conduct in the first place. Although Campbell tried to offer such a justificatory argument, he went nowhere near far enough, especially in providing a case for thinking that divine commands are not only sufficient but necessary for moral obligation. Given the role that this metaethical theory seems to play for many thinkers working in the area of biblical ethics, providing a serious philosophical case for divine command theory is an especially important task remaining not only for those in the Stone-Campbell traditions but also for those in other theological traditions that continue to emphasize the normative authority of revealed texts in deciding moral matters.

Despite the various shortcomings of his philosophical arguments, we can profit from Campbell nonetheless. One of the important features of Campbell's work was his emphasis on taking divine revelation seriously as sort of limiting constraint on, and supplement to, the usual arguments in natural theology. Although he emphasized the indispensability of divine revelation when it comes to thinking about God, this does not mean that he was opposed to natural theology as such or, alternatively, that he was simply indulging in mysterious irrationalism when he appealed to revelation. Rather, Campbell saw revelation and natural theology as standing in an intimate dialectical relation with one another. With his revealed-idea argument for God's existence, he tried to offer a natural theology argument for divine revelation. And he tried to offer serious, secular reasons for thinking that miraculous events occurred and, in turn, that they confirm the divine origin and truth of certain propositions contained in the biblical record. With all of that in hand, he then appealed to revelation as the final push for moving one from theism to Christian theism, and he relied on revelation to fill out the rest of his theology. But even if Campbell's arguments failed to close the loop successfully, natural theologians may be well advised to consider his basic strategy. If we indeed have good reasons to think that God exists and that certain miracles occurred, then perhaps we also have good reason to think that certain propositions are divinely revealed. And perhaps, as Campbell thought, we should take those propositions seriously and allow them to double back to influence how we engage in natural theology in the first place and in ramified natural theology moving forward.

A second feature of Campbell's thought worth highlighting involves his sustained resistance to anti-intellectual postures toward religion. He seemed frustrated by a constellation of attitudes he encountered among religious believers, a constellation that he often referred to under the heading of religious enthusiasm. Brought on by an intellectual gene he seems to have inherited from Locke, Campbell had a sort of allergic reaction to irrational fideism, the willingness on the part of some religious believers to wallow in obscurity and ambiguity, the reluctance of religious believers to justify their views by means of either argument or evidence, the tendency of some to disengage others who disagreed, and the inclination of many religious believers to simply punt in the face of difficult questions by retreating to personal, *mysterium tremendum* experiences. Campbell seems to have been deeply bothered by these intellectual vices.

And for good reason. Campbell understood well that religious beliefs rooted in little more than the blind passion of emotional highs and lows are easily dissolved in the face of the real struggles, suffering, and objections posed by those outside of the protective walls of one's own religious community. Further, he seems to have understood that those unsecured beliefs are ripe for abuse by the demagogic pulpiteer. Especially salient for Campbell was the fact that such an intellectually lazy posture toward one's religious life is simply unbiblical: he believed that Christians have a biblically specified obligation to know the reasons why they take their Christian views to be true and to be able to defend them against the objections posed by religious skeptics, agnostics, and atheists. For Campbell, controversy and argumentative exchange was not something to be avoided at all costs. For, in his view, truth has nothing to fear from inquiry, and religious believers can profit from the refining fire of opposition. Campbell's remedy for religious enthusiasm was to offer reasons for thinking God exists, to offer reasons for thinking that Jesus was resurrected, to make a case for divine revelation, and to understand the case against theism and respond to it thoughtfully. Although his arguments were not always successful, what he set out to accomplish was certainly worthwhile, and the model he offered as a Christian thinker is a worthy one for religious believers even today.

* * *

Alexander Campbell was one of the most respected figures of nineteenth-century America, and he is widely known for the important role he played in the American Restoration Movement that emerged during the Second Great Awakening. But while his legacy as a religious leader and theologian has been well noted, his contribution as a philosopher of religion has been underappreciated, if not entirely overlooked, even by those scholars affiliated with the Stone-Campbell Restoration traditions. My hope is that this book has helped to cast a new light on Campbell, one that will allow us to better understand this important American and his lasting influence. And while there is a host of more familiar names in the history of American philosophy—from Jonathan Edwards to Ralph Waldo Emerson to C. S. Peirce, William James, and John Dewey—Campbell merits at least an honorable mention when the story of philosophy of religion in American is told. Given his lasting influence as a religious thinker, and given his efforts to provide a philosophical backbone for the primitivist vision of Christianity his movement helped to promote, Alexander Campbell deserves to be remembered as a significant antebellum American philosopher of religion.

Notes

1. Campbell the Philosopher and His Philosophical Influences

1. Henry Clay's complete letter is quoted in Robert Richardson, *The Memoirs of Alexander Campbell, Embracing a View of the Origin, Progress and Principles of the Religious Reformation which He Advocated,* 2 vols. (Nashville: Gospel Advocate Company, 1956), 2:548n.

2. Benjamin Lyon Smith, *Alexander Campbell* (St. Louis: Bethany Press, 1930), 147.

3. For more on Campbell's education, see Frank Pack, "Alexander Campbell the Scholar," *Restoration Quarterly* 30, no. 2–3 (1988): 125–33.

4. For more on the history of the Stone-Campbell Restoration Movement, see Michael W. Casey and Douglas A. Foster, eds., *The Stone-Campbell Movement: An International Religious Tradition* (Knoxville: University of Tennessee Press, 2002); Douglas A. Foster, Paul M. Blowers, Anthony L. Dunnavant, and D. Newell Williams, eds., *The Encyclopedia of the Stone-Campbell Movement* (Grand Rapids, MI: Wm. B. Eerdmans Publishing, 2004); Leroy Garrett, *The Stone-Campbell Movement* (Joplin, MO: College Press Publishing, 2006); Richard M. Tristano, *The Origins of the Restoration Movement: An Intellectual History* (Atlanta: Glenmary Research Center, 1998); C. Leonard Allen and Richard T. Hughes, *Rediscovering Our Roots: The Ancestry of Churches of Christ* (Abilene: Abilene Christian University Press, 1988); Richard T. Hughes, *Reviving the Ancient Faith: The Story of Churches of Christ in America* (Abilene: Abilene Christian University Press, 2008); and C. Leonard Allen, *Things Unseen: Churches of Christ in (and after) the Modern Age* (Siloam Springs, AR: Leafwood, 2004). See also the relevant chapters in Nathan O. Hatch, *The Democratization of American Christianity* (New Haven, CT: Yale University Press, 1989); and Mark A. Noll, *A History of Christianity in the United States and Canada* (Grand Rapids, MI: Eerdmans, 2000). For a good study on Thomas Campbell, see Richard Phillips, "Thomas Campbell: A Reappraisal Based on Backgrounds," *Restoration Quarterly* 49 no. 2 (2007): 75–102.

5. Leslie Lyall Kingsbury, "The Philosophical Influences Bearing on Alexander Campbell and the Beginnings of the Disciples of Christ Movement" (PhD diss., University of Edinburgh, 1954), 46; emphasis added.

6. Thomas Campbell, *Declaration and Address of the Christian Association of Washington* (Washington, PA: Brown and Sample, 1809).

7. Peter A. Verkruyse, *Prophet, Pastor, and Patriarch: The Rhetorical Leadership of Alexander Campbell* (Tuscaloosa: University of Alabama Press, 2005), xi. R. Freeman Butts notes that "[b]etween 1800 and 1850 church membership increased ten times while the total population was increasing only five times." Butts, *A Cultural History of Western Education* (New York: McGraw Hill, 1955), 441. Quoted in James Leroy Shields Jr., "Alexander Campbell: A Synthesis of Faith and Reason (1823–1860)" (PhD diss., Syracuse University, 1974), 3.

8. Henry Webb, *In Search of Christian Unity: A History of the Restoration Movement* (Abilene: Abilene Christian University Press, 1990), 243. Quoted in Richard J. Cherok, *Debating for God: Alexander Campbell's Challenge to Skepticism in Antebellum America* (Abilene: Abilene Christian University Press, 2008), 36.

9. Cherok, *Debating for God*, 36.

10. Various other, smaller religious groups also claim a common heritage in the Stone-Campbell Restoration Movement.

11. This number represents a sum of the estimated total number of members of Churches of Christ (1.6 million in the United States), Independent Christian Churches/Churches of Christ (approximately 1 million, mainly in the United States), and the Disciples of Christ (roughly 700,000 in the United States and Canada). Because of the congregational governance of these churches, estimates on numbers tend to vary, and the estimates on numbers outside the United States are not entirely reliable. Data on the membership in the Churches of Christ and the Independent Christian Churches in the United States can be found at the Hartford Seminary Institute for Religion Research website, at http://hirr.hartsem.edu/research/fastfacts/fast_facts.thml#lasrgest. Data on the worldwide membership in the Churches of Christ can be found at the official website of the Christian Church (Disciples of Christ), at www.disciples.org/AboutTheDisciples/TheDisciplesToday/tabid/68/Default.aspx.

12. David Warren, "The Men of Glasgow: Influences upon the Campbells," *Restoration Quarterly* 51, no. 2 (2009): 65–79, at 73.

13. *Webster's Third New International Dictionary of the English Language* (1993), s.v. "campbellite." My thanks to Darryl Tippens for bringing this to my attention.

14. See, for example, Alexander Campbell, "Replication—No. I," *Christian Baptist* 4, no. 2 (September 1826): 271–72, at 271.

15. Selina Huntington Campbell, *Home Life and Reminiscences of Alexander Campbell by His Wife, Selina Huntington Campbell* (St. Louis: John Burns, 1882), 291–92.

16. Richardson, *Memoirs of Alexander Campbell,* 1:177.

17. For examples of his lecture topics, see Alexander Campbell, ed., *Popular Lectures and Addresses* (Philadelphia: James Challen and Son; Cincinnati: H. S. Bosworth; Bethany, VA: A. Campbell, 1866).

18. Some sources claim that one of Campbell's speeches lasted as long as twelve hours. See Kingsbury, "Philosophical Influences," 58. Clearly, there must have been some breaks taken here and there.

19. Terry Miethe, "The Social Ethics of Alexander Campbell," *Journal of the Evangelical Theological Society* 31, no. 3 (September 1988): 305–19, at 306.

20. Mark Twain, *The Autobiography of Mark Twain*, edited by Harriet Elinor Smith and Sharon Goetz (Berkeley: University of California Press, 2010), 1:457. For more on the encounter between Twain and Campbell—an encounter some think is probably fictional—see Miethe, "Social Ethics of Alexander Campbell," 305n3.

21. James Madison cited in Richardson, *Memoirs of Alexander Campbell,* 2:313.

22. Robert Frederick West, *Alexander Campbell and Natural Religion* (New Haven, CT: Yale University Press, 1948), 6.

23. See Alexander Campbell, *Delusions: An Analysis of the Book of Mormon with an Examination of Its Internal and External Evidences, and a Refutation of Its Pretenses to Divine Authority* (Boston: Benjamin H. Greene, 1832). First published as "Delusions" in *Millennial Harbinger,* 1st ser., 2, no. 2 (February 1831): 85–96.

24. West, *Alexander Campbell and Natural Religion,* 52.

25. Ibid., 45.

26. For the best historical account of Campbell's role in these debates, see Cherok, *Debating for God.* See also Bill J. Humble, *Campbell and Controversy* (Rosemead, CA: Old Path Books, 1952), 78–118; and James Noble Holm Jr., "Alexander Campbell's Debate with Robert Owen, April 1829: The Effect of a Rhetorical Event on the Speaker" (PhD diss., University of Michigan, 1976).

27. For more on Campbell's version of the New Testament, see Paul C. Gutjahr, *An American Bible: A History of the Good Book in the United States, 1777–1880* (Stanford: Stanford University Press, 1999), 101–5.

28. For more on Campbell's publications, see Gary Holloway, "Alexander Campbell as a Publisher," *Restoration Quarterly* 37, no. 1 (1995): 28–35.

29. See, for example, James Riley Estep Jr., "Alexander Campbell and the Education of Women," *Encounter* 58, no. 1 (Winter 1997): 73–92.

30. Clarence R. Athearn, *The Religious Education of Alexander Campbell: Morning Star of the Coming Reformation* (St. Louis: Bethany Press, 1928), 62.

31. Robert E. Lee's letter quoted in Selina Huntington Campbell, *Home Life*, 118.

32. See West, *Alexander Campbell and Natural Religion*, 209. West notes that Campbell said that nothing was more "anti-podal to the gospel than politics."

33. For more on the Virginia Constitutional Convention of 1829–30 and its participants, see David Pulliam, *The Constitutional Conventions of Virginia from Foundation of Commonwealth to Present Time* (Richmond, VA: John T. West, 1901); and Earl G. Swem and John W. Williams, *A Register of the General Assembly of Virginia, 1776–1918, and of the Constitutional Conventions* (Richmond, VA: Davis Bottom, 1918).

34. Jill Rogers, "The Reluctant Delegate: Alexander Campbell and the Statehood Movement in Western Virginia" (master's thesis, West Virginia University, 2002), 35–61.

35. Richardson, *Memoirs of Alexander Campbell,* 2:319.

36. For more on Campbell on slavery, see Ethelene Bruce White, "Jane Campbell McKeever (1800–1871): A Brief Biography with Comparison to Her Brother Alexander Campbell on the Issue of Slavery and Abolition," *Stone-Campbell Journal* 13, no. 1 (Spring

2010): 3–16; Jess O. Hall Jr., "The Long Shadow of Slavery: American Public Morality and the Stone-Campbell Restoration Movement," *Stone-Campbell Journal* 8, no. 1 (Spring 2005): 3–16; T. Brian Pendelton, "Alexander Campbell and Slavery: Gradualism and Anti-slavery Rhetoric in the *Millennial Harbinger*," *Restoration Quarterly* 42, no. 3 (2000): 149–54; Jess O. Hall Jr., "Ecclesiastical Politics on a Moral Powder Keg: Alexander Campbell and Slavery in the *Millennial Harbinger*," *Restoration Quarterly* 39, no. 2 (1997): 65–81; and Earl Eugene Eminhizer, "Alexander Campbell and James (Jonas) Hartzell Interpret the Bible on Slavery," *Iliff Review* 30, no. 1 (Winter 1973): 59–71.

37. See Alexander Campbell, "A Tract for the People of Kentucky," *Millennial Harbinger,* 3rd ser., 6, no. 5 (May 1849): 241–52.

38. Although I am unable to determine whether there was mutual influence, Campbell and Clay were named *together* when they were opposed at the time by Iveson L. Brookes in his *A Defence of Southern Slavery, against the Attacks of Henry Clay and Alexander Campbell, by a Southern Clergyman* (Hamburg, SC: Robinson and Carlisle, 1851).

39. See Alexander Campbell, "Address on War," in *Popular Lectures and Addresses,* 342–66, esp. at 362–63.

40. West, *Alexander Campbell and Natural Religion,* 210; see also Athearn, *Religious Education of Alexander Campbell,* 64–65.

41. Lee's letter quoted in Selina Huntington Campbell, *Home Life,* 118; emphasis in the original.

42. See, for example, Herbert Hovenkamp, *Science and Religion in America, 1800–1860* (Philadelphia: University of Pennsylvania Press, 1978), 82.

43. Edward H. Madden and Dennis W. Madden, "The Great Debate: Alexander Campbell vs. Robert Owen," *Transactions of the Charles S. Peirce Society* 18, no. 3 (Summer 1982): 207–26.

44. See, for example, the following books: S. Morris Eames, *The Philosophy of Alexander Campbell* (Bethany, WV: Bethany College, 1965); West, *Alexander Campbell and Natural Religion*; F. D. Kershner, ed., *The Philosophical Background of Alexander Campbell* (Indianapolis: Butler University Press, 1947); Harold L. Lunger, *The Political Ethics of Alexander Campbell* (St. Louis: Bethany Press, 1954); and Winfred Ernest Garrison, *Alexander Campbell's Theology: Its Sources and Historical Setting* (St. Louis: Christian Publishing, 1900). See also the following unpublished dissertations and theses: Billy Doyce Bowen, "Knowledge, the Existence of God, and Faith: John Locke's Influence on Alexander Campbell's Theology" (PhD diss., Michigan State University, 1978); Kingsbury, "Philosophical Influences"; James H. Ellerbrook, "The Influence of Thomas Reid on the Thought-Life of Alexander Campbell" (bachelor of divinity thesis, Butler University, 1947); George Harold Pratt, "The Philosophy of Alexander Campbell" (master's thesis, Phillips University, 1932); and S. Morris Eames, "The Philosophical Implications in the Theology of Alexander Campbell" (master's thesis, University of Missouri, 1941).

45. Madden and Madden, "Great Debate," 207.

46. As far as I know, the best and most comprehensive resource for accessing a healthy portion of Campbell's published work is Memorial University's "The Restoration Movement Pages," compiled and updated by Hans Rollman. This resource is available at http://www.mun.ca/rels/restmov/.

47. See Cherok, *Debating for God*, 11–12. Cherok notes that there is not much written on Campbell's debate with Owen; consequently, Campbell's role as an important antebellum apologist is largely forgotten today.

48. Alexander Campbell, "Concluding Remarks: Part of the Editor's History," *Christian Baptist*, 7, no. 12 (July 1830): 664–65, at 665. For a similar expression of regret, see also Alexander Campbell, "Reply to the Above," *Christian Baptist* 5, no. 3 (October 1827): 374–76, at 376.

49. Madden and Madden, "Great Debate," 207.

50. See, most notably, Edward Scribner Ames, "The Lockian Influence on Campbell," *Christian-Evangelist* (September 1938): 974–76; Thomas H. Olbricht, "The Rationalism of the Restoration," *Restoration Quarterly* 11, no. 2 (1968): 77–88; Michael Casey, "The Origins of the Hermeneutics of the Churches of Christ, Part Two: The Philosophical Background," *Restoration Quarterly* 31, no. 4 (1989): 193–206; John C. Nugent, "Was Alexander Campbell Enslaved to Scottish Baconianism?" *Stone-Campbell Journal* 12 (Spring 2009): 15–30. As for books from Restoration-related presses, see Garrison, *Alexander Campbell's Theology*; Athearn, *Religious Education of Alexander Campbell*; Kershner, *Philosophical Background of Alexander Campbell;* Lunger, *Political Ethics of Alexander Campbell*; Eames, *Philosophy of Alexander Campbell*; several of the essays in Kenneth Lawrence, ed., *Classic Themes of Disciples Theology: Rethinking the Traditional Affirmations of the Christian Church (Disciples of Christ)* (Fort Worth: Texas Christian University Press, 1986); some of the essays in L. Dale Richesin and Larry D. Bouchard, eds., *Interpreting Disciples: Practical Theology in the Disciples of Christ* (Fort Worth: Texas Christian University Press, 1987); several chapters in Hughes, *Reviving the Ancient Faith*; and several chapters in Allen, *Things Unseen.*

51. There are, of course, some obvious and noteworthy exceptions, including Texas Christian University, Butler University, Drake University, Chapman University, Transylvania University, Hiram College, and Pepperdine University (perhaps among some others).

52. West notes that "as a group, the Disciples have remained suspicious of theology and philosophy without becoming as proficient in them as Campbell was in his time. As an evidence of this, they have not produced a seasoned Christian theologian of distinction for a hundred years" (*Alexander Campbell and Natural Religion,* 219).

53. For more on Ames and Campbell's influence on Ames's religious naturalism and pragmatism, see J. Caleb Clanton and John Mark Gunter, "Edward Scribner Ames, Pragmatism, and Religious Naturalism," *Heythrop Journal* (forthcoming).

54. Ames, "Lockian Influence on Campbell," 974.

55. Ibid.

56. See Barton W. Stone et al., "The Last Will and Testament of the Springfield Presbytery," in Charles A Young, ed., *Historical Documents Advocating Christian Unity* (Chicago: Christian Century Publishing, 1904), 19–26, item 3; emphasis removed and added.

57. For an excellent treatment of the Fanning-Richardson affair, see Hughes, *Reviving the Ancient Faith,* 70–75. See also Allen, *Things Unseen,* 71–82.

58. Campbell quoted in Hughes, *Reviving the Ancient Faith,* 73. See also Alexander Campbell, "Christianity the True Philosophy," *Millennial Harbinger,* 4th ser., 7, no. 8 (1857): 481–85.

59. Alexander Campbell, "Introductory Lecture Delivered at the Organization of Bethany College, Nov. 2, 1841" in Alexander Campbell, ed., *Introductory Addresses, Delivered at the Organization of Bethany College, November 2d, 1841* (Bethany, VA: A. Campbell, 1841), 61–86, at 63–64.

60. See West, *Alexander Campbell and Natural Religion*, 219. West captures this point well: "[Campbell's] Disciples of Christ admirers had and still have difficulty in following his pattern. Their tendency has been to reject all theology and philosophy as proper subjects of reflective thought, without distinguishing the particular types of theology and philosophy which Campbell rejected. Their departure from Campbell is largely based upon their failure to discriminate between his formal words (and natural tendency to overstate the application of his principles) and his actual objectives and life program."

61. Richardson, *Memoirs of Alexander Campbell,* 1:33–34.

62. Garrett, *Stone-Campbell Movement*, 28.

63. For example, see Alexander Campbell, "Evidences of the Gospel—No. 1," *Millennial Harbinger,* 1st ser., 6, no. 5 (1835): 197–201, at 199; emphasis added.

64. See Campbell, "Introductory Lecture."

65. Kingsbury, "Philosophical Influences," 111–13; see also the extracts from the Bethany College catalog printed in Alexander Campbell, "Bethany College: The Course of Instruction and Text Books," *Millennial Harbinger,* 4th ser., 5, no. 4 (1855): 225–31.

66. See, for example, Alexander Campbell, "A Good Library," *Millennial Harbinger,* 1st ser., 5, no. 10 (1834): 490–93.

67. Hence, Campbell criticized his debating opponent Robert Owen for merely asserting his position, as opposed to providing argument. See, for example, Alexander Campbell and Robert Owen, *The Evidences of Christianity: A Debate between Robert Owen of New Lanark, Scotland and Alexander Campbell, President of Bethany College, Va., Containing an Examination of the "Social System" and All the Systems of Skepticism of Ancient and Modern Times, Held in the City of Cincinnati, in April 1829* (1892; reprint, Nashville: McQuiddy, 1912), 460. Hereafter cited as *Campbell-Owen Debate.*

68. Campbell quoted in Athearn, *Religious Education of Alexander Campbell*, 150.

69. Alexander Campbell, "The Social System and Deism—No. II," *Christian Baptist* 4, no. 11 (June 1827): 343–45, at 343–44; emphasis in original.

70. Alexander Campbell, "Religious Controversy," *Millennial Harbinger,* 1st ser., 1, no. 1 (January 1830): 40–44, at 40–41. Quoted in Cherok, *Debating for God*, 20.

71. Cherok, *Debating for God*, 76.

72. See Plato, *Gorgias*, translated and edited by W. D. Woodhead, in *The Collected Dialogues of Plato,* ed. Edith Hamilton and Huntington Cairns (Princeton, NJ: Princeton University Press, 1989), 229–307, at 241 [458a]. There Socrates says to Gorgias, "And what kind of man am I? One of those who would gladly be refuted if anything I say is not true, and would gladly refute another who says what is not true, but would be no less happy to be refuted myself than to refute, for I consider that a greater benefit, inasmuch as it is a greater boon to be delivered from the worst evils oneself than to deliver another."

73. Campbell quoted in Athearn, *Religious Education of Alexander Campbell*, 160.

74. See notes 43, 44, and 50, this chapter. See also Sydney Ahlstrom, *A Religious History of the American People* (New Haven, CT: Yale University Press, 1972), 449; Garrett, *Stone-Campbell Movement*, 24–29.

75. See, for example, Casey, "Origins of the Hermeneutics," 193. While acknowledging Campbell's eclecticism, Casey says that he "borrowed naïvely from [philosophers] to suit his theological scheme." By contrast, Garrison notes (in *Alexander Campbell's Theology*, 154–55), "In writing of his indebtedness to others for religious and theological ideas, he says that he was more indebted to their failures than to their successes. As the wreck of one ship may warn another from a dangerous coast, so he admitted he had been helped by the mistakes of earlier theologians." By extension, the same could be said of Campbell's philosophical influences.

76. Campbell, "Introductory Lecture," 70.

77. Ibid.

78. Alexander Campbell, "Extracts from the Due-West Telescope," *Millennial Harbinger*, 4th ser., 3, no. 4 (1853): 228–30, at 228.

79. Campbell, "Introductory Lecture," 64.

80. See, for instance, *Campbell-Owen Debate*, 281–82.

81. Campbell, "Introductory Lecture," 64. Apparently, Campbell adopted this high regard for Bacon from his teacher, George Jardine, while a student. See, for example, Alexander Campbell, "Lecture 67th, Feb. 23, 1809," Campbell Family Papers, Box 5, Lecture Notes at Glasgow University, transcribed by Earl Eugene Eminhizer, in the archives at the Disciples of Christ Historical Society, Nashville, Tennessee.

82. For more on Campbell's hermeneutics, as well as its Baconian influences, see Casey, "Origins of the Hermeneutics," esp. at 198–201. See also Michael Casey, *The Battle over Hermeneutics in the Stone Campbell Movement, 1800–1870* (Lewiston, NY: Edwin Mellon Press, 1998); Olbricht, "Rationalism of the Restoration"; C. Leonard Allen, "Baconianism and the Bible among the Disciples of Christ: James S. Lamar and the Organum of Scripture," *Church History* 55 (March 1986): 65–80; Allen, *Things Unseen*, 45–98; Nugent, "Was Alexander Campbell Enslaved"; Garrett, *Stone-Campbell Movement*, 23–24; Samuel C. Pearson, "Faith and Reason in Disciples Theology," in *Classic Themes of Disciples Theology: Rethinking the Traditional Affirmations of the Christian Church (Disciples of Christ)*, ed. Kenneth Lawrence (Fort Worth: Texas Christian University Press, 1986), 101–24, esp. at 102–4.

83. Francis Bacon, *Novum Organum* [1620], in *The Complete Essays of Francis*, ed. Henry Leroy Finch (New York: Washington Square Press, 1963), 178–264, esp. at 193–206.

84. Garrett, *Stone-Campbell Movement*, 24.

85. Much of the following sections on the Lockean and Scottish influence on Campbell's thinking follows Kingsbury's insightful comparative study of Campbell, Locke, and Reid, as well as Bowen's comparative study of Locke and Campbell.

86. Campbell quoted in Kingsbury, "Philosophical Influences," 359; emphasis added.

87. *Campbell-Owen Debate*, 281.

88. John Locke, *An Essay Concerning Human Understanding* (1689; reprint, Indianapolis: Hackett, 1996), 40 [bk. II.ii.2].

89. Alexander Campbell, "The Office of Reason in Reference to the Divine Revelation," *Millennial Harbinger*, 5th ser., 6, no. 8 (1863): 351–55.

90. Locke, *Essay*, 322–23 [IV.xvii.23–24]; see Alexander Campbell, "The Millennium—No. IV," *Millennial Harbinger*, 4th ser., 6, no. 3 (1856), 269–76, at 270. There, Campbell says, "Faith is not, in any case, incompatible with the highest reason. But it often transcends its

power, and out-measures its periphery" (270). For other instances of Campbell's view about the relationship between faith and reason, see Alexander Campbell, "Reason Examined by Interrogatories—No. I," *Millennial Harbinger*, 1st ser., 2, no. 11 (1831): 485–87; Alexander Campbell, "Reason Examined by Interrogatories—No. II," *Millennial Harbinger*, 1st ser., 3, no. 1 (1832): 8–10; Alexander Campbell, "Reason Examined by Interrogatories—No. III," *Millennial Harbinger*, 1st ser., 3, no. 3 (1832): 97–100; and Campbell, "Social System and Deism."

91. Kingsbury, "Philosophical Influences," 154–55.

92. See, for example, Campbell, "Replication—No. I," 271–72.

93. See Kingsbury, "Philosophical Influences," 139, 185, 187, 170, 189, 190, and 202, respectively.

94. See, for example, Alexander Campbell and John B. Purcell, *A Debate on the Roman Catholic Religion between Alexander Campbell, Bethany, Va., and the Right Reverend John B. Purcell, Bishop of Cincinnati* (Cincinnati: J. A. James and Co., 1837), 231. Hereafter cited as *Campbell-Purcell Debate.*

95. John Locke, *An Essay for the Understanding of St. Paul's Epistles, &c.* (London, 1733), vi. For Campbell's edited translation of the Bible, see Alexander Campbell, ed., *The Living Oracles, or the Sacred Writings of the Apostles and Evangelists of Jesus Christ Commonly Styled "The New Testament," Translated from the Original Greek by Doctors George Campbell, James McKnight and Philip Doddridge* (Nashville: Gospel Advocate, 1974). For Campbell's reflections on his edition of the Bible, see Alexander Campbell, "Historical Sketch of the Origin and Progress of the New Translation," *Millennial Harbinger*, 1st ser., 3, no. 6 (1832): 268–74; and Alexander Campbell, "Locke's Opinion of the Form in which the Scriptures Are Printed," *Millennial Harbinger*, 1st ser., 3, no. 6 (1832): 274–75. See also Gutjahr, *American Bible*, 103–4.

96. *Campbell-Owen Debate*, 281.

97. Richardson, *Memoirs of Alexander Campbell*, 1:33.

98. See John Locke, *The Second Treatise of Government and a Letter Concerning Toleration* (Mineola, NY: Dover Publications, 2002), 96–112 (chap. 19). See also Kingsbury, "Philosophical Influences," 196–98.

99. Kingsbury, "Philosophical Influences," 200–201.

100. For the most informative treatment of the content Campbell received from George Jardine's course at Glasgow, see Casey, "Origins of the Hermeneutics," 201–5. See also Alexander Campbell, Lecture Notes at Glasgow University, Campbell Family Papers, Box 5, in the archives at the Disciples of Christ Historical Society in Nashville, Tennessee.

101. Nugent tells the story that when Campbell was shipwrecked on his way to America, what he chose to save were his copies of philosophical treatises by the common sense philosophers. See Nugent, "Was Alexander Campbell Enslaved," 19.

102. Alexander Campbell, "Mr. Brantly's Views of Reformation and of New Version," *Christian Baptist* 7, no. 12 (1830): 662.

103. Campbell quoted in Eames, *Philosophy of Alexander Campbell*, 20.

104. Campbell, "Introductory Lecture," 65.

105. Ibid., 65–66.

106. Ellerbrook, "Influence of Thomas Reid," 45–56.

107. See Thomas Reid, *Essays on the Intellectual Powers,* in *Thomas Reid's Inquiry and Essays,* ed. Ronald E. Beanblossom and Keith Lehrer (Indianapolis: Hackett, 1983), 175–80. For a helpful discussion of Reid on this point, see Gideon Yaffe and Ryan Nichols, "Thomas Reid," in *The Stanford Encyclopedia of Philosophy,* ed. Edward N. Zalta, winter 2009 ed., http://plato.stanford.edu/archives/win2009/entries/reid/.

108. See Alexander Campbell, "Lecture 58th, February 8, 1809," in the Campbell Family Papers, Box 5, Lecture Notes at Glasgow University, in the archives at the Disciples of Christ Historical Society in Nashville, Tennessee. There, Campbell writes that "our knowledge of the material world is *immediate* or intuitive" (emphasis added). See also *Campbell-Owen Debate,* 160–61, where Campbell says, "*Sensation* is the name which philosophers have given to the exercise of these senses, or rather to the operation by them which makes us acquainted with the material world. *Perception* is the name given to those acts of the mind which discriminate the different sensations of impressions made upon our senses. . . . By this faculty we become acquainted with all things external" On this same point, see Melancthon, "No External World," *Millennial Harbinger,* 4th ser. 3, no. 9 (1853): 509–10. As the preface to this article, Campbell poses a rhetorical question: "I think it is more difficult to prove an internal world, than an external one. Yet some great men, and well educated in the common views of mankind, in their day have doubted both worlds. Shall we then, conclude, that because one philosopher affirms that there is no external world, and another that there is no internal world,—ergo, there is no world at all?" (509).

109. Casey, "Origins of the Hermeneutics," 199.

110. Reid, *Essays on the Intellectual Powers,* 151–59. See also James Beattie, *Essay on the Nature and Immutability of Truth in Opposition to Sophistry and Scepticism* (London: Edward and Charles Dilly, 1778), particularly pt. 1, chap. 2, sec. 9.

111. See, for example, Alexander Campbell, "Acts of Apostles: Analysis of Chapter VI," *Millennial Harbinger,* 3rd ser., 3, no. 8 (1846): 431–38, at 435.

112. Alexander Campbell, "To the Christian Messenger," *Christian Baptist* 5, no. 3 (1827): 379–81, at 380; emphasis added.

113. For more on his view of memory and how he vaguely attributes it to Reid, see Alexander Campbell, "The Philosophy of Memory and of Commemorative Institutions," in *Popular Lectures and Addresses,* 272–90, esp. at 273. See also Ellerbrook, "Influence of Thomas Reid," 89–95.

114. Kingsbury, "Philosophical Influences," 321.

115. The best treatment of Campbell's Reidian view of freedom is Madden and Madden, "Great Debate," 209–215. See also Kingsbury, "Philosophical Influences," 273–79 and 322.

116. Athearn, *Religious Education of Alexander Campbell,* 170.

117. For other Scottish influences on Campbell's religious movement, see Lynn A. McMillon, "Alexander Campbell's Early Exposure to Scottish Restorationism, 1808–1809," *Restoration Quarterly* 30, no. 2–3 (1988): 85–101.

118. John Cottingham, "Why Should Analytic Philosophers Do History of Philosophy" in *Analytic Philosophy and History of Philosophy,* ed. Tom Sorrel and G. A. J. Rogers (Oxford, UK: Clarendon Press, 2005), 25–41, at 37–38.

2. The Revealed-Idea Argument for the Existence of God

1. Bacon, "Of Atheism," in *The Complete Essays of Francis Bacon*, ed. Henry Leroy Finch (New York: Washington Square Press, 1963), 44-6, at 44.

2. See, for example, Karl Barth, *Church Dogmatics: A Selection*, trans. and ed. by G. W. Bromiley (Edinburgh: T. and T. Clark, 1961), 49.

3. For a helpful discussion of the distinction between natural and revealed theology, as well as the antipathy with which some theologians (such as Barth) have viewed the former, see Antony Flew, *God and Philosophy* (New York: Prometheus, 2005), 23–37. For different reasons, some Christian philosophers either reject traditional approaches to natural theology or express little optimism in them. See, for example, Paul K. Moser, *The Elusive God: Reorienting Religious Epistemology* (New York: Cambridge University Press, 2008), 25, 46–49.

4. For example, Campbell's close friend and biographer Robert Richardson describes Campbell as having made manifest "his opposition to the claims of natural theology." See Richardson, *Memoirs of Alexander Campbell*, 2:229–30. See also Athearn, *Religious Education of Alexander Campbell*, 51; Garrison, *Alexander Campbell's Theology*, 190–91 and 196; and Cherok, *Debating for God*, 36. The confusion about Campbell's view of natural theology is not directly the fault of the above authors, per se. For example, Cherok is correct in saying that Campbell is opposed to natural *religion*, but unfortunately Cherok does not give due emphasis to the distinction Campbell makes between natural *theology* and natural *religion*, which I explain below.

5. Alexander Campbell, "Notes on a Tour to New York—No. 6," *Millennial Harbinger*, 1st ser., 5, no. 2 (1834): 75–80, at 77.

6. *Campbell-Owen Debate*, 143.

7. Ibid., 91.

8. Campbell, "Introductory Lecture," 72.

9. Alexander Campbell, "Natural Theology—No. 4," *Millennial Harbinger*, 1st ser., 7, no. 11 (1836): 510–16, at 511n1.

10. Alexander Campbell, "The Deist's Corner," *Millennial Harbinger*, 1st ser., 3, no. 7 (1832), 310–11, at 311.

11. Garrison, *Alexander Campbell's Theology*, 190–91.

12. See, for example, Alexander Campbell, "Natural Theology—No. 1," *Millennial Harbinger*, 1st ser., 7, no. 6 (1836): 262–68; Alexander Campbell, "Natural Theology—No. 2," *Millennial Harbinger*, 1st ser., 7, no. 8 (1836): 370–75; Alexander Campbell, "Natural Theology—No. 3," *Millennial Harbinger*, 1st ser., 7, no. 10 (1836): 457–63; Campbell, "Natural Theology—No. 4," 510–16. See also West, *Alexander Campbell and Natural Religion*, 130–31, esp. at n16, which lists several other sources for Campbell's view on the distinction between natural theology and natural religion.

13. Alexander Campbell, "Address at the Annual Meeting of the Christian Missionary Society," in *Popular Lectures and Addresses*, 531–50, at 536.

14. See, for example, Campbell, "Natural Theology—No. 4," 512n2.

15. Ibid., 511n1; emphasis added.

16. *Campbell-Owen Debate*, 5–6. For a similar point about Campbell's commitment to answering skeptical challenges, see West, *Alexander Campbell and Natural Religion*, 90–91.

17. There are, of course, a few counterexamples to this claim. See, for example, M. R. Ayers, "Mechanism, Superaddition, and the Proof of God's Existence in Locke's Essay," *Philosophical Review* 90, no. 2 (April 1981): 210–51; Nicholas Wolterstorff, *John Locke and the Ethics of Belief* (New York: Cambridge University Press, 1996), 124–25; and M. A. Stewart, "Arguments for the Existence of God: The British Debate," in *The Cambridge History of Eighteenth-Century Philosophy*, ed. Knud Haakonssen (Cambridge: Cambridge University Press, 2006), 2:710–30.

18. Nicholas Wolterstorff, "Locke's Philosophy of Religion," in *The Cambridge Companion to Locke*, ed. Vere Chappell (New York: Cambridge University Press, 1994), 173–98, at 189.

19. Locke, *Essay*, 276 [bk. IV.x.6.i].

20. Lover of Just Reasoning, "Deism and the Social System—No. V," *Christian Baptist* 5, no. 3 (October 1827): 373–74. Campbell's response immediately follows this letter, on pages 374–76.

21. Campbell, "Reply to the Above," 376.

22. Ibid.

23. Ibid.; emphasis added.

24. Note that Locke argues in book 2 of the *Essay* that we construct our complex idea of God from the simple ideas provided to us in sensation and reflection. It is not until book 4 that Locke develops his cosmological argument.

25. Locke holds that our idea of God—like all of our other ideas—is derived of sensation and reflection. He says, for example, "For if we examine the *idea* we have of the incomprehensible supreme being, we shall find, that we come by it the same way [through sensation and reflection]; and that the complex *ideas* we have . . . of God . . . are made up of the simple *ideas* we receive from *reflection, v.g.* having from what we experiment in ourselves, got the *ideas* of existence and duration; of knowledge and power; of pleasure and happiness; and of several other qualities and powers, which it is better to have, than to be without; when we would frame an *idea* the most suitable we can to the supreme being, we enlarge every one of these with our *idea* of infinity; and so putting them together, make our complex *idea of God*." See Locke, *Essay*, 127 [bk. II.xxiii.33]; emphasis in original.

26. *Campbell-Owen Debate*, 125.

27. Ibid; emphasis in original.

28. Ibid., 376; emphasis added.

29. Ibid. In a different context, Campbell makes a similar point against deists who claim to have originated the idea of God through the use of reason: "Reasoning on what? the things that are made—but who made them? Thus it goes in a circle; they prove that there is a creator, from things created; and they prove that things are created, because there is a creator. Sagacious doctors! But pray, good doctors, where is the archetype or original . . . from which you were put in possession of the idea, where did you see any thing created by a mere exertion of Almighty power?" Campbell, "Replication—No. I," 271.

30. The main thrust of Campbell's criticism of Locke resembles the sort of criticism offered by Locke's contemporary, Bishop Edward Stillingfleet. Stillingfleet argues that if the original idea of God is not innate, then there is no way to explain how it emerges from sensation and reflection. In turn, he goes on to argue that the idea of God *is* innate, a view denied by both Locke and Campbell. On this point, see Bowen, "Knowledge," 72n152. For Stillingfleet's part in his exchange with Locke, see Edward Stillingfleet, *A Discourse in Vindication of the Doctrine of the Trinity: with an Answer to the Late Socinian Objections against it from Scripture, Antiquity and Reason* (London, 1697); Edward Stillingfleet, *The Bishop of Worchester's Answer to Mr. Locke's Letter, concerning Some Passages in Relation to his Essay of Humane Understanding, mention'd in the Late Discourse in Vindication of the Trinity* (London, 1697); and Edward Stillingfleet, *The Bishop of Worchester's Answer to Mr. Locke's Second Letter; Wherein his Notion of Ideas is Prov'd to be Inconsistent with it self, and with the Articles of Christian Faith* (London, 1698).

31. Campbell, "Reply to the Above," 376; emphasis added.

32. Ibid.

33. *Campbell-Owen Debate*, 91–92; emphasis added.

34. For a similar point about Campbell's take on Locke's cosmological argument, see Samuel C. Pearson Jr., "Enlightenment Influence on Protestant Thought in Early National America," *Encounter* 38, no. 3 (1977): 193–212, esp. at 206–7. See also Garrison, *Alexander Campbell's Theology*, 195–96; and West, *Alexander Campbell and Natural Religion*, 112.

35. *Campbell-Owen Debate*, 435.

36. Alexander Campbell, "Evidences of the Gospel—No. 2," *Millennial Harbinger*, 1st ser., 6, no. 7 (1835): 317–22, at 317.

37. Ibid. In his later years, he also moved in the direction of offering an ontological argument for God's existence. See, for example, Alexander Campbell, "Ontology and Deontology," *Millennial Harbinger*, 5th ser., 5, no. 5 (1862): 199–201, at 199–200.

38. Campbell, "Evidences of the Gospel—No. 1," 200–201.

39. See, for example, Bowen, "Knowledge," 63–73. I say "unsurprisingly" here because Campbell scholars frequently note the Lockean overtones to Campbell's thinking.

40. See, for example, Kingsbury, "Philosophical Influences," 248.

41. Bowen, "Knowledge," 4 and 44; Kingsbury, "Philosophical Influences," 248.

42. Royal Humbert, introduction to *A Compend of Alexander Campbell's Theology*, ed. Royal Humbert (St. Louis: Bethany Press, 1961), 14 and 87; Kingsbury, "Philosophical Influences," 248.

43. Cherok, *Debating for God*, 64.

44. I have also toyed with calling it the "idea-origin argument" or the "revealed-origin argument" for the same reasons.

45. *Campbell-Owen Debate*, 47–48.

46. Campbell, "Evidences of the Gospel—No. 1," 199–201.

47. *Campbell-Owen Debate*, 91.

48. Campbell, "Office of Reason," 352.

49. Ibid.

50. *Campbell-Owen Debate*, 47.

51. Paul Draper argues that Craig's *kalam* argument relies (in part) on the principle that whatever begins to exist *with* time must have a cause. See Paul Draper, "A Critique of the *Kalam* Cosmological Argument," in *Philosophy of Religion: An Anthology*, ed. Louis Pojman and Michael Rea, 5th ed. (Belmont, CA: Wadsworth, 2008), 45–51, esp. at 49–50. For Craig's formulations of the *kalam* argument, see William Lane Craig, "The Existence of God and the Beginning of the Universe," *Truth* 3 (1991): 85–96; William Lane Craig, *Reasonable Faith*, 3rd ed. (Wheaton, IL: Crossway, 2008), 111–56; see also William Lane Craig and Quentin Smith, *Theism, Atheism, and Big Bang Cosmology* (Oxford: Oxford University Press, 1993).

52. See, for example, Graham Oppy, "Uncaused Beginnings," *Faith and Philosophy* 27, no. 1 (January 2010): 61–71. For a similar criticism see Wes Morriston, "Must the Beginning of the Universe Have a Personal Cause? A Critical Examination of the *Kalam* Cosmological Argument," *Faith and Philosophy* 17, no. 2 (2000): 149–69; and J. L. Mackie, *The Miracle of Theism* (Oxford: Oxford University Press, 1982), 82–86.

53. See, for example, Craig's response to Oppy in William Lane Craig, "Reflections on 'Uncaused Beginnings,'" *Faith and Philosophy* 27, no. 1 (January 2010): 71–78.

54. Campbell, "Reply to the Above," 376.

55. In his famous 1948 BBC Radio debate with Frederick Copleston about the existence of God, Bertrand Russell says, "[T]he universe is just there, and that's all." The transcript of the debate on the argument from contingency is reprinted in Bertrand Russell, *Why I Am Not a Christian* (London: George Allen and Unwin, 1957).

56. Clarence Athearn disagrees and asserts that "Campbell disagreed with Locke that the mind was a tabula rasa." Athearn, *Religious Education of Alexander Campbell*, 180. Athearn contends that given his indebtedness to the Scottish common sense school, Campbell thought that we are somehow born with a "capital stock of general ideas" (179). Athearn's view here is predicated upon a serious misreading of Campbell's texts, and he quotes Campbell out of context when attempting to support this interpretation. When Campbell refers to the "stock" ideas in the passage Athearn quotes, he is clearly referring to ideas received already from sensation and reflection.

57. Alexander Campbell, "The Rank and Dignity of Man," *Millennial Harbinger*, 2nd ser., 2, no. 12 (1838): 529–46 at 529.

58. Ibid., 529.

59. Jeffrey Tlumak, *Classical Modern Philosophy* (New York: Routledge, 2007), 109.

60. Locke, *Essay*, 8 [bk. I.ii.4].

61. See, for example, *Campbell-Owen Debate*, 144, 148–51, and 160–63. See also Campbell, "Replication—No. I," 271; Alexander Campbell, "Essays on Man in His Primitive State, and under the Patriarchal, Jewish, and Christian Dispensations—No. IV: Primitive State—No. IV," *Christian Baptist* 6, no. 4 (November 1828): 494–95.

62. *Campbell-Owen Debate*, 149.

63. For a similar observation, see Garrison, *Alexander Campbell's Theology*, 191.

64. For a much more thorough analysis of Descartes's trademark argument, see Tlumak, *Classical Modern Philosophy*, 32–38. See also Bernard Williams, *Descartes: The Project of Pure Enquiry* (New York: Routledge, 2005), 115–47; and the chapter related to

the trademark argument in Anthony Kenny, *Descartes: A Study of His Philosophy* (New York: Random House, 1968).

65. See, for example, Campbell's references to Descartes's cogito argument in *Campbell-Owen Debate*, 44.

66. Rene Descartes, *Meditations on First Philosophy*, in *The Philosophical Writings of Descartes*, translated by John Cottingham, Robert Stoothoof, and Dugald Murdoch (Cambridge: Cambridge University Press, 1984), 2:35 [AT VII, 51–52].

67. *Campbell-Owen Debate*, 161.

68. Ibid.

69. Ibid.

70. Ibid., 151.Δ171

71. See David Hume, *An Enquiry Concerning Human Understanding*, ed. Eric Steinberg, 2nd ed. (Indianapolis: Hackett, 1993), 11 [§2.5]; Locke, *Essay*, 40 [bk. II.ii.2–3].

72. *Campbell-Owen Debate*, 122; see also 47–48.

73. Ibid., 48.

74. Ibid.

75. Ibid.

76. Whether Campbell imported this principle from Locke or Descartes, I do not know. But it is worth noting that Locke relies on it in his cosmological argument in book 4 of the *Essay*, and Locke's *Essay* was probably more influential than any other philosophical work on Campbell's thinking.

77. See, for example, William Rowe, *Philosophy of Religion*, 4th ed. (Belmont, CA: Wadsworth, 2007), 31–32.

78. *Campbell-Owen Debate*, 11–12.

79. For a similar view concerning the presupposition of the principle of sufficient reason, see Richard Taylor, *Metaphysics*, 4th ed. (Englewood Cliffs, NJ: Prentice Hall, 1992), 101.

80. Rowe, *Philosophy of Religion*, 32. See also Mackie, *Miracle of Theism*, 86–87.

81. For a helpful discussion of super-sense-perceptual experiences, see Jerome I. Gellman, "Mysticism and Religious Experience," in *The Oxford Handbook of Philosophy of Religion*, ed. William J. Wainwright (Oxford: Oxford University Press, 2005), 138–67. See also William J. Wainwright, "Mysticism and Religious Experience," in *Readings in Philosophy of Religion*, ed. Linda Zagzebski and Timothy D. Miller (Oxford, UK: Wiley-Blackwell, 2009), 123–36.

82. *Campbell-Owen Debate*, 125 and 151.

83. *Campbell-Owen Debate*, 113; emphasis added.

84. Alvin Plantinga, *Warranted Christian Belief* (New York: Oxford University Press, 2000), 172–79. Of course, Plantinga is following John Calvin here.

85. Hume, *Enquiry Concerning Human Understanding*, 11 [§II.6].

86. Locke, *Essay*, 127 [bk. II.xxiii.33].

87. One could push a similar sort of objection against Campbell by other means. For example, Richard Swinburne suggests that we get our idea of God (and his various attributes) through a reflection on simplicity: infinite power is a simpler idea than the idea of some extreme (but finite) amount of power, and the same holds for knowledge, and so

forth. See Richard Swinburne, *Is There a God* (New York: Oxford University Press, 1996), 43–47. Alternatively, following Anselmian perfect being theology, we might say that we construct the idea of the greatest conceivable being out of the materials empirically available to us.

3. From Theism to Christian Theism

1. Alexander Campbell, "The Confirmation of Testimony," *Millennial Harbinger*, 1st ser., 1, no. 1 (1830): 8–14, at 13–14; emphasis added.

2. See Campbell, ed., *The Living Oracles.*

3. For exceptions, see, for example, West, *Alexander Campbell and Natural Religion*, 133–45; Eames, *Philosophy of Alexander Campbell*, 43–46; Cherok, *Debating for God*, 85–86; Bowen, "Knowledge," 118–37; Kingsbury, "Philosophical Influences," 338–41; Pratt, "Philosophy of Alexander Campbell," 90–94; Eames, "Philosophical Implications," 61–67 and 87–89.

4. Alexander Campbell, "Supernatural Facts," in *Popular Lectures and Addresses*, 142–62, at 143.

5. Ibid., 143.

6. Ibid.

7. Alexander Campbell, "Tracts for the People—No. II," *Millennial Harbinger*, 3rd ser., 2, no. 11 (1845): 481–92, at 484.

8. Strictly speaking, Campbell thinks that only a supernatural agent could perform a miracle. Accordingly, human agents serve merely as the natural conduit through which the supernatural, miraculous power flows. However, because talking about "a person's being involved in the performance of a miracle" is overly cumbersome, for ease of reference here and after I just talk about human agents performing miracles.

9. See John Locke, *A Discourse of Miracles*, in *"The Reasonableness of Christianity" with "A Discourse of Miracles" and Part of "A Third Letter Concerning Toleration,"* ed. I. T. Ramsey (Stanford: Stanford University Press, 1958), 78–87.

10. Campbell, "Natural Theology—No. 4," 513n5; emphasis in original.

11. Campbell, "Tracts for the People," 484.

12. Locke, *Discourse of Miracles*, 80; emphasis added.

13. Campbell, "Tracts for the People—No. II," 484; emphasis added.

14. Campbell, "Natural Theology—No. 4," 513n5.

15. Campbell, "Tracts for the People—No. II," 484.

16. Campbell, "Supernatural Facts," 158; emphasis added.

17. Ibid., 157.

18. *Campbell-Owen Debate*, 201 and 312.

19. Ibid., 182.

20. See, for example, John Locke, *The Reasonableness of Christianity*, in *"The Reasonableness of Christianity" with "A Discourse of Miracles" and Part of "A Third Letter Concerning Toleration,"* ed. I. T. Ramsey (Stanford: Stanford University Press, 1958), 25–77, at 32–34.

21. *Campbell-Owen Debate*, 312; emphasis in original.

22. Campbell, "Confirmation of Testimony," 11 and 13.

23. See Locke, *Discourse of Miracles*, 84.

24. Campbell, "Natural Theology—No. 4," 513n5.

25. My setup here draws heavily from section 2 of Timothy McGrew, "Miracles," in *The Stanford Encyclopedia of Philosophy*, ed. Edward N. Zalta, Winter 2010 ed., http://plato.stanford.edu/archives/win2010/entries/miracles/.

26. For an example of a deductive argument for miracles, see William Paley, *A View of the Evidences of Christianity* (London: John W. Parker and Son, 1859). Cited in McGrew, "Miracles," 2.2.1.

27. For examples of a probabilistic argument for miracles, see Richard Swinburne, *The Concept of a Miracle* (London: Macmillan, 1970); Richard Swinburne, *The Coherence of Theism* (Oxford, UK: Clarendon Press, 1977); Richard Swinburne, *The Existence of God* (Oxford, UK: Clarendon Press, 1979); Richard Swinburne, ed., *Miracles* (New York: Macmillan, 1989); Richard Swinburne, *Revelation: From Metaphor to Analogy* (Oxford, UK: Clarendon Press, 1993); and Richard Swinburne, *The Resurrection of God Incarnate* (Oxford, UK: Clarendon Press, 2003). Cited in McGrew, "Miracles," 2.2.4.

28. For an example of an abductive or explanatory argument for miracles, see Gary Habermas, *The Historical Jesus* (Joplin, MO: College Press, 1996). Cited in McGrew, "Miracles," 2.2.3.

29. See, for instance, *Campbell-Owen Debate*, 322–27.

30. See, for example, Charles Leslie, *A Short and Easy Method with the Deists; Wherein the Certainty of the Christian Religion is Demonstrated by Infallible Proof from Four Rules, Which Are Incompatible to Any Imposture That Ever Yet Has Been or Can Possibly Be. In a Letter to a Friend* (London: R. and C. Rivington, 1801).

31. *Campbell-Owen Debate*, 183.

32. Ibid.; emphasis in original

33. Alexander Campbell, "Letters to Humphrey Marshal, Esq.—Letter II," *Millennial Harbinger*, 1st ser., 1, no. 12 (1830): 529–32, at 530.

34. *Campbell-Owen Debate*, 184.

35. Ibid.

36. Ibid.

37. Ibid., 203.

38. Ibid., 185; emphasis/capitalization in original.

39. See, in particular, ibid., 279–437. See also Alexander Campbell, *The Christian Preacher's Companion, or The Gospel Facts Sustained by the Testimony of Unbelieving Jews and Pagans* (Centerville, KY: R. B. Neal, 1891).

40. *Campbell-Owen Debate*, 309–10.

41. Ibid., 285, 305, 311–12, and 324–25.

42. Campbell, "Notes on a Tour to New York—No. 6," 79.

43. *Campbell-Owen Debate*, 325–26.

44. Campbell, "Philosophy of Memory," 290.

45. McGrew, "Miracles," 2.2.2.

46. Ibid.

47. Ibid.

48. John Earman, *Hume's Abject Failure: The Argument against Miracles* (New York: Oxford University Press, 2000), vii.

49. Craig, *Reasonable Faith*, 278.

50. Bart D. Ehrman, *The Historical Jesus,* audio/video lectures in "The Great Courses" series, (Chantilly, VA: The Teaching Company, 2000), pt. 2, 50, quoted in Craig, *Reasonable Faith*, 279n39.

51. Richard H. Popkin, introduction to *Dialogues Concerning Natural Religion* (with "Of the Immortality of the Soul," "Of Suicide," and "Of Miracles"), by David Hume, ed. Richard H. Popkin, 2nd ed. (Indianapolis: Hackett, 1998), vii–xx, at xix. For a brief history of the essay, see Earman, *Hume's Abject Failure,* 6–8.

52. Hume, *Enquiry Concerning Human Understanding,* 72. See also John Tolliston, *A Doctrine against Transubstantiation* (London: M. Flesher, 1685).

53. Hume, *Enquiry Concerning Human Understanding,* 73.

54. For a representative sample of the different interpretations of the main argument in Hume's essay, see Earman, *Hume's Abject Failure*; Mackie, *Miracle of Theism*, 13–29; Don Garrett, *Cognition and Commitment in Hume's Philosophy* (New York: Oxford University Press, 1997), 145–50; Swinburne, *Resurrection of God Incarnate,* 17–26; Peter van Inwagen, "Of 'Of Miracles,'" in *Philosophy of Religion: An Anthology,* ed. Louis Pojman and Michael Rea, 5th ed. (Belmont, CA: Wadsworth, 2008), 285–95; James E. Taylor, "Hume on Miracles: Interpretation and Criticism," *Philosophy Compass* 2, no. 4 (2007): 611–24; Anthony Flew, *Hume's Philosophy of Belief* (London: Routledge and Kegan Paul, 1961); C. D. Broad, "Hume's Theory of the Credibility of Miracles," *Proceedings of the Aristotelian Society* 17 (1916–17): 77–94; Robert Fogelin, "What Hume Actually Said about Miracles," *Hume Studies* 16 (1990): 81–86; Robert Fogelin, *A Defense of Hume on Miracles* (Princeton, NJ: Princeton University Press, 2003); Robert Larmer, "Interpreting Hume on Miracles," *Religious Studies* 45 (2009): 325–38; Benjamin F. Armstrong Jr., "Hume on Miracles; Begging-the-Question against Believers," *History of Philosophy Quarterly* 9 (1992): 319–28; Benjamin F. Armstrong Jr. "Hume's Actual Argument against Belief in Miracles," *History of Philosophy Quarterly* 12, no. 1 (January 1995): 65–76.

55. Earman, *Hume's Abject Failure*, 8.

56. For a classic argument against the possibility of miracles, see Baruch Spinoza, "Of Miracles," in *Theological-Political Treatise*, trans. Samuel Shirley, 2nd ed. (Indianapolis: Hackett, 2001), 71–85.

57. Hume, *Enquiry Concerning Human Understanding*, 73.

58. Ibid.

59. Ibid., 74.

60. Ibid., 76.

61. Ibid.

62. Ibid.

63. For a helpful discussion of the "straight rule of induction" that Hume follows, see Earman, *Hume's Abject Failure*, 22–24.

64. Hume, *Enquiry Concerning Human Understanding*, 77–78.

65. Ibid., 78.

66. Ibid.

67. Of course, Hume could have thought George Campbell's interpretation was so off base that there was no point in trying to correct it. But in my view, this seems very unlikely. See Larmer, "Interpreting Hume on Miracles," 336. Larmer notes that "Hume accepted an invitation to respond to [George] Campbell, but at no point in criticizing Campbell does he claim that Campbell has misunderstood what the argument of the essay is intended to establish. Hume's silence is inexplicable if he felt that all his respondents fundamentally missed the point of the essay, but makes good sense if . . . he did intend to assert that no amount of testimonial evidence could suffice to justify accepting a miracle report."

68. Campbell, "Supernatural Facts," 144.

69. Ibid., 154.

70. Earman, *Hume's Abject Failure*, 6; see also Larmer, "Interpreting Hume on Miracles," 326. For a useful discussion of George Campbell's critique of Hume's argument, see George N. Schlesinger, "Miracles and Probabilities," *Nous* 21, no. 2 (June 1987): 219–32, esp. at 219–21.

71. *Campbell-Owen Debate*, 274.

72. Campbell, "Supernatural Facts," 154.

73. *Campbell-Owen Debate*, 274.

74. George Campbell, *A Dissertation on Miracles; Containing an Examination of the Principles Advanced by David Hume, Esq., in an Essay on Miracles*, 4th ed. (Edinburgh: Mundell, Doig, and Stevenson, 1807), 34.

75. *Campbell-Owen Debate*, 272; see also George Campbell, *Dissertation on Miracles*, 34.

76. *Campbell-Owen Debate*, 272; see also George Campbell, *Dissertation on Miracles*, 34.

77. Campbell, "Supernatural Facts," 154–55; emphasis added. Note the similarity of Campbell's view here to George Campbell's view. George Campbell argues that Hume "is aware of the consequence: and therefore, in whatever sense he uses the term *experience* in proposing his argument, in prosecuting it, he, with great dexterity, shifts the sense, and, ere the reader is apprised, insinuates another. 'It is a miracle,' says [Hume], 'that a dead man should come to life, because that has never been observed in any age or country. There must therefore be an uniform experience against every miraculous event, otherwise the event would not merit that appellation.' Here the phrase, *an uniform experience against an event*, in the latter clause, is implicitly defined in the former, not what has never been observed BY US, but (mark his words) *what has never been observed* IN ANY AGE OR COUNTRY. Now what has been observed, and what has not been observed, in all ages and countries, pray how can you, Sir, or I, or any man, come to the knowledge of? Only I suppose by testimony, oral or written" (*Dissertation on Miracles*, 36–37; emphasis/capitalizations in original).

78. *Campbell-Owen Debate*, 273; emphasis in original. See also George Campbell, *Dissertation on Miracles*, 35.

79. Hume, "Of Miracles," 76.

80. Campbell, "Supernatural Facts," 155.

81. *Campbell-Owen Debate*, 273.

82. Campbell, "Supernatural Facts," 155; emphasis in original.

83. *Campbell-Owen Debate*, 276; emphasis and capitalization in original.

84. George Campbell, *Dissertation on Miracles*, 38; emphasis in original.

85. For more on this point, see Tony Pitson, "George Campbell's Critique of Hume on Testimony," *Journal of Scottish Philosophy* 4, no. 1 (2006): 1–15, at 2–3. See also Alexander Broadie, "Scottish Philosophy in the 18th Century," in *The Stanford Encyclopedia of Philosophy*, ed. Edward N. Zalta, Fall 2009 ed., http://plato.stanford.edu/archives/fall2009/entries/scottish-18th/, sec. 6.

86. Apparently, Campbell adopted this view, in part, from George Jardine. In his lecture notes, Campbell writes that "we must trust to testimony before we can reason about it. Children have a propensity to believe and rely upon the testimony of others. It is necessary [for] their improvement and happiness. Human testimony is the first truth. Children don't lie till they are taught from example, motive and alurements [*sic*]." See, for example, Alexander Campbell, "Lecture 61st, February 1809," Campbell Family Papers, Box 5, Lecture Notes at Glasgow University, in the archives at the Disciples of Christ Historical Society in Nashville, Tennessee.

87. *Campbell-Owen Debate*, 114.

88. Campbell, "Notes on a Tour to New York—No. 6," 78; emphasis in original.

89. For a similar claim, see C. S. Peirce, "The Scientific Attitude and Fallibilism," in *Philosophical Writings of Peirce*, ed. Justus Buchler (New York: Dover, 1995), 42–59, at 56. There, Peirce says, "The last philosophical obstacle to the advance of knowledge which I intend to mention is the holding that this or that law or truth has found its last and perfect formulation—and especially that the ordinary and usual course of nature never can be broken. 'Stones never fall from heaven,' said Laplace, although they had been falling upon inhabited ground every day from the earliest times. But there is no kind of inference which can lend the slightest probability to any such absolute denial of an unusual phenomenon."

90. van Inwagen, "Of 'Of Miracles,'" 292; emphasis added.

91. See Campbell's lecture notes from his class with George Jardine: "[N]o inference can be drawn from negative testimony." Alexander Campbell, "Lecture 61st, February 1809," Campbell Family Papers, Box 5, Lecture Notes at Glasgow University, in the archives at the Disciples of Christ Historical Society in Nashville, Tennessee.

92. Swinburne, *Resurrection of God Incarnate*, 24–26.

93. For a similar point, see Mackie, *Miracle of Theism*, 26–27.

94. Alexander Campbell, "Letters to Humphrey Marshal, Esq.—Letter III," *Millennial Harbinger*, 1st ser., 2, no. 1 (1831):16–18, at 18.

95. Ibid., 18.

4. On the Problem of Evil and the Problem of Divine Hiddenness

1. Mr. D, "To the Editor of the *Christian Baptist*," *Christian Baptist* 4, no. 2 (September 1826): 270–71.

2. Campbell, "Replication—No. I," 271. Mr. D's letter and Campbell's six replies were reprinted as a book some years later. See Alexander Campbell, *Letters to a Skeptic* (St. Louis: Christian Publishing, 1859). One of the replies was authored by Campbell's father, Thomas Campbell.

3. Campbell, "Replication—No. I," 271.

4. Ibid.

5. The few who have commented in any way on Campbell's response to the problem of evil include West, *Alexander Campbell and Natural Religion*, 83–89; Eames, *Philosophy of Alexander Campbell*, 53; Cherok, *Debating for God*, 37–40 and 45; and Mark Wiebe, "Alexander Campbell on Rationality and the Problem of Evil," paper presented at the American Academy of Religion, Northwest Regional Conference (2010) and at the Christian Scholars Conference, Pepperdine University (June 16, 2011), on file with the author. I am grateful to Wiebe for sharing his paper with me.

6. There are, of course, other ways of categorizing arguments from evil: for example, one might draw a distinction between internal problems of evil and external problems of evil. See William Lane Craig, "Theistic Critique of Atheism," in *The Cambridge Companion to Atheism*, ed. M. Martin (Cambridge: Cambridge University Press, 2007), 69–85. Alternatively, one might draw a distinction between a global argument from evil and various local arguments from evil. See Peter van Inwagen, *The Problem of Evil: The Gifford Lectures Delivered in the University of St. Andrews in 2003* (Oxford, UK: Clarendon Press, 2006), 8.

7. David Hume, *Dialogues Concerning Natural Religion*, ed. Richard H. Popkin, 2nd ed. (Indianapolis: Hackett, 1998), 63.

8. *Campbell-Owen Debate*, 460; emphasis in original. See also 303, where Campbell casts the problem in the following way: "A benevolent being could not create a world like this. See how badly it is planned, arranged, and adapted to the subsistence of animals. One part of it parched with a vertical sun; another bound in perpetual ice. One part of it dreary wastes, sandy deserts, and threefourths [*sic*] of the whole immense oceans."

9. Mr. D, "To the Editor of the Christian Baptist," 270; emphasis in original.

10. I take a few cues from Jeffrey Tlumak's discussion of Hume on evil in setting up this argument here. See Tlumak, *Classical Modern Philosophy*, 234–35.

11. Strictly speaking, premise L5 does not follow from premises L1–L4 unless we also assume that the existence of evil is not logically necessary and that there exist no good reasons for God to allow evil. On this point, see Nelson Pike, "God and Evil: A Reconsideration," *Ethics* 68, no. 2 (1958): 116–24, esp. at 119–20.

12. Campbell, "Replication—No. I," 272.

13. See, for example, Alexander Campbell, *The Christian System, in Reference to the Union of Christians, and a Restoration of Primitive Christianity as Plead in the Current Reformation*, 3rd ed. (Pittsburgh, PA: Forrester and Campbell, 1840), 30.

14. Campbell, "Replication—No. I," 272.

15. Alexander Campbell, "To Mr. D—A Skeptic—Replication—No. III," *Christian Baptist* 4, no. 4 (November 1826): 281–82, at 282.

16. Campbell, "Replication—No. I," 272; emphasis added.

17. Campbell here seems to assume that God cannot be a governor unless there is someone who is governed, and he further assumes that being governed without free agency is impossible. The implication of this view is that if God merely determined the world and the creatures in it, he would not be an actual governor but more like a puppet master.

18. Campbell, *Christian System*, 29–30; emphasis added.

19. For more on the distinction between a theodicy and a defense against the problem of evil, see Alvin Plantinga, *God, Freedom, and Evil* (Grand Rapids, MI: Eerdmans, 1977), 26–29.

20. J. L. Mackie, "Evil and Omnipotence," *Mind* 64, no. 254 (1955): 200–212, at 209; emphasis added.

21. Campbell, "To Mr. D—A Skeptic—Replication—No. III," 282.

22. For a similar point about omnipotence involving an interesting discussion of the so-called paradox of the stone, see George Mavrodes, "Some Puzzles Concerning Omnipotence," *Philosophical Review* 72 (1963): 221–23.

23. *Campbell-Purcell Debate*, 167–68.

24. See Alvin Plantinga's distinction between *weak* and *strong* actualization in Plantinga, *The Nature of Necessity* (Oxford: Oxford University Press, 1982), 173–84.

25. Plantinga, *God, Freedom, and Evil*, 30; emphasis in original.

26. For a full account of Plantinga's free will defense, see Plantinga, *God, Freedom, and Evil*, 7–64; and Plantinga, *Nature of Necessity*, 164–95.

27. See, for example, William Alston, "The Inductive Argument from Evil and the Human Cognitive Condition," in *The Evidential Argument from Evil*, ed. Daniel Howard-Snyder (Bloomington: Indiana University Press, 1996), 97–125, at 97 and 121; Daniel Howard-Snyder, introduction to Howard-Snyder, *Evidential Argument from Evil*, xi–xx, at xiii; Alvin Plantinga, "Epistemic Probability," in Howard-Snyder, *Evidential Argument from Evil*, 69–96, at 71n3; and Peter van Inwagen, "The Problem of Evil, the Problem of Air, and the Problem of Silence," in Howard-Snyder, *Evidential Argument from Evil*, 151–74, at 151. These sources are quoted in Graham Oppy, "Argument from Moral Evil," *International Journal of Philosophy of Religion* 56 (2004): 59–87, at 82n3.

28. There are, of course, some notable exceptions to this trend. Representative examples include David O'Connor, "A Reformed Problem of Evil and the Free Will Defense," *International Journal of Philosophy of Religion* 39, no. 1 (1996): 33–63; Michael Tooley, "Alvin Plantinga and the Argument from Evil," *Australasian Journal of Philosophy* 58 (1980): 360–76. See also Oppy, "Argument from Moral Evil"; Richard Gale, "Some Difficulties in Theistic Treatments of Evil," in Howard-Snyder, *Evidential Argument from Evil*, 206–18, esp. at 206.

29. This kind of argument is sometimes also referred to as an "inductive" or "probabilistic" argument from evil.

30. Rowe, *Philosophy of Religion*, 120.

31. Ibid.

32. Ibid. For a representative sample of Rowe's other, more technical formulations of, and reflections on, the evidential argument from evil, see William Rowe, "The Problem of Evil and Some Varieties of Atheism," *American Philosophical Quarterly* 16 (1979): 335–41; William Rowe, "The Evidential Argument from Evil: A Second Look," in Howard-Snyder, *Evidential Argument from Evil*, 262–85; William Rowe, "Reply to Plantinga," *Nous* 32, no. 4 (1998): 545–52; and William Rowe, "Friendly Atheism, Skeptical Theism, and the Problem of Evil," *International Journal of Philosophy of Religion* 59 (2006): 79–92.

33. Campbell, *Christian System*, 29–30.

34. Peter van Inwagen rejects premise E1; see van Inwagen, *Problem of Evil*, chap. 6.

35. Of course, not everyone agrees. See, for example, Stephen J. Wykstra, "The Humean Obstacle to Evidential Arguments from Suffering: On Avoiding the Evils of 'Appearance,'" *International Journal of Philosophy of Religion* 16 (1984): 73–93. Wykstra argues that Rowe is not even entitled to the *appears* claim here.

36. For a representative sample of different skeptical theist responses to the evidential problem of evil, see Wykstra, "Humean Obstacle"; William Alston, "The Inductive Argument from Evil and the Human Cognitive Condition"; Kirk Durston, "The Consequential Complexity of History and Gratuitous Evil," *Religious Studies* 39 (2000): 65–80; and Michael Bergmann, "Skeptical Theism and Rowe's New Evidential Argument from Evil," *Nous* 35 (2001): 278–96. For an excellent overview of the issue and a comprehensive review of the surrounding literature, see Justin P. McBrayer, "Skeptical Theism," *Philosophy Compass* 5 (2010): 611–23.

37. See Stephen Wykstra, "Rowe's Noseeum Arguments from Evil," in Howard-Snyder, *Evidential Argument from Evil*, 126–51. This label has become virtually industry standard in the literature since 1996.

38. For an interesting discussion of the pedagogical uses of obscurity, see Mason Marshall and Aaron M. Clark, "Is Clarity Essential to Good Teaching," *Teaching Philosophy* 33, no. 3 (2010): 271–89.

39. Proponents of skeptical theism have offered a variety of illustrations to knock home a similar point. Wykstra, for example, argues that if one is looking for a dog in her garage and does not see it there, she would be justified in concluding that there is no dog in the garage, given that she could reasonably expect to see the dog, if it were actually there. But the same is not true of, say, a flea: she could not reasonably expect to see the flea in the garage, *even if* it is there. Accordingly, she would not be justified in concluding that, simply because she does not see a flea when she looks in the garage, there is not one there. See Wykstra, "Rowe's Noseeum Arguments from Evil," 126–27. Another approach is to rely on a parent-child analogy: a child's limited knowledge makes him unable to detect the reasons why his parents would subject him to a painful course of medical treatment. Accordingly, the child would not be justified in concluding that because he cannot detect his parents' reasons for allowing him to suffer, there are none. Because both the dog-flea illustration and the parent-child analogy have been subject to considerable debate in recent years, I have tried to circumvent this controversy by means of the teacher-student anal-

ogy above. See also the analogies offered by William Alston, "Some (Temporarily) Final Thoughts on Evidential Arguments from Evil," in Howard-Snyder, *Evidential Argument from Evil*, 311–32, esp. at 317–18.

40. See Plantinga: "Why suppose that if God *does* have a good reason for permitting evil, that the theist would be the first to know? Perhaps God has a good reason, but that reason is too complicated for us to understand. Or perhaps He has not revealed it for some other reason" (*God, Freedom, and Evil*, 10).

41. See, for example, *Campbell-Owen Debate*, 139–40. There, Campbell argues that we have no way of knowing God's full set of reasons for sentencing the damned to eternal punishment in hell. While it might appear to us that such punishment is unmerciful—hence incompatible with God's nature—this is because we do not have access to all the reasons that led God to punish them in the first place. While we might understand certain features of God's justice or mercy, we do not understand those properties fully. Nor do we fully understand the relationship between God's various properties. Hence, the Divine character—in terms of both God's individual properties and the complex of properties that he possesses—is beyond human comprehension. Accordingly, many of the reasons God may have for doing something may well be beyond our ability to grasp.

42. *Campbell-Owen Debate*, 391.

43. See Alexander Campbell, "Mysteries of Providence," *Millennial Harbinger*, 3rd ser., 4, no. 12 (1847): 704–9, at 705. There he comments that "Providence, in its scheme and development, has . . . presented its proportions of mysteries, no less inscrutable than those of Nature and Revelation." For a similar point, see Alexander Campbell, "Life and Death," *Millennial Harbinger*, 3rd ser., 1, no. 11 (1844): 529–74, at 547.

44. *Campbell-Owen Debate*, 374.

45. Ibid.

46. Ibid.

47. Ibid.

48. Ibid.; emphasis added.

49. For a list of the most common objections to skeptical theism, as well as a corresponding bibliography, see McBrayer, "Skeptical Theism," 616–19. McBrayer organizes these objections as follows: skeptical theism is inconsistent with moral facts; skeptical theism is inconsistent with inductive reasoning; skeptical theism is inconsistent with trust in God; skeptical theism is inconsistent with commonsense epistemology; skeptical theism is inconsistent with common knowledge; skeptical theism is inconsistent with metaethical knowledge; and skeptical theism is inconsistent with moral deliberation/moral knowledge. The charge that skeptical theism is inconsistent with commonsense epistemology may pose a particularly difficult problem for Campbell to the extent that he seems to be sympathetic with several features of Reid's commonsense philosophy at times, as mentioned in chapter 1. For a particularly helpful discussion on the possible tension between commonsense epistemology and skeptical theism, see Trent Dougherty, "Epistemological Considerations Concerning Skeptical Theism," *Faith and Philosophy* 25, no. 2 (2008): 172–76. See also Jonathan D. Matheson, "Epistemological Considerations Concerning Skeptical

Theism: A Response to Dougherty," *Faith and Philosophy* 28, no. 3 (2011): 323–31; and Trent Dougherty, "Further Epistemological Considerations Concerning Skeptical Theism," *Faith and Philosophy* 28, no. 3 (2011): 332–40.

50. Several philosophers have raised similar concerns about skeptical theism. For a few examples of these kind of arguments, see Michael Almeida and Graham Oppy, "Sceptical Theism and Evidential Arguments from Evil," *Australasian Journal of Philosophy* 81, no. 4 (2003): 496–516; William Hasker, "The Sceptical Solution to the Problem of Evil," in *Providence, Evil, and the Openness of God*, ed. William Hasker (London: Routledge, 2004), 43–57; Jeff Jordan, "Does Skeptical Theism Lead to Moral Skepticism?" *Philosophy and Phenomenological Research* 72 (2006): 403–16; Mark Piper, "Skeptical Theism and the Problem of Moral Aporia," *International Journal for Philosophy of Religion* 62 (2007): 65–79; Ira Schnall, "Skeptical Theism and Moral Skepticism," *Religious Studies* 43 (2007): 49–69; and Steven Maitzen, "Skeptical Theism and Moral Obligation," *International Journal for Philosophy of Religion* 65, no. 2 (2009): 93–103.

51. For a similar view, see Michael Bergmann and Michael Rea, "In Defence of Sceptical Theism: A Reply to Almeida and Oppy," *Australasian Journal of Philosophy* 83, no. 2 (2005): 241–51, esp. at 244. There, Bergmann and Rea argue that "theists very typically believe that God has commanded his creatures to behave in certain ways; and they also very typically believe that God's commands provide all-things-considered reasons to act. Thus, a sceptical theist will very likely not find it the least bit plausible to think that [the central commitments of skeptical theism] leave us without an all-things-considered reason to prevent harm to others" in cases like *B*.

52. To be sure, there are other potentially viable decision procedures that do not require speculation about God's reasons for allowing *B*.

53. For likely objections, see McBrayer, "Skeptical Theism," 619. One of the difficulties with this view, according to McBrayer, is as follows: "First, even if successful, it only applies to theists. Is the skeptical theist willing to say that non-theists who don't know of God's command have reason to allow rape to occur?" In response to this concern, I suspect that Campbell would simply bite the bullet but push the point that the nontheist now has a reason for accepting divine revelation.

54. Russell quoted in Al Seckel, preface to *Bertrand Russell on God and Religion*, ed. Al Seckel (Amherst, NY: Prometheus Books, 1986), 13–33, at 11.

55. For a discussion of the similarities and mutual independence of the argument from evil and the argument from divine hiddenness, see J. L. Schellenburg, "The Hiddenness Problem and the Problem of Evil," *Faith and Philosophy* 27, no. 1 (2010): 45–60. See also Peter van Inwagen, "What Is the Problem of the Hiddenness of God?" in *Divine Hiddenness: New Essays*, ed. Daniel Howard-Snyder and Paul K. Moser (Cambridge: Cambridge University Press, 2002), 24–32, at 24–25.

56. Alexander Campbell, "Deism and the Social System—No. IV," *Christian Baptist* 5, no. 2 (September 1827): 364–66, at 365–66.

57. For an excellent overview of the issues involved in the problem of divine hiddenness, see Daniel Howard-Snyder and Paul K. Moser, "Introduction: The Hiddenness of God," in Howard-Snyder and Moser, *Divine Hiddenness*, 1–23. Also see the several essays contained in that volume for a range of views related to the problem of divine hiddenness.

58. By *evidence* here, I am following J. L. Schellenberg's statement that evidence "refers to anything that can serve as a ground of belief, and so not only to propositions that provide the basis for deductive and inductive inference but also to nonpropositional, experiential evidence in which belief may be directly (noninferentially) grounded" (*Divine Hiddenness and Human Reason*, paperback ed. [Ithaca, NY: Cornell University Press, 2006], 33).

59. See ibid., esp. 83–92 . J. L. Schellenberg, "What the Hiddenness of God Reveals: A Collaborative Discussion," in Howard-Snyder and Moser, *Divine Hiddenness*, 24–32; J. L. Schellenberg, "The Hiddenness Argument Revisited (I)," *Religious Studies* 41, no. 2 (2005): 201–15; and J. L. Schellenberg, "The Hiddenness Argument Revisited (II)," *Religious Studies* 41, no. 2 (2005): 287–303.

60. Campbell, "Deism and the Social System—No. IV," 365; emphasis added.

61. There are some interesting similarities between Campbell's view here and certain features of Michael Murray's "soul-making" response to the argument from divine hiddenness. See Michael Murray, "Deus Absconditus," in Howard-Snyder and Moser, *Divine Hiddenness*, 62–82.

62. Campbell, "Social System and Deism—No. II," 343; emphasis added.

63. Ibid.

64. *Campbell-Owen Debate*, 470; emphasis added.

65. See, for example, *Campbell-Owen Debate*, 189–90, 213, and 382. See also Alexander Campbell, "Evidences of the Gospel—No. 3," *Millennial Harbinger*, 1st ser., 6, no. 10 (1835): 470–72, at 470.

66. Alexander Campbell, "Notes on a Tour to New York—No. 5," *Millennial Harbinger*, 1st ser., 5, no. 1 (1834): 36–40, at 39.

67. Ibid.

68. This sort of view is hardly unique to Campbell, as it has been offered by many historically important religious thinkers, including, notably, Jonathan Edwards. See, for example, William J. Wainwright, "Jonathan Edwards and the Hiddenness of God," in Howard-Snyder and Moser, *Divine Hiddenness*, 98–119. Wainwright notes that in Edwards's view, "[o]nly the truly benevolent . . . are equipped to reason rightly about divine things" (101). Accordingly, blindness to divine matters results "not so much from a defect of the reasoning powers as from a fault of the disposition" (Wainwright quoting Edwards, ibid., 103). For a similar treatment of the issue, see also Paul K. Moser, "Cognitive Idolatry and Divine Hiding," in Howard-Snyder and Moser, *Divine Hiddenness,* 120–47, esp. at 135–36.

69. Campbell quoted in Garrison, *Alexander Campbell's Theology*, 219; see also *Campbell-Owen Debate*, 66–67, 153, 222–23, and 420. See also Eames, *Philosophy of Alexander Campbell*, 60–62; and West, *Alexander Campbell and Natural Religion*, 76–78.

70. *Campbell-Owen Debate*, 66–67; see also Campbell, "Deism and the Social System—No. IV," 365.

71. *Campbell-Owen Debate*, 153.

72. Ibid.

73. For a useful discussion on Campbell's view of the role of will in forming beliefs, see Eames, *Philosophy of Alexander Campbell,* 60–62. Eames argues that Campbell thinks "we can reason only when we 'decide' to reason; and we can perform the act of judging in

much the same way as by previous determination we decide to eat supper or go to bed" (61).

74. Campbell, "Deism and the Social System—No. IV," 365.

75. See also Alexander Campbell, "On the Importance of Uniting the Moral with the Intellectual Culture of the Mind," in *Popular Lectures and Addresses*, 453–84, esp. at 471. There Campbell says, "Were it not a matter of fact, forcing itself upon our daily observation, that there is a possibility of intellectual culture without moral culture, one might be induced, from speculative reasonings [*sic*], to conclude that in cultivating the mind he was cultivating the morals of youth. To the philosophic Christian it is impossible to study nature without seeing God in every law and in every arrangement of nature. The Christian philosopher will therefore be apt to conclude that the knowledge of nature and the knowledge of God are not only intimately, but, in some degree, inseparably, connected; yet society, as it now exists, presents to him the phenomenon of an avowed atheistic philosopher—of one who not only studies nature without seeing God the Supreme Architect and Lawgiver of nature, but of one who, while he boasts of the knowledge of nature, denies the existence of the God of nature. This being possible, it must not be thought incredible that we may have a system of intellectual culture without any moral influence, or that the intellectual powers of youth may in some degree be highly cultivated, while the moral powers are in no respect improved."

76. Ludwig Wittgenstein, *Philosophical Investigations*, trans. G. E. M. Anscombe (Oxford, UK: Blackwell, 2001), 166 [II.xi].

77. Campbell, "Office of Reason," 352.

78. Campbell, "Evidences of the Gospel—No. 2," 317.

79. Ibid.; emphasis added.

80. Alexander Campbell, "Letters to Humphrey Marshal, Esq.—No. I," *Millennial Harbinger*, 1st ser., 1, no. 1 (1830): 513–17, at 514; emphasis added.

81. Campbell, *Christian System*, 17.

82. Ibid., 18.

83. Campbell, "Social System and Deism—No. II," 343.

84. Again, note the similarity of Campbell's view to that of Jonathan Edwards. Wainwright summarizes Edwards's view on the role sin plays in distorting one's assessment of the evidence of God's existence: "What is needed isn't more evidence or a fuller revelation but a new heart to appreciate the evidence and revelation we have" ("Jonathan Edwards," 104).

5. On Revelation, Divine Commands, and Morality

1. Alexander Campbell, "Is Moral Philosophy an Inductive Science?" in *Popular Lectures and Addresses*, 95–124, at 99.

2. Alexander Campbell, "Morality of Christians—No. I," *Millennial Harbinger*, 2nd ser., 2, no. 1 (1838): 5–8, at 8.

3. The few exceptions include Eames, *Philosophy of Alexander Campbell*, 51–66; Lunger, *Political Ethics of Alexander Campbell*, 66–76; Miethe, "Social Ethics of Alexander Campbell," 307–10; and John L. Morrison, *Alexander Campbell: Educating the Moral Person* (Thousand Oaks, CA: privately published, 1991), 103–76.

4. Campbell, "Is Moral Philosophy an Inductive Science?," 99.

5. Campbell, "Introductory Lecture," 79.

6. Ibid.

7. Alexander Campbell, "Address on the Responsibilities of Men of Genius," in *Popular Lectures and Addresses*, 73–94, at 73–74; emphasis added.

8. Campbell, "Is Moral Philosophy an Inductive Science?," 95; emphasis added.

9. Ibid., 100.

10. Ibid., 116.

11. Ibid.

12. Ibid., 117.

13. Ibid.

14. Ibid.

15. Ibid.

16. Ibid.

17. Ibid.

18. Ibid.

19. Ibid., 118.

20. Ibid., 124.

21. Ibid.

22. Ibid., 121.

23. Ibid., 108.

24. Ibid., 116.

25. Ibid.; emphasis added.

26. See, for example, Joseph Butler, *Five Sermons Preached at the Rolls Chapel and a Dissertation upon the Nature of Virtue*, edited by Stephen L. Darwall (Indianapolis: Hackett, 1983), 29–30.

27. See, for example, David Hume, *A Treatise of Human Nature*, in *David Hume: Moral Philosophy*, ed. Geoffrey Sayre-McCord (Indianapolis: Hackett, 2006), 12–181, at 77–81 [bk. III.1.ii]. See also Rachel Cohon, "Hume's Moral Philosophy," in *The Stanford Encyclopedia of Philosophy*, ed. Edward N. Zalta, Fall 2010 ed., http://plato.stanford.edu/archives/fall2010/entries/hume-moral/.

28. Alexander Campbell, "What Is Education, in Its Full Import," *Millennial Harbinger*, 5th ser., 5, no. 3 (1862): 109–13, at 110.

29. Ibid., 110.

30. Alexander Campbell, "Address on Colleges," in *Popular Lectures and Addresses*, 291–310, at 303.

31. Lunger, *Political Ethics of Alexander Campbell*, 26.

32. Cited in ibid., 27.

33. Campbell, *Christian System*, 125; emphasis added.

34. Ibid., 91.

35. See, for example, Immanuel Kant, *Grounding for the Metaphysics of Morals* (with "On a Supposed Right to Lie Because of Philanthropic Concerns") translated by James W. Ellington, 3rd ed. (Indianapolis: Hackett, 1993), 24–25 [II.416–18].

36. Campbell, *Christian System*, 91.

37. See, for example, Mark Timmons, *Moral Theory: An Introduction* (Lanham, MD: Rowman and Littlefield, 2002), 23–35, esp. at 24–25. By contrast, Robert Adams does not view divine command theory as a theory of value and thus limits his own version to a theory of right conduct. See, for example, Robert Adams, *Finite and Infinite Goods: A Framework for Ethics* (New York: Oxford University Press, 1999).

38. Campbell, "Address on the Responsibilities of Men of Genius," 78.

39. Ibid., 79.

40. Ibid.

41. Ibid.

42. Ibid.

43. Campbell, "Address on Colleges," 303.

44. Ibid.; emphasis added.

45. Ibid.; emphasis/capitalization in the original.

46. Alexander Campbell, "Morality of Christians—No. III," *Millennial Harbinger*, 2nd ser., 2, no. 3 (1838): 97–101, at 97; emphasis added.

47. Alexander Campbell, "Slavery and the Fugitive Slave Law," *Millennial Harbinger*, 4th ser., 1, no. 4 (1851): 201–6, at 201.

48. See, for example, James Beattie, *Elements of Moral Science*, vol. 2, 3rd ed. (Edinburgh: Archibald Constable and Co. and John Fairbairn, 1817), 77.

49. Alexander Campbell and John Walker, *Infant Sprinkling Proved to Be a Human Tradition; Being the Substance of a Debate on Christian Baptism between Mr. John Walker, a Minister of the Secession, and Alexander Campbell, V.D.M., a Regular Baptist Minister* (Stubenville, OH: James Wilson, 1820), 46. Hereafter cited as *Campbell-Walker Debate*.

50. *Campbell-Walker Debate*, 46; emphasis added.

51. Ibid., 47; emphasis added.

52. Ibid., 46.

53. Ibid.

54. Ibid., 47.

55. Campbell, "Morality of Christians—No. I," 5; emphasis added.

56. Plato, *Euthyphro*, in *Plato: Five Dialogues*, translated by G. M. A. Grube and revised by John M. Cooper, 2nd ed. (Indianapolis: Hackett, 2002), 1–20, at 12 [10a].

57. The layout of this section draws heavily from Timmons, *Moral Theory*, 23–35.

58. This sort of complaint is commonly raised as an objection to divine command theories of ethics. See, for example, James Rachels and Stuart Rachels, *The Elements of Moral Philosophy*, 6th ed. (New York: McGraw-Hill, 2010), 52; Timmons, *Moral Theory*, 27–30; Robert Young, "Theism and Morality," in *Divine Commands and Morality*, ed. Paul Helm (Oxford: Oxford University Press, 1981), 154–64, at 154–56; Alasdair MacIntyre, "Atheism and Morals," in *The Religious Significance of Atheism*, ed. Alasdair MacIntyre and Paul Ricoeur (New York: Columbia University Press, 1970), 34–36.

59. Timmons, *Moral Theory*, 28–29.

60. Alexander Campbell, "Is Capital Punishment Sanctioned by Divine Authority?" in *Popular Lectures and Addresses*, 311–41, at 313.

61. See, for example, Timmons, *Moral Theory*, 30–32.

62. Campbell, "What Is Education, in its Full Import,"110; emphasis added.

63. This discussion pulls heavily from Timmons, *Moral Theory*, 30–32.

64. Timmons, *Moral Theory*, 31.

65. James Simpson, *Necessity of Popular Education, as a National Object; with Hints on the Treatment of Criminals, and Observations on Homicidal Insanity* (Boston: Marsh, Capen and Lyon, 1834), 289.

66. Alexander Campbell, "On the Importance of Uniting the Moral with the Intellectual Culture of the Mind," *Millennial Harbinger*, 1st ser. (extra), 7, no. 9 (1836): 579–99, at 589; emphasis in original.

Bibliography

Adams, Robert. *Finite and Infinite Goods: A Framework for Ethics*. New York: Oxford University Press, 1999.

Ahlstrom, Sydney. *A Religious History of the American People*. New Haven, CT: Yale University Press, 1972.

Allen, C. Leonard. "Baconianism and the Bible among the Disciples of Christ: James S. Lamar and the Organum of Scripture." *Church History* 55 (March 1986): 65–80.

———. *Things Unseen: Churches of Christ in (and after) the Modern Age*. Siloam Springs, AR: Leafwood, 2004.

Allen, C. Leonard, and Richard T. Hughes. *Rediscovering Our Roots: The Ancestry of Churches of Christ*. Abilene: Abilene Christian University Press, 1988.

Almeida, Michael, and Graham Oppy. "Sceptical Theism and Evidential Arguments from Evil." *Australasian Journal of Philosophy* 81, no. 4 (2003): 496–516.

Alston, William. "The Inductive Argument from Evil and the Human Cognitive Condition." In *The Evidential Argument from Evil,* edited by Daniel Howard-Snyder, 97–125. Bloomington: Indiana University Press, 1996.

———. "Some (Temporarily) Final Thoughts on Evidential Arguments from Evil." In *The Evidential Argument from Evil,* edited by Daniel Howard-Snyder, 311–32. Bloomington: Indiana University Press, 1996.

Ames, Edward Scribner. "The Lockian Influence on Campbell." *Christian-Evangelist* (September 1938): 974–76.

Armstrong, Benjamin F., Jr. "Hume on Miracles: Begging-the-Question against Believers." *History of Philosophy Quarterly* 9 (1992): 319–28.

———. "Hume's Actual Argument against Belief in Miracles." *History of Philosophy Quarterly* 12, no. 1 (January 1995): 65–76.

Athearn, Clarence R. *The Religious Education of Alexander Campbell: Morning Star of the Coming Reformation*. St. Louis: Bethany Press, 1928.

Ayers, M. R. "Mechanism, Superaddition, and the Proof of God's Existence in Locke's Essay." *Philosophical Review* 90, no. 2 (1981): 210–51.

Bacon, Francis. *Novum Organum*. 1620. In *The Complete Essays of Francis Bacon*, 179–264. Edited by Henry Leroy Finch. New York: Washington Square Press, 1963.

———. "Of Atheism." In *The Complete Essays of Francis Bacon*, 44–46. Edited by Henry Leroy Finch. New York: Washington Square Press, 1963.

Barth, Karl. *Church Dogmatics: A Selection*. Edited and translated by G. W. Bromiley. Edinburgh: T. and T. Clark, 1961.

Beattie, James. *Elements of Moral Science*. Vol. 2. 3rd ed. Edinburgh: Archibald Constable and Co. and John Fairbairn, 1817.

———. *Essay on the Nature and Immutability of Truth in Opposition to Sophistry and Scepticism*. London: Edward and Charles Dilly, 1778.

Bergmann, Michael. "Skeptical Theism and Rowe's New Evidential Argument from Evil." *Nous* 35 (2001): 278–96.

Bergmann, Michael, and Michael Rea. "In Defence of Sceptical Theism: A Reply to Almeida and Oppy." *Australasian Journal of Philosophy* 83, no. 2 (2005): 241–51.

Bowen, Billy Doyce. "Knowledge, the Existence of God, and Faith: John Locke's Influence on Alexander Campbell's Theology." PhD dissertation, Michigan State University, 1978.

Broad, C. D. "Hume's Theory of the Credibility of Miracles." *Proceedings of the Aristotelian Society* 17 (1916–17): 77–94.

Broadie, Alexander. "Scottish Philosophy in the 18th Century." In *The Stanford Encyclopedia of Philosophy*, edited by Edward N. Zalta. Fall 2009 ed. http://plato.stanford.edu/archives/fall2009/entries/scottish-18th/.

Brookes, Iveson L. *A Defence of Southern Slavery, against the Attacks of Henry Clay and Alexander Campbell, by a Southern Clergyman*. Hamburg, SC: Robinson and Carlisle, 1851.

Butler, Joseph. *Five Sermons Preached at the Rolls Chapel and a Dissertation upon the Nature of Virtue*. Edited by Stephen L. Darwall. Indianapolis: Hackett, 1983.

Butts, R. Freeman. *A Cultural History of Western Education*. New York: McGraw Hill, 1955.

Campbell, Alexander. "Acts of Apostles: Analysis of Chapter VI." *Millennial Harbinger*, 3rd ser., 3, no. 8 (1846): 435–38.

———. "Address at the Annual Meeting of the Christian Missionary Society." In *Popular Lectures and Addresses*, edited by Alexander Campbell, 531–50. Philadelphia: James Challen and Son, 1866.

———. "Address on Colleges." In *Popular Lectures and Addresses,* edited by Alexander Campbell, 291–310. Philadelphia: James Challen and Son, 1866.

———. "Address on the Responsibilities of Men of Genius." In *Popular Lectures and Addresses,* edited by Alexander Campbell, 73–94. Philadelphia: James Challen and Son, 1866.

———. "Address on War." In *Popular Lectures and Addresses,* edited by Alexander Campbell, 342–66. Philadelphia: James Challen and Son, 1866.

———. "Bethany College: The Course of Instruction and Text Books." *Millennial Harbinger,* 4th ser., 5, no. 4 (1855): 225–31.

———. "Christianity the True Philosophy." *Millennial Harbinger,* 4th ser., 7, no. 8 (1857): 481–85.

———. *The Christian Preacher's Companion, or The Gospel Facts Sustained by the Testimony of Unbelieving Jews and Pagans.* Centerville, KY: R. B. Neal, 1891.

———. *The Christian System, in Reference to the Union of Christians, and a Restoration of Primitive Christianity as Plead in the Current Reformation.* 3rd ed. Pittsburgh, PA: Forrester and Campbell, 1840.

———. "Concluding Remarks: Part of the Editor's History." *Christian Baptist* 7, no. 12 (July 1830): 664–65.

———. "The Confirmation of Testimony." *Millennial Harbinger,* 1st ser., 1, no. 1 (1830): 8–14.

———. "Deism and the Social System—No. IV." *Christian Baptist* 5, no. 2 (September 1827): 364–66.

———. "The Deist's Corner." *Millennial Harbinger,* 1st ser., 3, no. 7 (1832): 310–11.

———. "Delusions." *Millennial Harbinger,* 1st ser., 2, no. 2 (February 1831): 85–91.

———. *Delusions: An Analysis of the Book of Mormon with an Examination of Its Internal and External Evidences, and a Refutation of Its Pretenses to Divine Authority.* Boston: Benjamin H. Greene, 1832.

———. "Essays on Man in His Primitive State, and under the Patriarchal, Jewish, and Christian Dispensations—No. IV: Primitive State—No. IV." *Christian Baptist* 6, no. 4 (November 1828): 494–95.

———. "Evidences of the Gospel—No. 1." *Millennial Harbinger,* 1st ser., 6, no. 5 (1835): 197–201.

———. "Evidences of the Gospel—No. 2." *Millennial Harbinger,* 1st ser., 6, no. 7 (1835): 317–22.

———. "Evidences of the Gospel—No. 3." *Millennial Harbinger,* 1st ser., 6, no. 10 (1835): 470–72.

———. “Extracts from the Due-West Telescope.” *Millennial Harbinger,* 4th ser., 3, no. 4 (1853): 228–30.

———. “A Good Library.” *Millennial Harbinger,* 1st ser., 5, no. 10 (1834): 490–93.

———. “Historical Sketch of the Origin and Progress of the New Translation.” *Millennial Harbinger,* 1st ser., 3, no. 6 (1832): 268–74.

———. “Introductory Lecture Delivered at the Organization of Bethany College, Nov. 2, 1841.” In *Introductory Addresses, Delivered at the Organization of Bethany College, November 2d, 1841,* edited by Alexander Campbell, 61–86. Bethany, VA: A. Campbell, 1841.

———. “Is Capital Punishment Sanctioned by Divine Authority?” In *Popular Lectures and Addresses,* edited by Alexander Campbell, 311–41. Philadelphia: James Challen and Son, 1866.

———. “Is Moral Philosophy an Inductive Science?” In *Popular Lectures and Addresses,* edited by Alexander Campbell, 95–124. Philadelphia: James Challen and Son, 1866.

———. “Lecture 58th, February 8, 1809.” Lecture Notes at Glasgow University, Campbell Family Papers, Box 5. Archives of Disciples of Christ Historical Society, Nashville, Tennessee.

———. “Lecture 61st, February 1809.” Lecture Notes at Glasgow University, Campbell Family Papers, Box 5. Archives of Disciples of Christ Historical Society, Nashville, Tennessee.

———. “Lecture 67th, February 23, 1809.” Lecture Notes at Glasgow University, Campbell Family Papers, Box 5. Archives of Disciples of Christ Historical Society, Nashville, Tennessee.

———. *Letters to a Skeptic*. St. Louis: Christian Publishing, 1859.

———. “Letters to Humphrey Marshal, Esq.—No. I.” *Millennial Harbinger,* 1st ser., 1, no. 11 (1830): 513–17.

———. “Letters to Humphrey Marshal, Esq.—Letter II.” *Millennial Harbinger,* 1st ser., 1, no. 12 (1830): 529–32.

———. “Letters to Humphrey Marshal, Esq.—Letter III.” *Millennial Harbinger,* 1st ser., 2, no. 1 (1831): 16–18.

———. “Life and Death.” *Millennial Harbinger,* 3rd ser., 1, no. 11 (1844): 529–74.

———, ed. *The Living Oracles, or the Sacred Writings of the Apostles and Evangelists of Jesus Christ Commonly Styled “The New Testament,” Translated from the Original Greek by Doctors George Campbell, James McKnight and Philip Doddridge*. Nashville: Gospel Advocate, 1974.

———. “Locke’s Opinion of the Form in which the Scriptures Are Printed.” *Millennial Harbinger,* 1st ser., 3, no. 6 (1832): 274–75.

———. "The Millennium—No. IV." *Millennial Harbinger,* 4th ser., 6, no. 3 (1856): 269–76.

———. "Morality of Christians—No. I." *Millennial Harbinger,* 2nd ser., 2, no. 1 (1838): 5–8.

———. "Morality of Christians—No. III." *Millennial Harbinger,* 2nd ser., 2, no. 3 (1838): 97–101.

———. "Mr. Brantly's Views of Reformation and of New Version." *Christian Baptist* 7, no. 12 (1830): 660–64.

———. "Mysteries of Providence." *Millennial Harbinger,* 3rd ser., 4, no. 12 (1847): 704–9.

———. "Natural Theology—No. 1." *Millennial Harbinger,* 1st ser., 7, no. 6 (1836): 262–68.

———. "Natural Theology—No. 2." *Millennial Harbinger,* 1st ser., 7, no. 8 (1836): 370–75.

———. "Natural Theology—No. 3." *Millennial Harbinger,* 1st ser., 7, no. 10 (1836): 457–63.

———. "Natural Theology—No. 4." *Millennial Harbinger,* 1st ser., 7, no. 11 (1836): 510–16.

———. "Notes on a Tour to New York—No. 5." *Millennial Harbinger,* 1st ser., 5, no. 1 (1834): 36–40.

———. "Notes on a Tour to New York—No. 6." *Millennial Harbinger,* 1st ser., 5, no. 2 (1834): 75–80.

———. "The Office of Reason in Reference to the Divine Revelation." *Millennial Harbinger,* 5th ser., 6, no. 8 (1863): 351–55.

———. "On the Importance of Uniting the Moral with the Intellectual Culture of the Mind." *Millennial Harbinger,* 1st ser. (extra), 7, no. 9 (1836): 579–99.

———. "On the Importance of Uniting the Moral with the Intellectual Culture of the Mind." In *Popular Lectures and Addresses,* edited by Alexander Campbell, 453–84. Philadelphia: James Challen and Son, 1866.

———. "Ontology and Deontology." *Millennial Harbinger,* 5th ser., 5, no. 5 (1862): 199–201.

———. "The Philosophy of Memory and of Commemorative Institutions." In *Popular Lectures and Addresses,* edited by Alexander Campbell, 272–90. Philadelphia: James Challen and Son, 1866.

———, ed. *Popular Lectures and Addresses*. Philadelphia: James Challen and Son; Cincinnati: H. S. Bosworth; Bethany, VA: A. Campbell, 1866.

———. "The Rank and Dignity of Man." *Millennial Harbinger,* 2nd ser., 2, no. 12 (1838): 529–46.

———. "Reason Examined by Interrogatories—No. I." *Millennial Harbinger,* 1st ser., 2, no. 11 (1831): 485–87.

———. "Reason Examined by Interrogatories—No. II." *Millennial Harbinger,* 1st ser., 3, no. 1 (1832): 8–10.

———. "Reason Examined by Interrogatories—No. III." *Millennial Harbinger,* 1st ser., 3, no. 3 (1832): 97–100.

———. "Religious Controversy." *Millennial Harbinger,* 1st ser., 1, no. 1 (1830): 40–44.

———. "Replication—No. I." *Christian Baptist* 4, no. 2 (September 1826): 271–72.

———. "Reply to the Above." *Christian Baptist* 5, no. 3 (October 1827): 374–76.

———. "Slavery and the Fugitive Slave Law." *Millennial Harbinger,* 4th ser., 1, no. 4 (1851): 201–6.

———. "The Social System and Deism—No. II." *Christian Baptist* 4, no. 11 (June 1827): 343–45.

———. "Supernatural Facts." In *Popular Lectures and Addresses,* edited by Alexander Campbell, 142–62. Philadelphia: James Challen and Son, 1866.

———. "To Mr. D—A Skeptic—Replication—No. III." *Christian Baptist* 4, no. 4 (November 1826): 281–82.

———. "To the Christian Messenger." *Christian Baptist* 5, no. 3 (1827): 379–81.

———. "A Tract for the People of Kentucky." *Millennial Harbinger,* 3rd ser., 6, no. 5 (May 1849): 241–52.

———. "Tracts for the People—No. II." *Millennial Harbinger,* 3rd ser., 2, no. 11 (1845): 481–92.

———. "What Is Education, in Its Full Import." *Millennial Harbinger,* 5th ser., 5, no. 3 (1862): 109–13.

Campbell, Alexander, and Robert Owen. *The Evidences of Christianity: A Debate between Robert Owen of New Lanark, Scotland, and Alexander Campbell, President of Bethany College, Va., Containing an Examination of the "Social System" and All the Systems of Skepticism of Ancient and Modern Times, Held in the City of Cincinnati, in April 1829.* Nashville: McQuiddy, 1912. Cited in the notes as *Campbell-Owen Debate.*

Campbell, Alexander, and John B. Purcell. *A Debate on the Roman Catholic Religion between Alexander Campbell, Bethany, Va., and the Right Reverend John B. Purcell, Bishop of Cincinnati.* Cincinnati: J. A. James and Co., 1837. Cited in notes as *Campbell-Purcell Debate.*

Campbell, Alexander, and John Walker. *Infant Sprinkling Proved to Be a Human Tradition; Being the Substance of a Debate on Christian Baptism between Mr. John Walker, a Minister of the Secession, and Alexander Campbell, V.D.M., a Regular Baptist Minister.* Stubenville, OH: James Wilson, 1820. Cited in notes as *Campbell-Walker Debate.*

Campbell, George. *A Dissertation on Miracles; Containing an Examination of the Principles Advanced by David Hume, Esq., in an Essay on Miracles*. 4th ed. Edinburgh: Mundell, Doig, and Stevenson, 1807.

Campbell, Selina Huntington. *Home Life and Reminiscences of Alexander Campbell by His Wife, Selina Huntington Campbell*. St. Louis: John Burns, 1882.

Campbell, Thomas. *Declaration and Address of the Christian Association of Washington*. Washington, PA: Brown and Sample, 1809.

Casey, Michael. *The Battle over Hermeneutics in the Stone Campbell Movement, 1800–1870*. Lewiston, NY: Edwin Mellon Press, 1998.

———. "The Origins of the Hermeneutics of the Churches of Christ, Part Two: The Philosophical Background." *Restoration Quarterly* 31, no. 4 (1989): 193–206.

Casey, Michael W., and Douglas A. Foster, eds. *The Stone-Campbell Movement: An International Religious Tradition*. Knoxville: University of Tennessee Press, 2002.

Cherok, Richard J. *Debating for God: Alexander Campbell's Challenge to Skepticism in Antebellum America*. Abilene: Abilene Christian University Press, 2008.

Clanton, J. Caleb, and John Mark Gunter. "Edward Scribner Ames, Pragmatism, and Religious Naturalism: A Critical Assessment." *Heythrop Journal*, forthcoming.

Cohon, Rachel. "Hume's Moral Philosophy." In *The Stanford Encyclopedia of Philosophy*, edited by Edward N. Zalta. Fall 2010 ed. http://plato.stanford.edu/archives/fall2010/entries/hume-moral/.

Cottingham, John. "Why Should Analytic Philosophers Do History of Philosophy." In *Analytic Philosophy and History of Philosophy*, edited by Tom Sorrel and G. A. J. Rogers, 25–41. Oxford, UK: Clarendon Press, 2005.

Craig, William Lane. "The Existence of God and the Beginning of the Universe." *Truth* 3 (1991): 85–96.

———. *Reasonable Faith*. 3rd ed. Wheaton, IL: Crossway, 2008.

———. "Reflections on 'Uncaused Beginnings.'" *Faith and Philosophy* 27, no. 1 (January 2010): 71–78.

———. "Theistic Critique of Atheism." In *The Cambridge Companion to Atheism*, edited by M. Martin, 69–85. Cambridge, UK: Cambridge University Press, 2007.

Craig, William Lane, and Quentin Smith. *Theism, Atheism, and Big Bang Cosmology*. Oxford, UK: Oxford University Press, 1993.

Descartes, Rene. *Meditations on First Philosophy*. Vol. 2 of *The Philosophical Writings of Descartes*. Translated and edited by John Cottingham, Robert Stoothoof, and Dugald Murdoch. Cambridge, UK: Cambridge University Press, 1984.

Dougherty, Trent. "Epistemological Considerations Concerning Skeptical Theism." *Faith and Philosophy* 25, no. 2 (2008): 172–76.

———. "Further Epistemological Considerations Concerning Skeptical Theism." *Faith and Philosophy* 28, no. 3 (2011): 332–40.

Draper, Paul. "A Critique of the *Kalam* Cosmological Argument." In *Philosophy of Religion: An Anthology,* edited by Louis Pojman and Michael Rea, 45–51. 5th ed. Belmont, CA: Wadsworth, 2008.

Durston, Kirk, "The Consequential Complexity of History and Gratuitous Evil." *Religious Studies* 39 (2000): 65–80.

Eames, S. Morris. "The Philosophical Implications in the Theology of Alexander Campbell." Master's thesis, University of Missouri, 1941.

———. *The Philosophy of Alexander Campbell*. Bethany, WV: Bethany College, 1965.

Earman, John. *Hume's Abject Failure: The Argument against Miracles*. New York: Oxford University Press, 2000.

Ehrman, Bart D. *The Historical Jesus*. Audio/video lectures in "The Great Courses" series. Chantilly, VA: The Teaching Company, 2000.

Ellerbrook, James H. "The Influence of Thomas Reid on the Thought-Life of Alexander Campbell." Bachelor of divinity thesis, Butler University, 1947.

Eminhizer, Earl Eugene. "Alexander Campbell and James (Jonas) Hartzell Interpret the Bible on Slavery." *Iliff Review* 30, no. 1 (Winter 1973): 59–71.

Estep, James Riley, Jr. "Alexander Campbell and the Education of Women." *Encounter* 58, no. 1 (Winter 1997): 73–92.

Flew, Antony. *God and Philosophy*. New York: Prometheus, 2005.

———. *Hume's Philosophy of Belief*. London: Routledge and Kegan Paul, 1961.

Fogelin, Robert. *A Defense of Hume on Miracles*. Princeton, NJ: Princeton University Press, 2003.

———. "What Hume Actually Said about Miracles." *Hume Studies* 16, no. 1 (1990): 81–86.

Foster, Douglas A., Paul M. Blowers, Anthony L. Dunnavant, and D. Newell Williams, eds. *The Encyclopedia of the Stone-Campbell Movement*. Grand Rapids, MI: Wm. B. Eerdmans Publishing, 2004.

Gale, Richard. "Some Difficulties in Theistic Treatments of Evil." In *The Evidential Argument from Evil,* edited by Daniel Howard-Snyder, 206–18. Bloomington: Indiana University Press, 1996.

Garrett, Don. *Cognition and Commitment in Hume's Philosophy*. New York: Oxford University Press, 1997.

Garrett, Leroy. *The Stone-Campbell Movement*. Joplin, MO: College Press Publishing, 2006.

Garrison, Winfred Ernest. *Alexander Campbell's Theology: Its Sources and Historical Setting*. St. Louis: Christian Publishing, 1900.

Gellman, Jerome I. "Mysticism and Religious Experience." In *The Oxford Handbook of Philosophy of Religion*, edited by William J. Wainwright, 138–67. Oxford, UK: Oxford University Press, 2005.

Gutjahr, Paul C. *An American Bible: A History of the Good Book in the United States, 1777–1880*. Stanford: Stanford University Press, 1999.

Habermas, Gary. *The Historical Jesus*. Joplin, MO: College Press, 1996.

Hall, Jess O., Jr. "Ecclesiastical Politics on a Moral Powder Keg: Alexander Campbell and Slavery in the *Millennial Harbinger*." *Restoration Quarterly* 39, no. 2 (1997): 65–81.

———. "The Long Shadow of Slavery: American Public Morality and the Stone-Campbell Restoration Movement." *Stone-Campbell Journal* 8, no. 1 (Spring 2005): 3–16.

Hasker, William. "The Sceptical Solution to the Problem of Evil." In *Providence, Evil, and the Openness of God*, edited by William Hasker, 43–57. London: Routledge, 2004.

Hatch, Nathan O. *The Democratization of American Christianity*. New Haven, CT: Yale University Press, 1989.

Holloway, Gary. "Alexander Campbell as a Publisher." *Restoration Quarterly* 37, no. 1 (1995): 28–35.

Holm, James Noble, Jr. "Alexander Campbell's Debate with Robert Owen, April 1829: The Effect of a Rhetorical Event on the Speaker." PhD dissertation, University of Michigan, 1976.

Hovenkamp, Herbert. *Science and Religion in America, 1800–1860*. Philadelphia: University of Pennsylvania Press, 1978.

Howard-Snyder, Daniel. Introduction to *The Evidential Argument from Evil*, edited by Daniel Howard-Snyder, xi–xx. Bloomington: Indiana University Press, 1996.

Howard-Snyder, Daniel, and Paul K. Moser. "Introduction: The Hiddenness of God." In *Divine Hiddenness*, edited by Daniel Howard-Snyder and Paul K. Moser, 1–23. Cambridge, UK: Cambridge University Press, 2002.

Hughes, Richard T. *Reviving the Ancient Faith: The Story of Churches of Christ in America*. Abilene: Abilene Christian University Press, 2008.

Humbert, Royal. Introduction to *A Compend of Alexander Campbell's Theology*, edited by Royal Humbert, 7–16. St. Louis: Bethany Press, 1961.

Humble, Bill J. *Campbell and Controversy*. Rosemead, CA: Old Path Books, 1952.

Hume, David. *Dialogues Concerning Natural Religion*. Edited by Richard H. Popkin. 2nd ed. Indianapolis: Hackett, 1998.

———. *An Enquiry Concerning Human Understanding*. Edited by Eric Steinberg. 2nd ed. Indianapolis: Hackett, 1993.

———. *A Treatise of Human Nature*. In *David Hume: Moral Philosophy*, edited by Geoffrey Sayre-McCord, 12–181. Indianapolis: Hackett, 2006.

Jordan, Jeff. "Does Skeptical Theism Lead to Moral Skepticism?" *Philosophy and Phenomenological Research* 72 (2006): 403–16.

Kant, Immanuel. *Grounding for the Metaphysics of Morals* (with "On a Supposed Right to Lie Because of Philanthropic Concerns"). Translated by James W. Ellington. 3rd ed. Indianapolis: Hackett, 1993.

Kenny, Anthony. *Descartes: A Study of His Philosophy*. New York: Random House, 1968.

Kershner, F. D., ed. *The Philosophical Background of Alexander Campbell*. Indianapolis: Butler University Press, 1947.

Kingsbury, Leslie Lyall. "The Philosophical Influences Bearing on Alexander Campbell and the Beginnings of the Disciples of Christ Movement." PhD dissertation, University of Edinburgh, 1954.

Larmer, Robert. "Interpreting Hume on Miracles." *Religious Studies* 45 (2009): 325–38.

Lawrence, Kenneth, ed. *Classic Themes of Disciples Theology: Rethinking the Traditional Affirmations of the Christian Church (Disciples of Christ)*. Fort Worth: Texas Christian University Press, 1986.

Leslie, Charles. *A Short and Easy Method with the Deists; Wherein the Certainty of the Christian Religion Is Demonstrated by Infallible Proof from Four Rules, Which Are Incompatible to Any Imposture That Ever Yet Has Been or Can Possibly Be. In a Letter to a Friend*. London: R. and C. Rivington, 1801.

Locke, John. *A Discourse of Miracles*. In *"The Reasonableness of Christianity" with "A Discourse of Miracles" and Part of "A Third Letter Concerning Toleration,"* 78–87. Edited by I. T. Ramsey. Stanford: Stanford University Press, 1958.

———. *An Essay Concerning Human Understanding*. 1689. Reprint, Indianapolis: Hackett, 1996.

———. *An Essay for the Understanding of St. Paul's Epistles, &c*. London, 1733.

———. *The Reasonableness of Christianity*. In *"The Reasonableness of Christianity" with "A Discourse of Miracles" and Part of "A Third Letter Concerning Toleration,"* 78–87. Edited by I. T. Ramsey. Stanford: Stanford University Press, 1958.

———. *The Second Treatise of Government and a Letter Concerning Toleration*. Mineola, NY: Dover Publications, 2002.

Lover of Just Reasoning. "Deism and the Social System—No. V." *Christian Baptist* 5, no. 3 (October 1827): 373–74.

Lunger, Harold L. *The Political Ethics of Alexander Campbell*. St. Louis: Bethany Press, 1954.

MacIntyre, Alasdair. "Atheism and Morals." In *The Religious Significance of Atheism*, edited by Alasdair MacIntyre and Paul Ricoeur. New York: Columbia University Press, 1970.

Mackie, J. L. "Evil and Omnipotence." *Mind* 64, no. 254 (1955): 200–212.

———. *The Miracle of Theism*. Oxford, UK: Oxford University Press, 1982.

Madden, Edward H., and Dennis W. Madden. "The Great Debate: Alexander Campbell vs. Robert Owen." *Transactions of the Charles S. Peirce Society* 18, no. 3 (1982): 207–26.

Maitzen, Steven. "Skeptical Theism and Moral Obligation." *International Journal of Philosophy of Religion* 65, no. 2 (2009): 93–103.

Marshall, Mason, and Aaron M. Clark. "Is Clarity Essential to Good Teaching." *Teaching Philosophy* 33, no. 3 (2010): 271–89.

Matheson, Jonathan D. "Epistemological Considerations Concerning Skeptical Theism: A Response to Dougherty." *Faith and Philosophy* 28, no. 3 (2011): 323–31.

Mavrodes, George. "Some Puzzles Concerning Omnipotence." *Philosophical Review* 72 (1963): 221–23.

McAllister, L. G. "Fact and Fiction in Disciples History." *Discipliana* 39 (Winter 1979): 52.

McBrayer, Justin P. "Skeptical Theism." *Philosophy Compass* 5 (2010): 611–23.

McGrew, Timothy. "Miracles." In *The Stanford Encyclopedia of Philosophy*, edited by Edward N. Zalta. Winter 2010 ed. http://plato.stanford.edu/archives/win2010/entries/miracles/.

McMillon, Lynn A. "Alexander Campbell's Early Exposure to Scottish Restorationism, 1808–1809." *Restoration Quarterly* 30, no. 2–3 (1988): 85–101.

Melancthon, [?]. "No External World." *Millennial Harbinger*, 4th ser., 3, no. 9 (1853): 509–10.

Miethe, Terry. "The Social Ethics of Alexander Campbell." *Journal of the Evangelical Theological Society* 31, no. 3 (September 1988): 305–19.

Morrison, John L. *Alexander Campbell: Educating the Moral Person*. Thousand Oaks, CA: privately published, 1991.

Morriston, Wes. "Must the Beginning of the Universe Have a Personal Cause? A Critical Examination of the *Kalam* Cosmological Argument." *Faith and Philosophy* 17, no. 2 (2000): 149–69.

Moser, Paul K. "Cognitive Idolatry and Divine Hiding." In *Divine Hiddenness: New Essays*, edited by Daniel Howard-Snyder and Paul K. Moser, 120–48. Cambridge, UK: Cambridge University Press, 2002.

———, *The Elusive God: Reorienting Religious Epistemology*. New York: Cambridge University Press, 2008.

Mr. D [name unknown]. "To the Editor of the *Christian Baptist*." *Christian Baptist* 4, no. 2 (September 1826): 270–71.

Murray, Michael. "Deus Absconditus." In *Divine Hiddenness: New Essays*, edited by Daniel Howard-Snyder and Paul K. Moser, 62–82. Cambridge, UK: Cambridge University Press, 2002.

Noll, Mark A. *A History of Christianity in the United States and Canada*. Grand Rapids, MI: Eerdmans, 2000.

Nugent, John C. "Was Alexander Campbell Enslaved to Scottish Baconianism?" *Stone-Campbell Journal* 12 (Spring 2009): 15–30.

O'Connor, David. "A Reformed Problem of Evil and the Free Will Defense." *International Journal of Philosophy of Religion* 39, no. 1 (1996): 33–63.

Olbricht, Thomas H. "The Rationalism of the Restoration." *Restoration Quarterly* 11, no. 2 (1968): 77–88.

Oppy, Graham. "Argument from Moral Evil." *International Journal of Philosophy of Religion* 56 (2004): 59–87.

———. "Uncaused Beginnings." *Faith and Philosophy* 27, no. 1 (January 2010): 61–71.

Pack, Frank. "Alexander Campbell the Scholar." *Restoration Quarterly* 30, no. 2–3 (1988): 125–33.

Paley, William. *A View of the Evidences of Christianity*. London: John W. Parker and Son, 1859.

Pearson, Samuel C., Jr. "Enlightenment Influence on Protestant Thought in Early National America." *Encounter* 38, no. 3 (1977): 193–212.

Pearson, Samuel C. "Faith and Reason in Disciples Theology." In *Classic Themes of Disciples Theology: Rethinking the Traditional Affirmations of the Christian Church (Disciples of Christ)*, edited by Kenneth Lawrence, 101–24. Fort Worth: Texas Christian University Press, 1986.

Peirce, C. S. "The Scientific Attitude and Fallibilism." In *Philosophical Writings of Peirce*, 42–59. Edited by Justus Buchler, New York: Dover, 1995.

Pendelton, T. Brian. "Alexander Campbell and Slavery: Gradualism and Anti-slavery Rhetoric in the *Millennial Harbinger*." *Restoration Quarterly* 42, no. 3 (2000): 149–54.

Phillips, Richard. "Thomas Campbell: A Reappraisal Based on Backgrounds." *Restoration Quarterly* 49, no. 2 (2007): 75–102.

Pike, Nelson. "God and Evil: A Reconsideration." *Ethics* 68, no. 2 (1958): 116–24.

Piper, Mark. "Skeptical Theism and the Problem of Moral Aporia." *International Journal for Philosophy of Religion* 62 (2007): 65–79.

Pitson, Tony. "George Campbell's Critique of Hume on Testimony." *Journal of Scottish Philosophy* 4, no. 1 (2006): 1–15.

Plantinga, Alvin. "Epistemic Probability." In *The Evidential Argument from Evil*, edited by Daniel Howard-Snyder, 69–96. Bloomington: Indiana University Press, 1996.

———. *God, Freedom, and Evil*. Grand Rapids, MI: Eerdmans, 1977.

———. *The Nature of Necessity*. Oxford, UK: Oxford University Press, 1982.

———. *Warranted Christian Belief*. New York: Oxford University Press, 2000.

Plato. *Euthyphro*. In *Plato: Five Dialogues*, 1–20. Translated by G. M. A. Grube and revised by John M. Cooper. 2nd ed. Indianapolis: Hackett, 2002.

———. *Gorgias*. Translated and edited by W. D. Woodhead. In *The Collected Dialogues of Plato*, edited by Edith Hamilton and Huntington Cairns, 229–307. Princeton, NJ: Princeton University Press, 1989.

Popkin, Richard H. Introduction to *Dialogues Concerning Natural Religion*, by David Hume, vii–xx. Edited by Richard H. Popkin. 2nd ed. (Indianapolis: Hackett, 1998).

Pratt, George Harold. "The Philosophy of Alexander Campbell." Master's thesis, Phillips University, 1932.

Pulliam, David. *The Constitutional Conventions of Virginia from Foundation of Commonwealth to Present Time*. Richmond, VA: John T. West, 1901.

Rachels, James, and Stuart Rachels. *The Elements of Moral Philosophy*. 6th ed. New York: McGraw-Hill, 2010.

Reid, Thomas. *Essays on the Intellectual Powers*. In *Thomas Reid's Inquiry and Essays*, edited by Ronald E. Beanblossom and Keith Lehrer, 127–295. Indianapolis: Hackett, 1983.

Richardson, Robert. *The Memoirs of Alexander Campbell, Embracing a View of the Origin, Progress and Principles of the Religious Reformation which He Advocated*. 2 vols. Nashville: Gospel Advocate Company, 1956.

Richesin, L. Dale, and Larry D. Bouchard, eds. *Interpreting Disciples: Practical Theology in the Disciples of Christ*. Fort Worth: Texas Christian University Press, 1987.

Rogers, Jill. "The Reluctant Delegate: Alexander Campbell and the Statehood Movement in Western Virginia." Master's thesis, West Virginia University, 2002.

Rowe, William. "The Evidential Argument from Evil: A Second Look," in *The Evidential Argument from Evil,* edited by Daniel Howard-Snyder, 262–85. Bloomington: Indiana University Press, 1996.

———. "Friendly Atheism, Skeptical Theism, and the Problem of Evil." *International Journal of Philosophy of Religion* 59 (2006): 79–92.

———. *Philosophy of Religion.* 4th ed. Belmont, CA: Wadsworth, 2007.

———. "The Problem of Evil and Some Varieties of Atheism." *American Philosophical Quarterly* 16 (1979): 335–41.

———. "Reply to Plantinga." *Nous* 32, no. 4 (1998): 545–52.

Russell, Bertrand. *Why I Am Not a Christian.* London: George Allen and Unwin, 1957.

Schellenburg, J. L. *Divine Hiddenness and Human Reason.* Paperback ed. Ithaca, NY: Cornell University Press, 2006.

———. "The Hiddenness Argument Revisited (I)." *Religious Studies* 41, no. 2 (2005): 201–15.

———. "The Hiddenness Argument Revisited (II)." *Religious Studies* 41, no. 2 (2005): 287–303.

———. "The Hiddenness Problem and the Problem of Evil." *Faith and Philosophy* 27, no. 1 (2010): 45–60.

———. "What the Hiddenness of God Reveals: A Collaborative Discussion." In *Divine Hiddenness,* edited by Daniel Howard-Snyder and Paul K. Moser, 24–32. Cambridge, UK: Cambridge University Press, 2002.

Schlesinger, George N. "Miracles and Probabilities." *Nous* 21, no. 2 (June 1987): 219–32.

Schnall, Ira. "Skeptical Theism and Moral Skepticism." *Religious Studies* 43 (2007): 49–69.

Seckel, Al. Preface to *Bertrand Russell on God and Religion,* edited by Al Seckel, 13–33. Amherst, NY: Prometheus Books, 1986.

Shields, James Leroy, Jr. "Alexander Campbell: A Synthesis of Faith and Reason (1823–1860)." PhD dissertation, Syracuse University, 1974.

Simpson, James. *Necessity of Popular Education, as a National Object; with Hints on the Treatment of Criminals, and Observations on Homicidal Insanity.* Boston: Marsh, Capen and Lyon, 1834.

Smith, Benjamin Lyon. *Alexander Campbell.* St. Louis: Bethany Press, 1930.

Spinoza, Baruch. "Of Miracles." In *Theological-Political Treatise,* translated by Samuel Shirley, 71–85. 2nd ed. Indianapolis: Hackett, 2001.

Stewart, M. A. "Arguments for the Existence of God: The British Debate." In *The Cambridge History of Eighteenth-Century Philosophy,* edited by Knud Haakonssen, 2:710–30. Cambridge, UK: Cambridge University Press, 2006.

Stillingfleet, Edward. *The Bishop of Worchester's Answer to Mr. Locke's Letter, concerning Some Passages in Relation to his Essay of Humane Understanding, mention'd in the Late Discourse in Vindication of the Trinity*. London, 1697.

———. *The Bishop of Worchester's Answer to Mr. Locke's Second Letter; Wherein his Notion of Ideas is Prov'd to be Inconsistent with it self, and with the Articles of Christian Faith*. London, 1698.

———. *A Discourse in Vindication of the Doctrine of the Trinity: with an Answer to the Late Socinian Objections against it from Scripture, Antiquity and Reason*. London, 1697.

Stone, Barton W., et al. "The Last Will and Testament of the Springfield Presbytery." In *Historical Documents Advocating Christian Unity*, edited by Charles A. Young, 19–26. Chicago: Christian Century Publishing, 1904.

Swem, Earl G., and John W. Williams. *A Register of the General Assembly of Virginia, 1776–1918, and of the Constitutional Conventions*. Richmond, VA: Davis Bottom, 1918.

Swinburne, Richard. *The Coherence of Theism*. Oxford, UK: Clarendon Press, 1977.

———. *The Concept of a Miracle*. London: Macmillan, 1970.

———. *The Existence of God*. Oxford, UK: Clarendon Press, 1979.

———. *Is There a God*. New York: Oxford University Press, 1996.

———, ed. *Miracles*. New York: Macmillan, 1989.

———. *The Resurrection of God Incarnate*. Oxford, UK: Clarendon Press, 2003.

———. *Revelation: From Metaphor to Analogy*. Oxford, UK: Clarendon Press, 1993.

Taylor, James E. "Hume on Miracles: Interpretation and Criticism." *Philosophy Compass* 2, no. 4 (2007): 611–24.

Taylor, Richard. *Metaphysics*. 4th ed. Englewood Cliffs, NJ: Prentice Hall, 1992.

Timmons, Mark. *Moral Theory: An Introduction*. Lanham, MD: Rowman and Littlefield, 2002.

Tlumak, Jeffrey. *Classical Modern Philosophy*. New York: Routledge, 2007.

Tolliston, John. *A Doctrine against Transubstantiation*. London: M. Flesher, 1685.

Tooley, Michael. "Alvin Plantinga and the Argument from Evil." *Australasian Journal of Philosophy* 58 (1980): 360–76.

Tristano, Richard M. *The Origins of the Restoration Movement: An Intellectual History*. Atlanta: Glenmary Research Center, 1998.

Twain, Mark. *The Autobiography of Mark Twain*. Edited by Harriet Elinor Smith and Sharon Goetz. Berkeley: University of California Press, 2010.

van Inwagen, Peter. "Of 'Of Miracles.'" In *Philosophy of Religion: An Anthology,* edited by Louis Pojman and Michael Rea, 285–295. 5th ed. Belmont, CA: Wadsworth, 2008.

———. *The Problem of Evil: The Gifford Lectures Delivered in the University of St. Andrews in 2003*. Oxford, UK: Clarendon Press, 2006.

———. "The Problem of Evil, the Problem of Air, and the Problem of Silence." In *The Evidential Argument from Evil,* edited by Daniel Howard-Snyder, 151–74. Bloomington: Indiana University Press, 1996.

———. "What Is the Problem of the Hiddenness of God?" In *Divine Hiddenness: New Essays,* edited by Daniel Howard-Snyder and Paul K. Moser, 24–32. Cambridge, UK: Cambridge University Press, 2002.

Verkruyse, Peter A. *Prophet, Pastor, and Patriarch: The Rhetorical Leadership of Alexander Campbell*. Tuscaloosa: University of Alabama Press, 2005.

Wainwright, William J. "Jonathan Edwards and the Hiddenness of God." In *Divine Hiddenness: New Essays,* edited by Daniel Howard-Snyder and Paul K. Moser, 98–119. Cambridge, UK: Cambridge University Press, 2002.

———. "Mysticism and Religious Experience." In *Readings in Philosophy of Religion,* edited by Linda Zagzebski and Timothy D. Miller, 123–36. Oxford, UK: Wiley-Blackwell, 2009.

Warren, David. "The Men of Glasgow: Influences upon the Campbells." *Restoration Quarterly* 51, no. 2 (2009): 65–79.

Webb, Henry. *In Search of Christian Unity: A History of the Restoration Movement*. Abilene: Abilene Christian University Press, 1990.

West, Robert Frederick. *Alexander Campbell and Natural Religion*. New Haven, CT: Yale University Press, 1948.

White, Ethelene Bruce. "Jane Campbell McKeever (1800–1871): A Brief Biography with Comparison to Her Brother Alexander Campbell on the Issue of Slavery and Abolition." *Stone-Campbell Journal* 13, no. 1 (Spring 2010): 3–16.

Wiebe, Mark. "Alexander Campbell on Rationality and the Problem of Evil." Paper presented at the American Academy of Religion, Northwest Regional Conference (2010) and at the Christian Scholars Conference, Pepperdine University (June 16, 2011), on file with the author.

Williams, Bernard. *Descartes: The Project of Pure Enquiry*. New York: Routledge, 2005.

Wittgenstein, Ludwig. *Philosophical Investigations*. Translated by G. E. M. Anscombe. Oxford, UK: Blackwell, 2001.

Wolterstorff, Nicholas. *John Locke and the Ethics of Belief*. New York: Cambridge University Press, 1996.

———. "Locke's Philosophy of Religion." In *The Cambridge Companion to Locke,* edited by Vere Chappell, 173–98. New York: Cambridge University Press, 1994.

Wykstra, Stephen J. "The Humean Obstacle to Evidential Arguments from Suffering: On Avoiding the Evils of 'Appearance.'" *International Journal of Philosophy of Religion* 16 (1984): 73–93.

———. "Rowe's Noseeum Arguments from Evil." In *The Evidential Argument from Evil,* edited by Daniel Howard-Snyder, 126–51. Bloomington: Indiana University Press, 1996.

Yaffe, Gideon, and Ryan Nichols. "Thomas Reid." In *The Stanford Encyclopedia of Philosophy,* edited by Edward N. Zalta. Winter 2009 ed. http://plato.stanford.edu/archives/win2009/entries/reid/.

Young, Robert. "Theism and Morality." In *Divine Commands and Morality,* edited by Paul Helm, 154–64. Oxford, UK: Oxford University Press, 1981.

Index

The Philosophy of Religion of Alexander Campbell was designed and typeset on a Macintosh OS 10.6.8 computer system using CS5 InDesign software. The body text is set in 10/13.5 Minion Pro and display type is set in ITC Tiffany Std. This book was designed and typeset by Barbara Karwhite and manufactured by Thomson-Shore, Inc.